P9-CFL-425

SAVEUR
COOKS

AUTHENTIC AMERICAN

SAVEUR
COOKS

AUTHENTIC AMERICAN

Celebrating the Recipes and Diverse Traditions of Our Rich Heritage

BY THE EDITORS OF SAVEUR MAGAZINE

CHRONICLE BOOKS
SAN FRANCISCO

This Chronicle Books LLC edition published in 2007.

Text copyright © 1998 by Meigher Communications, L.P.
All rights reserved. No part of this book may be reproduced in any form
without written permission from the publisher.
Page 309 constitutes a continuation of the copyright page.

ISBN 978-0-8118-5524-2

The Library of Congress has cataloged the previous edition as follows:

Saveur cooks authentic American / by the editors of Saveur magazine.
     p. cm.
     Includes index.
     ISBN 0-8118-2160-9
     1. Cookery, American. I. Saveur.
TX715.S273   1998
641.5973-DC21

     98-19344
     CIP
     r98

Manufactured in China.

Designed by Jill Armus, Toby Fox, and Michael Grossman

Distributed in Canada by Raincoast Books
9050 Shaughnessy Street
Vancouver, British Columbia V6P 6E5

10 9 8 7 6 5 4 3 2 1

Chronicle Books LLC
680 Second Street
San Francisco, California 94107

www.chroniclebooks.com

Acknowledgments

ONE WINTER WEEKEND in 1993, a tiny group of us sat in a room and, pooling our collective hopes and experience, invented SAVEUR. I am happy to report that, four years later, this same tiny band—Colman Andrews, Editor; Christopher Hirsheimer, Executive Editor; Michael Grossman, Creative Director; and myself—is bringing you our first cookbook. This time, however, we had lots of superb help—from, to begin with, SAVEUR Art Director Jill Armus; Toby Fox, Acting Art Director; María Millán, Photography Editor; Ann McCarthy, Assistant Managing Editor; Catherine Tillman, Associate Editor; Jill Bigelow, Assistant Editor; Nanette Maxim, Copy Editor; Ann Powell, Editorial Consultant; production wizards Melissa Moss and Betsey Barnum; and our freelance editor for this project, Erin Kelly. There were others who couldn't help but help: Connie McCabe, Corinne Trang, Kate Nowell-Smith, David Goldstein, Karen Ferries, Jennifer Herman, Maura Egan, John Haney, Barbara Pratt, Jenny Chung, Matthew Bates, Julia Michry, and Chad Tomlinson. Since this entire group also kept their day jobs (and didn't miss putting out a single issue of the magazine), I can't thank them enough for their inventiveness, attention to detail, humor, and grace under pressure.

The recipes in this book come from real-life American stories, some of them ours, others from the family histories of the writers and photographers whose dedication makes SAVEUR the award-winning magazine it is. Photography credits appear on page 308. The writers are: Pam Anderson, R.W. Apple Jr., Eugenia Bone, Gene Bourg, Miles Chapin, Marion Cunningham, John Mercuri Dooley, Mary Ann Eagle, March Egerton, Allison Engel, Amy Ephron, Meryle Evans, Judith M. Fertig, Barbara Freda, Perry Garfinkel, Robbin Gourley, Lori Gray, Rebecca Gray, David Grinstead/Laura McCallum, Cynthia Hacinli, Barbara Hagerty, Josefina Howard, Schuyler Ingle, Warren Kalbacker, David Karp, John Kehoe, Peggy Knickerbocker, Diane Kochilas, Eric Lawlor, Linda L. Leake, Leslie Li, Monte Mathews, Thomas McNamee, Sarah Gray Miller, Mitch Omer, Marlene Parrish, Charles Perry, Kaui Philpotts, Stephanie Pierson, Elizabeth Schneider, Sally Schneider, Warren Schultz, William Sertl, Brian Silverman, Sandy Szwarc, John Thorne, Sallie Tisdale, William Woys Weaver, Clifford A. Wright, and Cathy Young.

To our agent, Cullen Stanley, and to counsel, Bennett Ashley at Janklow & Nesbit, we extend profound thanks; and to Bill LeBlond, our editor at Chronicle Books, as well. This would not, however, be a Meigher publication without those who make our company as unique as it is: Special thanks to our Chairman, Chris Meigher; President, Doug Peabody; and Publishing Director, Joe Armstrong—as well as to SAVEUR's Publisher, David Kahn, and the rest of our wonderfully spirited crew. —DOROTHY KALINS, *Editor-in-Chief*, SAVEUR

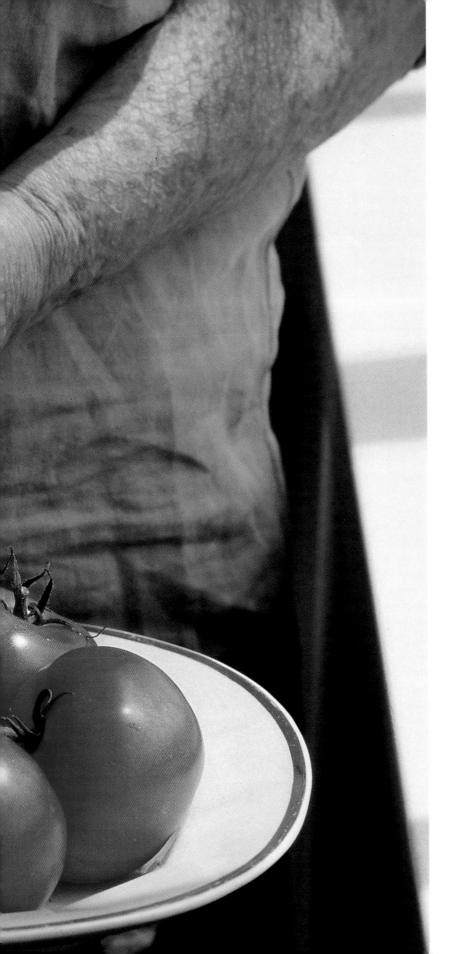

Table of Contents

The Family Meal

Husband, wife, and kids convene in Wyncote Township, Pennsylvania, in 1969, top, for the ultimate American suburban culinary ritual: a backyard barbecue. The Wong family has dinner at home in Minneapolis in 1937, bottom. Facing page, Professor Albert W. Rankin and family enjoy summer supper on the porch of their Wright County, Minnesota, farm in 1908.

In a society that has made a virtue of mobility and an icon of individualism, we Americans today look increasingly to food—not just recipes, but the rhyme and reason behind the things we eat—for stability and communality. Food becomes our most visceral, and most satisfying, link, not only with our pasts but with each other.

A year before SAVEUR first appeared—our pilot issue was dated Summer 1994—we tested the waters with a series of those highly unscientific but invariably thought-provoking market-research fishing expeditions known as "focus groups". In our case, this meant assembling demographically desirable potential readers in a room, showing them copies of a French culinary magazine that anticipated at least some of what we wanted to do ourselves, and asking them if they'd buy such a publication—if, that is, it were in English and offered plenty of American stories. Flipping past glorious, evocative photographs of black-dressed grandmothers stirring iron pots, apron-clad market workers hawking mounds of purple baby artichokes and dark wild mushrooms, honest bistro chefs perspiring at their ovens, and hardy, ruddy farmers cradling baby lambs (raised for their flavor, it might be noted, and not their cuddliness), a woman in one focus group announced "I'd love a magazine like this if it had American food in it—but we don't have people and products

abundance of foodstuffs that go into it, is immensely varied—cornucopian—and is often, calumny notwithstanding, some of the best in the world.

The truth is that Americans can be wonderful cooks—energetic, imaginative, and solidly grounded in sound technique. Because we have inherited a plurality of processes, tastes, and traditions, we are not slaves to any one of them; the stylistic tyrannies of many Asian and European cuisines were left behind along with harsher, more literal tyrannies. As a result, we have become great culinary tinkerers, happily inventing and redefining dishes. Long before anyone had heard of "Pacific Rim" or "fusion" cooking, we were assimilating and adapting flavors not just from our own ethnic backgrounds but from all over the world—so that chow mein, gnocchi with pesto, chiles rellenos, and Swedish coffee bread, say, can truly be considered every bit as American as baked beans, seafood gumbo, fried chicken, and apple pie.

At the same time (ironically, perhaps, but not unreasonably), we've also developed an appetite for the traditions of the past, and sought them out in our own family histories, or borrowed them from others. Realizing that we're not obliged to observe the foodways of our ancestors, we voluntarily embrace them, finding another kind of culinary freedom in reviving old dishes, old food ideas.

From Land and Sea

Men gather around an open pit to baste meat—enough to feed whole European villages—in a turn-of-the-century version of a Missouri barbecue, top. The 16th-century Indian village of Secotan in coastal North Carolina, with corn and tobacco plantings, as depicted by John White, bottom. Facing page, women cook clams and lobster on a Maine beach in the late 19th century.

*Communal
Tables*

The most famous
early American feast,
of course, was "The
First Thanksgiving",
as imagined, top, by
Pennsylvania artist
Jennie Brownscombe
in 1914. The pointed
pen (perhaps Thomas
Nast's) saluted
American diversity
with "Uncle Sam's
Thanksgiving Dinner"
in 1869, bottom.
Facing page, a com-
munal table at the
Immigrants' Dining
Hall at the Ellis Island
(New York) Immigra-
tion Station in 1906.

in its turn, if our streets weren't exactly paved with gold, they were certainly lined with food shops. And if the goods these establishments dispensed weren't always immediately affordable, at least they were *there*. They were something to strive for; they were tomorrow night's dinner if not tonight's.

The American cornucopia, after all, spilling over with bursting-ripe fruit and bright vegetables beneath a smiling sun, has long been a symbol of our nation's richness. Everything grew here, or could be raised or fished or hunted. There were no empty larders or barren tables in the New World—at least not in the mythology.

This is not to say that immigrants came to the American table empty-handed. On the contrary, they brought not just Grandma's recipes, but their basic culinary processes, their tastes, their food traditions. Some of these they adapted to new ingredients or to the new realities of American life; others they clung to as cultural talismans, with the tenacious nostalgia of the uprooted. Either way, they enriched our gastronomy.

The culinary calumny about America used to be that, while we had the raw materials, we didn't know what to do with them. American food was bland, overcooked, underseasoned; it was canned or frozen; it was hamburgers. The truth, of course, is that our cuisine, like the

INTRODUCTION

WE ARE ALL immigrants here, or the children of immigrants—even those "native" Americans whose ancestors walked down from Siberia. And as each generation of newcomers to this country discovered

The Knoxville (Tennessee) Market House in 1925, left. Once the city's hub, with its meat, seafood, and produce stands, it burned down in 1959.

like this in America." "Yes we do!" I wanted to shout from behind the mirrored glass that separated me from the proceedings. *"Yes we do!"*

In a sense, proving that one woman wrong has been part of our mission since we launched SAVEUR. There were plenty of other food magazines around when we made our debut. Some were devoted to illustrated cooking techniques and painstakingly detailed recipes; others were concerned with light, low-fat, "healthy" cuisine; still others praised trendy new restaurants and "superstar" chefs, and told readers how to set their tables, where to dine out in Melbourne and Aspen and Seoul, and how to buy wines by numerical score.

What there wasn't, and what we believed there ought to be, was a magazine that considered food in a larger context—a magazine that celebrated the world's great and good dishes, both casual and elaborate, but that also revealed where they came from, and who first made them, and why. Information of this kind, it seemed to us, was at least as important to the integrity and authenticity of a dish (and, by extension, to how good it would taste) as the number of teaspoons of this or ounces of that involved in its successful manufacture. To put it another way, we wanted to create a magazine about the multitude of ways in which food is connected to just about everything

Food from Home

Top, Juanita and Esperanza Garcia making tortillas on Haymarket Plaza in San Antonio, Texas, in 1937. A butcher and his wife turn out linguiça, a spicy Portuguese sausage, at their New Bedford, Massachusetts, shop in 1940, bottom. Facing page, an "Italian, eating his national dish", according to the archival caption on this photo, taken on Washington Street in Manhattan in 1919.

Trading Tastes

The culinary melting pot illustrated by a Brooklyn street scene from 1960, top. Chicago's bustling South Water Street Market in 1914, bottom. Facing page, the Black Hawk Barbecue restaurant in Kansas City in 1938, with proprietors VeEssa Spivey (in black dress) and her husband, William (to her left).

else in life, and in which it in turn connects *us*—to our families, to our heritage, to our world.

The cover of each issue of SAVEUR—whose name, incidentally, is pronounced approximately "sa-VUR", and means "flavor" or "taste"—invites readers to "Savor a world of authentic cuisine". For us, that world begins at home. While we've investigated kitchens and met (and learned from) cooks in nearly every corner of the globe, we've always reserved a special place in our magazine, and in our hearts, for the cooking of our neighbors, our families, our domestic culinary predecessors—of our fellow Americans. With the help of wonderful writers and photographers who share our gastronomic point of view, we've discovered rich local food traditions, impeccable world-class ingredients, whole communities held together by the way they cook and eat—and, yes, more than a few black-clad grandmothers, bountiful markets, honest chefs, and lamb-cradling farmers as well.

In our process of discovery, we've also found a breadth and depth to American cooking that even we, at our most optimistic and chauvinistic, scarcely could have imagined. It seems only fitting, then, that our first SAVEUR cookbook should be devoted to "Authentic America"—to the people, the places, the food; to the real thing, American-style. —COLMAN ANDREWS, *Editor*, SAVEUR

SOUPS

"PLYMOUTH, Massachusetts, is a community that takes chowder pretty seriously. There are chowder societies, chowder festivals, chowder-themed boat races, and even (or so my grandmother Ruth always believed) a chowder day: Wednesday. In this part of New England, chowder is more than a soup; it's a way of life."

—MILES CHAPIN ON CHOWDER *(SEE RECIPE ON PAGE 33)*

RECIPES

Summer Vegetable Soup

SERVES 6

LIKE ITALY'S minestrone and other classic vegetable soups, this dish depends for its success on the use of a variety of the freshest, most flavorful vegetables available.

6 cups vegetable stock
    (recipe follows)
1 large carrot, peeled and
    diced
¼ lb. green beans, trimmed
    and cut into 1" pieces
1 small bulb fennel,
    thinly sliced (tops
    reserved for garnish)
6 small red or white new
    potatoes, sliced
2 small yellow or green
    summer squash, diced
Salt and freshly ground
    black pepper
6 sprigs fresh parsley
6 sprigs fresh chervil

VEGETABLE STOCK:

3 tbsp. extra-virgin
    olive oil
2 medium yellow onions,
    peeled and chopped
6 cloves garlic, crushed
    and peeled (see Note)
1 large leek, trimmed
    and chopped
1 large carrot, chopped
2 stalks celery, chopped
1 bulb fennel, chopped
3 plum tomatoes
1 cup dry white wine
5 sprigs parsley
6 black peppercorns
1 bay leaf
Salt

1. Bring stock to a simmer in a large pot over medium heat. Add carrots, beans, fennel, potatoes, and squash to stock, then cover and gently simmer until vegetables are soft, about 20 minutes. Season to taste with salt and pepper. Ladle into individual bowls and garnish with reserved fennel tops and parsley and chervil sprigs.

VEGETABLE STOCK: Heat oil in a large pot over medium-low heat, add onions, garlic, leeks, carrots, celery, fennel, and tomatoes and cook, stirring frequently, for 15 minutes. Add wine, 7 cups water, parsley, peppercorns, and bay leaf. Bring to a boil, skimming off any foam. Reduce heat to low, then cover and simmer for 45 minutes. Remove from heat then strain stock and discard solids. Season to taste with salt. If not using immediately, refrigerate or freeze. Makes about 6 cups.

NOTE: *Peeling Garlic*—Separate cloves from head, then lay them on a cutting board and crush with the flat side of a knife blade. The papery peel will easily pull away from the garlic clove.

Indoor Foraging

Waiting in an outdoor kitchen in West Marin, California, for Evan Shively, a forager for several restaurants, SAVEUR executive editor Christopher Hirsheimer anticipated someone out of Tolkien—a tiny hobbit wearing a mushroom hat. Instead, in walked a handsome prince with a basketful of his morning's harvest: fresh green nettles, wild chives, and two kinds of woodsy mushrooms. Later, he'd chop the nettles and chives and wrap them in ravioli, and slice the mushrooms to top a thin-crust pizza. Somehow the wild freshness of the raw materials made both taste particularly good. Foraging—searching for edible (and preferably delicious) wild flora and their issue—has become something of a fad these days. More than one American restaurant employs a forager to supplement its organic produce and artisanal breads and cheeses—and even noted French chefs (like Jean-Georges Vongerichten, who owns several of Manhattan's best restaurants) go foraging regularly. We've found that the forager's approach can be adapted to more conventional food-gathering: Whether at a farmers' market or a regular supermarket, make shopping an adventure—a search for hidden treasures. Select your food with an eye for the fresh, the seasonal, and the flavorful. And if you find something special, go wild.

Call Me Butter Bean

L ima beans have a pretty dismal reputation. Though tiny and faint of color, their cold and mushy specter looms large in many a childhood dinner-table memory. To get over this negative association, try thinking of the lima as a "butter bean". The colonists, who discovered it here, called it that because of its creamy texture and sweet flavor. In England and in the American South, it often still goes by that name. (We know it as the lima in honor of the capital of Peru, near which one type of lima bean was first cultivated.) There are two basic varieties of lima beans: *Phaseolus limensis*, the large lima, also known as the Madagascar, Burma, or Cape bean or Cape pea, and *Phaseolus lunatus*, the smaller one, also called the baby lima, sieva bean, or civet bean. The larger variety is slightly nuttier in flavor. Most limas are sold frozen or dried, simply because the fresh ones are hard to shell. They used to be hard to harvest too, because they climbed up tall poles. In the late 1880s, though, a mutant plant growing like a bush was discovered, and today most commercial limas—the vast majority of them are fordhooks, grown in California—are the bushy type.

Lima Bean Soup

SERVES 8

WE CREATED this thick, rich, satisfying soup—which can be served as a kind of lima-bean vichyssoise—in the hopes that it would help convert limaphobes to the earthy flavors of this much maligned vegetable.

3 tbsp. butter
1 medium yellow onion, peeled and chopped
4 cups baby lima beans, fresh or frozen
2 large potatoes, peeled and diced
8 cups chicken stock (recipe follows)
Salt and freshly ground white pepper
¼ cup chopped fresh mint leaves
½ cup crème fraîche (optional)

CHICKEN STOCK:
1 3-lb. chicken
2 carrots, chopped
2 stalks celery, chopped
1 medium yellow onion, peeled and chopped
6 black peppercorns
Salt

1. Melt butter in a heavy saucepan over medium heat. Add onions and cook, stirring often, until soft, about 10 minutes.

2. Increase heat to high, add lima beans, potatoes, and chicken stock, then cover and bring to a boil. Reduce to medium heat and simmer until potatoes are soft, about 15 minutes. Using a slotted spoon, remove ½ cup of the vegetables and set aside for garnish. Continue to cook remaining vegetables until they are easily mashed against the side of the pot.

3. Purée vegetables with the stock in a food processor. Strain, then season to taste with salt and pepper. Serve hot or cold, garnished with reserved vegetables, mint leaves, and, if you like, crème fraîche. The soup will thicken when chilled; thin to desired consistency with cold chicken stock or water.

CHICKEN STOCK: Place the chicken, carrots, celery, onions, and peppercorns in a large stockpot with 3 quarts of water. Bring to a boil over medium-high heat. Reduce heat to low and simmer, uncovered, 2–3 hours, occasionally skimming foam. (After 1 hour, you may remove chicken, pick meat from the bones to reserve for another use, and return carcass to the pot.) Remove from heat, then strain stock and discard solids. Season to taste with salt. If not using immediately, refrigerate or freeze. Makes 8 cups (2 quarts).

Cranberry Bean Soup

SERVES 6

WHEN WRITER Eugenia Bone accompanies her father, Ed Giobbi (facing page and right)—himself author of several classic books on Italian cooking—on shopping trips to Arthur Avenue, she reconnects with her family's roots, and sometimes picks up the fixings for this favorite bean soup.

4 tbsp. extra-virgin olive oil

2 small yellow onions, peeled and chopped

2 small carrots, peeled and chopped

2 stalks celery, chopped

5 cloves garlic, peeled and minced

3 tbsp. finely chopped fresh parsley

3 tbsp. finely chopped fresh basil

1½ lbs. plum tomatoes, peeled and seeded (see page 56, step 1) and chopped

2 cups dried cranberry beans

1 bay leaf

1 tbsp. chopped fresh sage leaves

Salt and freshly ground black pepper

1. Heat oil in a large pot over medium-low heat. Add onions, carrots, and celery and cook until soft, about 15 minutes. Add garlic and 1 tbsp. each of parsley and basil. Cook for another 10 minutes.

2. Add tomatoes and cook 10 minutes more, then add beans, 4 cups water, bay leaf, and sage. Simmer soup over medium heat (adding more water if necessary) until beans are very tender, about 1½ hours. Add remaining parsley and basil and season to taste with salt and pepper.

Italy in New York

Arthur Avenue, the great Italian market street in the Bronx, just northeast of Manhattan, may look a bit down at the heels, but it's alive with activity. There are more than 200 Italian businesses packed into seven blocks. Shops spill out into the street, displaying food, crockery, and knickknacks. A deli owner packs his Cadillac with fresh-made ricotta and mozzarella, as a young man in butcher's whites totes a quarter of a cow's carcass down the street on his shoulders. Grandpas sit at outdoor cafés, sipping espresso macchiato and reading *Il Giornale* while grandmas with complicated braids argue over the dates of baptisms and weddings held generations ago. Butcher shops make a dozen kinds of sausage and sell rabbit and goat. Produce is varied and crisply fresh; mushrooms are wild.

King Squash

If you want to get technical about it, there's no such thing as a pumpkin—or, to put it another way, *pumpkin* is just another name for certain kinds of squash (often big, round, orange varieties). As much as 10,000 years ago, what we may now call pumpkins were cultivated in Mexico, specifically for the seeds (which are high in protein). Today, in the United States, scores if not hundreds of varieties are grown. They come in many forms—palm-size ones and ones too big to lift, sugar-sweet and tart varieties, species colored not just orange but blue, yellow, and red (like the French-bred rouge d'Étampes pictured above). Some of the most flavorful pumpkins have green or even white exteriors—for instance, the very sweet delicata. Jack-o'-lantern pumpkins (often the fibrous variety known as the Connecticut field pumpkin) may carve up nicely for Halloween, but, though edible, they aren't really the ones you want to eat. Since 1929, the commercial eating pumpkin of choice in America has been the dickinson—which is the one sold in cans, and thus the one that most often ends up in pies. For soup, almost any variety but the Connecticut field pumpkin will do just fine.

Pumpkin Soup with Sage

SERVES 6

PUTTING PUMPKINS in pie, however traditional (and satisfying) that may be, isn't the only good thing to do with them—as this autumnal soup deliciously demonstrates. Look for small, sweet pumpkins like the jack-be-little or delicata—or substitute butternut squash.

1 small pie pumpkin, about 5 lbs.
4 tbsp. extra-virgin olive oil
6 tbsp. unsalted butter
2 medium yellow onions, peeled and finely chopped
2 cloves garlic, peeled and minced
4–6 cups chicken stock (see page 26)
Salt and freshly ground black pepper
Vegetable oil
18 fresh sage leaves
9 shallots, peeled and halved lengthwise

1. Preheat oven to 350°. Quarter and seed pumpkin, rub flesh with olive oil, and bake on a baking sheet until tender, about 30 minutes. Set aside and allow to cool.

2. Melt 4 tbsp. butter in a heavy stockpot over medium heat. Add onions and garlic and cook, stirring frequently, until onions are soft, about 15 minutes. Meanwhile, scrape flesh from pumpkin. Add to onions and garlic and cook for another 5 minutes.

3. Add 4 cups stock to pot and simmer for 30 minutes. Purée soup in a food processor until smooth, then return it to pot. If necessary, thin with additional stock. Season to taste with salt and pepper, then cover soup and keep warm over lowest heat.

4. Meanwhile, heat about 1 cup vegetable oil in a small pan over medium heat. When oil is hot, fry sage leaves until crisp. Drain leaves on paper towels. Discard oil or reserve for another use.

5. In the same pan, melt remaining 2 tbsp. butter over medium heat and cook shallots until soft and golden, about 15 minutes. To serve, ladle soup into individual bowls and garnish each serving with 3 shallot halves and 3 fried sage leaves.

A

B

C

D

E

F

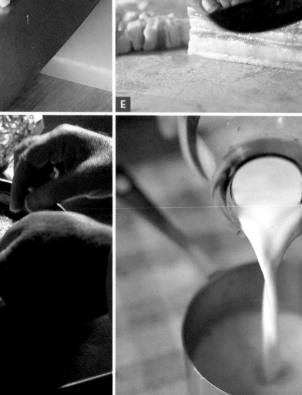

G

H

I

Chuck's Three-Day Fish Chowder

SERVES 6–8

CHUCK DAVIS'S all-fish version of New England clam chowder takes three days, he says, "because it takes that long for the 'sludge' and fat to separate, so I get a clear stock."

1 2½-lb. haddock or cod
   (yielding 1 lb. of filets)

FOR CHOWDER BASE:
4 cloves garlic, peeled
4 stalks celery
1 large white onion, peeled
⅓ lb. salt pork
1 bay leaf
1 tsp. chopped fresh thyme
   leaves
Reserved fish filets

FOR FISH CHOWDER:
4 cups fish stock (recipe
   follows)
2 lbs. red potatoes, peeled
   and diced
Cooked vegetables and fish
1 cup milk
1 cup heavy cream
Salt
Tabasco
Cooked salt pork
Paprika

FISH STOCK:
1 fish skeleton (see above,
   step one)
1 small yellow onion, peeled
   and chopped
2 stalks celery, chopped
2 small carrots, chopped
⅔ cup dry white wine
2 sprigs fresh parsley
1 sprig fresh thyme
1 bay leaf
1 tsp. black peppercorns

1. On day one, clean fish and filet (**A**). Refrigerate filets for chowder, then rinse skeleton for stock. Prepare stock according to recipe below. Set aside and allow to cool to room temperature, then refrigerate.

2. On day two, prepare chowder base. Mince garlic, dice celery (**C**) and onion (**D**), and set aside. Dice salt pork (**E**), then cook in a skillet over medium-low heat until crisp, about 20 minutes. Remove pork from skillet, drain on paper towels (**F**), and reserve for garnish. In the same skillet, add garlic, celery, onions, bay leaf, and thyme to rendered fat and cook over low heat until soft, about 20 minutes. Add fish, skin up, and ½ cup water. Cover, simmer for 4 minutes, then peel skin off fish (**G**). Refrigerate fish and vegetables.

3. On day three, prepare fish chowder. Skim fat from stock. Slowly pour stock into a large pot, leaving "sludge" behind. Add potatoes and cooked vegetables to stock. Set aside fish. Cover and simmer over medium heat until soft, about 20 minutes. Stir in milk and cream (**H**), then flake fish into chowder. Simmer (do not boil) until hot. Discard bay leaf. Season to taste with salt and Tabasco. Ladle into bowls (**I**), top with salt pork, and sprinkle with paprika.

FISH STOCK: Put fish skeleton, cut into 4" lengths including head and tail, into a large pot. Add onions, celery, carrots, wine, parsley, thyme, bay leaf, peppercorns, and 10 cups water. Bring to a boil over high heat, then reduce heat to low and simmer for 40 minutes, skimming fat and foam. Strain first through a colander, to separate bones and vegetables (**B**), then through a colander lined with cheesecloth, to catch any finer bits. Discard solids. Return stock to pot and reduce by half over medium heat. Makes 4 cups.

Family in a Bowl

A ctor/writer Miles Chapin's ancestors stepped ashore at Plymouth Rock almost 400 years ago, and the woods and ponds of that part of southeastern Massachusetts feel to him like his family's common ground—a place where he is deeply rooted. Though now an urban New Yorker, he still brings his wife and daughter to the Plymouth house he's summered in since childhood and introduces them to the things that make him feel so connected to New England. Sometimes, Chapin reports, the relationship he is so consciously helping to forge between his wife, their daughter, and his history becomes stronger over something as simple as a bowl of chowder. In fact, he says, perhaps nothing summarizes his feelings about the region more purely than this time-honored, tradition-bound soup. Chapin's chowder guru is his cousin Chuck Davis, whose family-famous fish chowder was eaten on special occasions throughout Chapin's childhood. Chuck makes a "manly" chowder, which means he adds wine and herbs for a complex, rich result.

Lobster and Corn Chowder

SERVES 8

CARY WHEATON, owner of Full Moon restaurant in Cambridge, Massachusetts, vacations down the coast at the seaside town of Westport, where lobster and corn are abundant. One summer there, she was inspired to create this unusual chowder for her friends and neighbors.

In the Soup

In the delicious limbo between soup and stew lies the definitively American concoction known as chowder. (Some scholars believe chowder to be French-Canadian in origin and suggest that it is named for the three-legged cauldron, or *chaudière*, in which it was made.) In New England, which is chowder country, recipes for this soup are a matter of highly impassioned and divergent opinion, even within families. There are virtually instant chowders and those that take three days to make (see previous page). There are chowders innocent of herbs and chowders containing unexpected greenery (like dill). Chowder may be thickened with cornstarch, flour, puréed potato, even crushed oyster crackers. The liquid may be milk or cream (or neither, as in the tomatoey Manhattan version, considered heretical by most New Englanders). And, of course, not all chowders are made with clams; cod, shrimp, lobster, and even corn chowders have their partisans.

Salt
2 2-lb. live lobsters
1 stalk celery, coarsely chopped
1 medium carrot, coarsely chopped
1 sprig fresh parsley
1 bay leaf
5 black peppercorns
¼ lb. salt pork, diced
3 medium yellow onions, peeled and diced
3 cloves garlic, peeled and minced
1½ lbs. red potatoes, peeled and cut into ½" cubes
4 cups fresh corn kernels (cut from about 6 ears)
3 cups half-and-half
Cayenne
Freshly ground white pepper

1. Bring a large pot of salted water to a boil over medium-high heat. Add lobsters and cook for 8–10 minutes. Remove lobsters, then strain cooking liquid into a large bowl or another pot. Rinse lobsters in cold water, then remove meat from shells, reserving shells but discarding tomalley and coral. Cut meat into small pieces and set aside. Return shells and 10 cups reserved cooking liquid to pot.

2. Add celery, carrots, parsley, bay leaf, and peppercorns to cooking liquid. Cover and simmer over low heat for 1½ hours. Strain stock through a fine sieve, then return stock to the same pot, discarding shells and remaining solids. Cook over medium-high heat until reduced to 6 cups, about 10 minutes.

3. Cook salt pork in a medium pan over medium-low heat, stirring occasionally, until crisp, about 20 minutes. Remove salt pork, drain on paper towels, and set aside to use as garnish. In the same pan, add onions and garlic to the rendered fat and cook over low heat until soft, about 20 minutes.

4. Add onion mixture, potatoes, and corn to reduced stock, then increase heat to medium and simmer until potatoes are tender, about 10 minutes. Stir in half-and-half and a dash of cayenne and return to a simmer. Add lobster meat and simmer (do not boil) until heated through, 3–5 minutes. Season to taste with salt and pepper. Ladle into bowls and top with reserved salt pork.

Aunt Gillie's Matzo Ball Soup

SERVES 6–8

CHICKEN SOUP is a universal panacea—invoked by many cultures as a cure for colds and broken hearts alike. With matzo balls added, it becomes a meal—and a must for any traditional Jewish-American Passover Seder. This recipe comes from Gillie Feuer of Long Island, New York.

FOR SOUP:
1 3-lb. chicken
3 carrots, halved
2 medium yellow onions, peeled and halved
5 stalks celery, with leaves, halved
3 parsnips, halved
2 leeks, well cleaned, white parts only
1 head garlic, unpeeled, split
4 stalks fresh dill
1 bunch parsley, washed

FOR MATZO BALLS:
1 medium yellow onion, peeled and halved
8 eggs
8 tbsp. margarine, melted and slightly cooled
2½ cups matzo meal
2 tbsp. finely chopped parsley
Salt and freshly ground black pepper
Small dill sprigs

1. For soup, combine chicken, carrots, onions, celery, parsnips, leeks, garlic, dill, and parsley in a large stockpot with water to cover. Bring just to a boil over medium-high heat. Skim foam. Reduce heat to low and simmer for 2½ hours. Strain and discard solids (chicken may be reserved for another use), then cool to room temperature. Refrigerate for at least 3 hours, then remove any solidified fat from surface.

2. For matzo balls, grate enough onion to yield about 2 tbsp. and set aside the rest. In a large bowl, combine grated onion, eggs, margarine, matzo meal, parsley, and ¼ cup water or chicken soup (**A**). Mix well, season with salt and pepper and set aside to rest for at least 30 minutes.

3. Wet hands and roll dough in your palms into 24 2" balls (**B**) (they will expand as they cook). Meanwhile, bring a large pot of water to a boil. Add 2 tbsp. salt and remaining onion. Drop matzo balls into water one at a time. (They won't stick together if the pot is large enough.) Reduce heat, cover, and simmer 30–40 minutes (**C**). Drain, remove to a plate and cover, until ready to use. (Matzo balls will keep up to 3 days in the refrigerator.)

4. To serve, heat soup over medium heat and season to taste with salt and pepper. Add matzo balls and heat through. Garnish with dill sprigs.

Cajun Matzos?

he matzo ball, a classic of the Eastern European Jewish kitchen, was invented by resourceful cooks to comply with the ban on leavened wheat products during the holiday of Passover. Often made of little more than hand-ground matzo meal plus chicken fat, eggs, and a bit of onion, matzo balls were originally called just *kneidel*—Yiddish for dumpling. Their more familiar name came into common use in the late 1930s, and American regional influences and personal tastes have since resulted in a myriad of variations. Cookbook author Joan Nathan writes of a Dallas version made with pecans and a Louisiana improvisation that uses hot pepper and scallions! A small but vocal splinter group of East Coast cooks always adds a couple of tablespoons of seltzer to the recipe, to keep the dumplings fluffy. And some folks even sneak a little vodka into the batter, perhaps to give extra levity to their Passover festivities.

Saimin

SERVES 4

AT FIRST GLANCE, saimin may look more Japanese than American, but in the definitively American cultural mix of Hawaii, this noodle soup is daily fare.

1 lb. fresh saimin, somen, or other fine white-flour noodles (see Note)

4 cups dashi (recipe follows)

1 bunch spinach, washed thoroughly and chopped

4 oz. kamaboko (Japanese fish cake), thinly sliced

8 oz. char sui (Chinese roasted pork), thinly sliced

6 scallions, trimmed and chopped

Soy sauce

DASHI:

1 oz. wide-cut konbu (dried kelp)

4 cups dried bonito flakes

1. Bring a large pot of water to a boil over high heat. Add noodles and cook until tender but firm, about 3 minutes. Drain noodles and divide evenly between 4 large, deep soup bowls.

2. While noodles cook, heat dashi over medium heat until just simmering but not boiling. Evenly divide spinach between the bowls of noodles, then ladle about 1 cup dashi into each bowl. Garnish soup with slices of fish cake and pork. Scatter scallions on top, dividing these ingredients evenly between the bowls. Serve with soy sauce.

NOTE: *Buying Japanese Ingredients*— Saimin, somen, and other Japanese noodles, as well as kamaboko, konbu, and instant dashi (an acceptable substitute for homemade), are widely available in Asian markets. Char sui may be found in Asian markets and in Chinese restaurants.

DASHI: Wipe any dirt off konbu, then place in a medium saucepan with 6 cups cold water. Bring to a simmer over medium heat, then reduce heat to low and cook—never allowing stock to return to a simmer—until konbu is soft, about 2 minutes. Remove and discard konbu, then increase heat to high to bring stock to a full boil. Add ¼ cup cold water to lower temperature of stock, then add bonito flakes. Do not stir. Return to a boil, then immediately remove pot from heat. (If bonito flakes boil more than a few seconds, stock will be too strong.) Allow bonito flakes to settle, skim foam, then carefully pour stock through a sieve lined with cheesecloth and discard remaining solids. Use stock immediately. Makes about 4 cups.

Pineapple Pizza It Ain't

L ong before mainland chefs started tossing lemongrass and soy sauce into everything and chattering about the "Pacific Rim", Hawaiians were enjoying true multicultural cuisine—much of it derived from the unpretentious home cooking of immigrants from China, Japan, Korea, the Philippines, Puerto Rico, and the Portuguese islands of Madeira and the Azores. Sam Choy (above) has cooked "local food"—as Hawaiians call their daily fare—all his life. He started as a kid, helping his Chinese father to stage Saturday luaus for as many as 800 people at a time. He grew up to become executive chef at one of Hawaii's many resort hotels, and then, in 1991, opened his own Sam Choy's Restaurant in Kona, on the big island of Hawaii. Choy is a large, generous man, spilling over with goodwill. You know instantly that at his table you can count on bounty, warmth, and flavor. At heart, he says, he simply loves to feed people—construction workers, fishermen, retired couples from the mainland, pretty young local girls—anyone who happens by to sample his bright saimin noodle soup and other specialties. "I just love to cook," says Choy. "I get in a kitchen, put my head down, and the next thing I know it's tomorrow."

A Moveable Soup

I n the early 1870s, seeking to sell millions of acres of vacant Kansas grassland it had acquired, the Santa Fe Railroad advertised good soil at bargain prices ($2 to $5 per acre). This sounded pretty good to the Mennonites, a European religious sect that had long struggled to find a place to work and worship in peace, traveling en masse from the Netherlands (their beliefs were derived from 16th-century Dutch Anabaptism) to Prussia and southern Russia. In 1874, groups of Mennonites began trickling into Kansas. Pioneers settled near the South Cottonwood River, establishing towns like Newton, Moundridge, and Goessell, 30 miles or so north of Wichita. They built huts, dug wells, and planted their crops—everything from potatoes to mulberry bushes to a hearty strain of winter wheat native to the shores of the Black Sea. This grain proved so well adapted to the soil and climate of its new home that it transformed the landscape of Kansas. Today, a sense of religious and cultural identity remains strong among Kansas Mennonite families. Youngsters stay on the family farm instead of heading off to grad school or to see the world. And the cooking gets passed down from generation to generation, inevitably evolving but remaining true to the spirit of the past.

Beef Borscht

SERVES 6–8

THE MENNONITES learned to make many types of borscht while in religious exile in Russia in the late 18th and early 19th centuries. Over time, after they reached the United States, they tailored the recipes. This version is hearty with beef and cabbage—but has no beets at all.

3 tbsp. butter
1 lb. beef chuck, cut into 1" pieces
2 medium yellow onions, peeled and chopped
1 small green cabbage, shredded
8 cups beef stock (recipe follows)
1 28-oz. can whole tomatoes with juice
2 tbsp. finely chopped fresh dill
1¼ lbs. red bliss potatoes, peeled and diced
Salt and freshly ground black pepper

BEEF STOCK:
8 lbs. beef bones, cracked
3 carrots, peeled and chopped
3 medium yellow onions, peeled and chopped
3 stalks celery, chopped
2 tbsp. tomato paste
2 cups red or white wine (optional)
2 plum tomatoes, chopped
2 cloves garlic, crushed and peeled
2 bay leaves
10 black peppercorns
3 sprigs fresh parsley
Salt

1. Heat 1 tbsp. butter in a large pot over high heat. Add beef and brown for about 1 minute. Transfer beef to a bowl and set aside. Reduce heat to medium, add 1 tbsp. butter and the onions and cook, stirring often, until onions start to soften, about 10 minutes.

2. Add remaining 1 tbsp. butter and the cabbage and cook, stirring occasionally, until cabbage begins to wilt, about 10 minutes. Add stock and bring to a simmer over medium-high heat. Lower heat to medium-low, return beef to pot, and add tomatoes with juice and dill. Cover and simmer for 1½ hours.

3. Add potatoes and continue cooking until tender, about 30 minutes. Season to taste with salt and pepper and serve.

BEEF STOCK: Preheat oven to 400°. Put beef bones in a large roasting pan. Roast bones until brown, about 1 hour, then add carrots, onions, celery, and tomato paste. Mix well and continue roasting until vegetables are well browned, about 40 minutes. Place roasting pan on top of stove and transfer bones and vegetables to a large stockpot. Heat roasting pan over medium-high heat, add 2 cups wine or water, then scrape up browned bits from bottom of pan. Simmer for about 1 minute, then add deglazing liquid to stockpot. Add tomatoes, garlic, bay leaves, peppercorns, parsley, and 4 quarts water. Simmer over medium-low heat, skimming occasionally, for 3 hours. Remove from heat then strain stock and discard solids. Season to taste with salt. If not using immediately, refrigerate or freeze. Makes 12 cups (3 quarts).

2

SALADS

"THE SALINAS VALLEY in north-central California, renowned for its agricultural vigor, produces hundreds of thousands of pounds of greens each year—including one with a distinctive red hue: radicchio, the

Italian chicory whose marbleized bur-gundy-and-white leaves now appear on smart tables all over America. Recently, in a Salinas Valley field, I picked up a head of it. In my hand, it looked like a brilliant, precious jewel. In a way, I thought, it is."

—PEGGY KNICKERBOCKER ON RADICCHIO (*SEE RECIPE ON PAGE 51*)

RECIPES

Iceberg Wedge with Blue Cheese Dressing

SERVES 2–4

THIS IS ONE OF iceberg-lover Marion Cunningham's favorite ways to serve this unfairly scorned lettuce. Another is with a classic Thousand Island dressing, an American variation on Russian dressing—perhaps named for the archipelago of pickles, eggs, and greens it contains.

FOR SALAD:
1 head iceberg lettuce

FOR DRESSING:
½ cup sour cream
½ cup mayonnaise
2 scallions, minced
2–3 tbsp. lemon juice
½ cup blue cheese, crumbled
Freshly ground black
* pepper*

1. For salad, remove core from an iceberg lettuce by banging core end of lettuce sharply on a counter. Then grab core, twist, and pull. It will separate cleanly. Plunge cored head of iceberg forcefully into a sinkful of cold water. Drain, wrap in a towel, and refrigerate overnight.

2. For dressing, combine sour cream, mayonnaise, scallions, and lemon juice in a bowl and mix well. Stir in cheese, cover with plastic wrap, then refrigerate for at least 4 hours.

3. To serve, cut lettuce into 4 large wedges, spoon dressing over it, and season generously with pepper.

VARIATION: *Thousand Island Dressing*—Mix together 1 cup mayonnaise, ½ cup ketchup, 1 chopped hard-cooked egg, 2 tbsp. pickle relish, 1 tbsp. minced scallion, and 1 tbsp. minced fresh parsley in a small bowl. Season to taste with salt and pepper. Use immediately or refrigerate. Makes about 1½ cups.

Iceberg Lovers, Unite!

There is no handsomer or more solid Cabbage Lettuce in cultivation," claimed a W. Atlee Burpee & Co. seed catalogue from 1894. They're talking about iceberg, cursed iceberg, the butt of jokes, the bane of all true "gourmets". "Hah!" responds cookbook writer Marion Cunningham (below) when she hears iceberg ridiculed. "Iceberg would smile if it could—for the truth is that, round and crisp, it is a perfect creation. It is sturdy but has a surprisingly delicate flavor. Unlike some of the frail field lettuces that wilt, swoon, and have the vapors readily, iceberg is stalwart. It's a close friend of every sandwich of note—hamburger, peanut butter, cheese, club, tuna, deviled egg, and more. And it's very cosmopolitan. It figures in the popular Chinese preparation of minced squab in lettuce leaves, and in petits pois à la française, among other imports. It is equally at home on the aristocratic or the peasant table." Iceberg is more than a century old. Burpee discovered it on its Fordhook Farm in Doylestown, Pennsylvania. When it was tasted, it was unusually crisp and "sweet" (in the sense of mild). Today there are countless varieties of iceberg. The California Iceberg Lettuce Commission says that iceberg is more correctly called "crisp-head" lettuce, incidentally. That's why Cunningham's informal association of iceberg lovers is called the Head-Lettuce Club. "We are now 17 members strong," she reports. "That doesn't count my dog, Rover, who positively loves the stuff—especially when dunked in meat drippings. He wouldn't touch arugula with a ten-foot pole."

The Vitamin Vegetable

S pinach was first cultivated in Persia, for the enjoyment of cats. Really. Later, it moved to China, India, and Nepal; the Moors brought it to Spain, and it spread across the rest of Europe from there. The French gave dishes made with spinach the fancy moniker florentine in honor of Catherine de Médicis, who was said to have eaten the green at every meal. By the 17th century, there were at least ten varieties of spinach grown in Europe. It made the journey to the New World, either with Columbus or on the *Mayflower*. Our appreciation of it in this country is un-Medician, to say the least. The image of spinach seems to have been forever tarnished by Carl Rose's oft-quoted 1928 *New Yorker* cartoon (small child at dinner table to mother: "I say it's spinach, and I say to hell with it"). Its reputation as "the broom of the stomach" and "the vitamin vegetable" probably hasn't helped, either. How can anybody seriously enjoy a vegetable that's so obviously good for you? No wonder Americans don't eat more than about half a pound of spinach a year per person.

Spinach Salad

THREE KINDS OF SPINACH are commonly sold in this country: crinkly savoy, the commonest strain; flat leaf, preferred for salads; and semi-savoy, a cross between the two. No matter which kind you use, make sure to wash it very well. Nothing ruins spinach more than residual grit.

2 lbs. fresh spinach
6 slices bacon
1 tbsp. brown sugar
Red wine vinegar
4 large mushrooms, sliced
2 hard-cooked eggs, diced
Freshly ground black
   pepper

1. Trim spinach of thick stems and wilted or yellowed leaves and wash thoroughly (see Note). Pat dry with paper towels or dry in a salad spinner.

2. Fry bacon in a heavy skillet over medium heat until golden brown and crisp, about 15 minutes. Remove bacon from skillet and drain on paper towels.

3. To make the dressing, strain bacon fat through a sieve, wipe out skillet with a paper towel, and return fat to skillet. Add brown sugar to fat, stir over low heat until dissolved, then add red wine vinegar to taste, up to 1 tbsp.

4. Put spinach, mushrooms, and eggs in a salad bowl. Crumble bacon on top and then pour warm dressing over the salad. (Dressing should be not quite hot enough to wilt spinach.) Toss a few times to evenly coat spinach leaves. Season to taste with freshly ground black pepper.

NOTE: *Washing Spinach*—Spinach may look clean, but it must be thoroughly washed to remove ever-present grit. After trimming, plunge spinach into a large bowl or sinkful of cold water, swish it around (grit will sink to the bottom), then lift it out and put it in a colander. Rinse bowl or sink and repeat process with fresh water several times until no grit remains and spinach is truly clean.

Radicchio Slaw

SERVES 4

CALIFORNIA RADICCHIO grower Lucio Gomiero (facing page, right) likes his head radicchio sliced into a slaw with fennel. He sometimes marinates treviso in olive oil for up to two weeks, then serves it as a salad with grated hard-cooked eggs. We like it both ways.

2 large heads radicchio, cored and thinly sliced
1 bulb fennel, thinly sliced, with tops reserved for garnish
2 scallions, minced
2 tbsp. extra-virgin olive oil
¼ cup mayonnaise
Juice of half a lemon
Salt and freshly ground black pepper

1. Toss radicchio, fennel, and scallions together in a large bowl until well mixed. Cover with plastic wrap and refrigerate until ready to dress.

2. Whisk oil into mayonnaise in a small bowl, then add lemon juice and salt and pepper to taste.

3. To keep slaw from getting soggy, dress salad just before serving—pour dressing over slaw and toss to mix well. Adjust seasoning to taste and garnish with fennel tops.

VARIATION: *Marinated Radicchio*— Combine 1 cup white wine vinegar, 3 cups water, 5 black peppercorns, ½ tsp. salt, and 1 bay leaf in a large pot and bring to a boil over medium heat. Cut 6 heads of treviso radicchio lengthwise into quarters. Blanch wedges, a few at a time, for 1–2 minutes. Blot dry with a towel, squeezing gently to remove as much moisture as possible. Arrange wedges in layers in a glass or ceramic dish. Add about ½ cup extra-virgin olive oil, then cover with plastic wrap and refrigerate overnight, or for up to 2 weeks. Before serving, bring to room temperature, season with salt and pepper, and garnish with 2 finely grated hard-cooked eggs. Serves 4.

Chicory Chic

In Italy, the first appearance of radicchio each fall is cause for celebration—and the winter's harvest is considered even better. In America, radicchio is grown and enjoyed year-round because the climate in California's coastal valleys is consistently mild. Some connoisseurs claim that California radicchio is better than its Italian forebear, because it's less bitter. "California is like heaven for radicchio," says Lucio Gomiero, co-owner of European Vegetable Specialties, one of the state's largest radicchio growers. One year, he boasts, "We even sent some to Italy when they ran short." Radicchio as we know it was developed in the late 1860s, from various chicory varieties in northern Italy's Veneto region, by Francesco Van Den Borre, a Belgian garden consultant. The two most common radicchio varieties today are rosa di chioggia, with its tight, red-and-white cabbage-shaped head, and radicchio di treviso, with a vertical shape, like a Belgian endive. Both are named for towns in the Veneto.

Playing the Market

L iving in Santa Monica, California, in the late 1980s and early '90s, SAVEUR editor Colman Andrews was a regular at the weekly farmers' markets set up around the city. "There was always so much great stuff," he recalls, "that I'd buy whatever looked wonderful and worry about what I was going to do with it later. Sometimes I'd just cook what needed cooking, chop the rest, and then toss it all together in the salad bowl. That's how this salad was born."

Cooked and Raw Vegetable Salad

SERVES 6–8

USE THE INGREDIENT LIST here as a guide, but buy whichever fresh vegetables look best at the market. Add shredded prosciutto and grated cheese if you wish.

⅓ cup extra-virgin olive oil
½ cup pine nuts
6 large shallots, peeled and thinly sliced
1 yellow bell pepper
2 lbs. fresh peas, shelled, to yield 2 cups
½ lb. green beans, trimmed and cut into 1"–2" pieces
1 bunch watercress, washed and chopped
3 bunches mâche, washed and trimmed (or 1 head baby bibb lettuce, washed and torn into pieces)
Leaves from 1 bunch celery
3 small stalks celery, sliced paper-thin
1 fennel bulb, trimmed and finely chopped
1 cup coarsely chopped fresh basil leaves
1 cup coarsely chopped fresh parsley
4 scallions, white parts only, finely chopped
Juice of 1 lemon
Salt and freshly ground black pepper

1. Heat 1 tbsp. oil in a small skillet over medium heat. Add pine nuts and cook, stirring constantly, until brown, about 2 minutes. Drain on paper towels and set aside.

2. Return skillet to heat and, if necessary, add more oil. Add shallots and cook, stirring occasionally, until golden, about 15 minutes. Drain on paper towels. Set aside.

3. Meanwhile, char bell pepper over a flame or under a broiler, turning to blacken all over. Place in a paper bag, close tightly, and steam for 15 minutes. Rub off and remove skin, cut in half, discard core and seeds, and dice. Set aside.

4. Bring a medium pot of salted water to a boil. Add peas and beans, reduce heat to medium-low, and cook briefly so that both peas and beans retain a little crunch, about 4 minutes. Drain in colander and stop the cooking process by running under cold water. Pat dry.

5. Combine pine nuts, shallots, bell pepper, peas, beans, watercress, mâche, celery leaves, celery, fennel, basil, parsley, and scallions in a salad bowl. Mix together lemon juice and remaining 3–4 tbsp. oil in a small mixing bowl and drizzle over salad. Toss well and season to taste with salt and pepper.

A B
C D

Parsley Salad

SERVES 6

IN ITALY, PARSLEY is so ubiquitous in food that people who keep turning up everywhere are said to be "like parsley, found in every sauce". In America, it's usually relegated to mere garnish status. That seems a pity, especially when you taste it in this bright salad, inspired by one served at Gustaf Anders in Santa Ana, California.

FOR SALAD:
4 cups packed curly
  parsley leaves
4 oz. parmigiano-
  reggiano, coarsely grated
1½ cups oil-packed
  sun-dried tomatoes,
  julienned
1 clove garlic, peeled and
  minced

FOR DRESSING:
½ cup packed basil leaves
¾ cup extra-virgin
  olive oil
¼ cup rice wine vinegar
Salt and freshly ground
  black pepper
1 shallot, peeled and
  minced
1 clove garlic, peeled and
  minced

1. For salad, carefully wash parsley leaves to remove any dirt, then dry well, either in a salad spinner or by placing the leaves in a clean, thin dish towel and wringing out moisture. Put parsley in a salad bowl, add 3 oz. parmigiano-reggiano, and toss well. Add sun-dried tomatoes and garlic and toss again, until salad is well mixed.

2. For dressing, wash basil leaves to remove any dirt or grit, then dry well and put in the bowl of a food processor. Add oil and vinegar and season to taste with salt and pepper. Process until smooth.

3. Stir shallots and garlic into dressing. Drizzle dressing over salad and toss until greens are evenly coated. Adjust seasonings to taste, then divide between 6 salad plates. Garnish with remaining 1 oz. parmigiano-reggiano.

Parsley, Top to Toe

Fresh parsley is so readily available and easy to store and use, we can't imagine why anyone buys the dried, flavorless spice-rack kind. Here's a fresh-parsley primer:

FLAT VS. CURLY: (A) Flat-leaf, or Italian, parsley has a strong, fresh, "green" flavor that's generally preferred in cooking. Where texture is important, as in salads, curly parsley shines.

SAVE AND CHOP: (B) Wash and dry parsley thoroughly, then refrigerate, wrapped in damp paper towels inside a plastic bag, for up to a week. When chopping, add a pinch of salt to keep it from sticking to knife and cutting board.

FRIED PARSLEY: (C) A superb, surprising side dish. Mix flour with just enough white wine to make a thin batter. Coat parsley sprigs and fry in hot oil until crisp and golden (less than a minute).

THE ROOTS: (D) Tasting a bit like celeriac (and more delicate than parsnips), parsley root flavors winter soups and stews, and is delicious cooked and puréed—and sliced raw into salads.

Jersey Tomatoes

I f you mention tomatoes to some East Coast connoisseurs, they'll sigh, "Ah, *Jersey* tomatoes." Others maintain that they're not what they used to be. What's the story? Tomatoes, in fact, are no longer the big business they once were in New Jersey, but they can still taste unusually intense and tomatoey—and growers have recently organized to try to protect their precious pomodoro's reputation. Why should these tomatoes be different from any other state's? Some say it's New Jersey's long growing season and the magical mix of sun and rain—conditions said to mimic those of Peru and Ecuador, where the tomato originated—that produce such superior fruit.

Stuffed Tomatoes

SERVES 4–6

TOMATOES CAN BE STUFFED with any kind of rice, but we prefer risotto rice, like Italy's arborio, for rice salads. Other rices turn grainy when refrigerated, but arborio stands up to the cold and keeps its creamy texture.

---

6 ripe tomatoes
Coarse salt
2 cups cooked fresh or
    frozen baby lima beans
1 cup cooked rice
1 cup shredded arugula
¼ cup chopped fresh
    parsley
¼ cup chopped fresh chives
6 tbsp. extra-virgin
    olive oil
2–3 tbsp. lemon juice
Freshly ground black
    pepper

1. Blanch tomatoes in a large pot of boiling water for 30 seconds. Slip off skins and cut off the top quarter of each tomato on the stem end, reserving tops. Carefully scoop out and reserve seeds and flesh. Lightly salt tomatoes inside and out. Turn upside down and allow to drain.

2. Combine reserved tomato seeds and flesh, lima beans, rice, arugula, parsley, and chives in a medium bowl. Drizzle 4 tbsp. olive oil and 2 tbsp. lemon juice into the lima mixture, add a few grinds of pepper, and mix lightly. Adjust seasoning to taste with lemon juice, salt, and pepper.

3. Fill tomato shells with lima bean mixture. Place tomatoes on a platter, replace tops, and scatter any leftover beans around them. Drizzle with remaining olive oil.

Halibut Salad

SERVES 4

A FORMER CHEF at the Glacier Bay Country Inn in Gustavus, Alaska, created this salad to use up leftover halibut. The same recipe also works well, we've found, with leftover salmon—and it makes a great sandwich: On crusty white bread, it's tuna salad gone to heaven.

Extra-virgin olive oil
1 1-lb. halibut steak, about ¾" thick
½ cup mayonnaise
2 stalks celery, finely chopped
3 scallions (white parts only), chopped
3 sprigs fresh dill, chopped
Salt and freshly ground black pepper

1. Lightly coat a medium skillet with oil and heat over medium-high heat. Sear halibut steak until browned, 3–5 minutes per side. Allow halibut to cool, then flake into large pieces and set aside.

2. Mix together mayonnaise, celery, scallions, and dill in a medium bowl and season to taste with salt and pepper. Fold in flaked fish and adjust seasonings. Use as a sandwich filling or serve as a salad.

VARIATION: *Steamed Halibut*—Add 2 bay leaves, 5 black peppercorns, half a lemon thinly sliced, and 1 cup dry white wine to a large pot. Fit pot with a rack and add enough water to come just below the rack. Bring to a boil over medium heat, place halibut on rack, cover, and steam until fish is opaque, about 15 minutes. Allow to cool, then flake into large pieces. Use in place of seared halibut.

Smoked in Sitka

At the Salmon River Smokehouse, in Gustavus (above), owner Aimée Youmans—who graduated from UC Berkeley and lived in Australia before settling here—smokes line-caught fish, including halibut and salmon, over fragrant Sitka black alder wood. Her result is excellent, with vivid fish flavor showing through a sweet veil of smoke. Though our Alaskan halibut salad is made with fresh, not smoked, fish, we always associate it with her—because we had it for lunch at the Glacier Bay Country Inn right after we met her—while we still had the scent of alder wood lingering in our nostrils.

Delicious Simplicity

James Beard was the father of modern American food culture—a great teacher and writer and an excellent cook. He was one of our first (and remained one of our most eloquent) champions of good, fresh ingredients, properly and simply prepared. Beard came to food through the stage door: Oregon-born, he found himself in New York as a failed actor and opera singer, and turned to catering as a way to make do. The hors d'oeuvres he served led to an offer from a publisher, and in 1940, his first book, *Hors d'Oeuvres and Canapés*, appeared. Beard's 1946 cooking show, *I Love to Eat!*, made him the first successful television chef. In his *Fireside Cook Book* (1949), he first made the quintessentially Beardian point that food was both a necessity and an art—a civilizing power. *The James Beard Cookbook* (1959) was unpretentious without being lowbrow. It preached flavorful food prepared with local, seasonal ingredients to a postwar America reveling in the scientific "advances" of frozen and premade foods.

Beard wrote 22 books in all, founded a cooking school, and influenced countless chefs and writers. He died in 1985, but a foundation in his name (and in his old town house on West 12th Street in Manhattan) lives on, as does his influence. James Beard was an arbiter not just of food but of culture in the larger sense.

Lobster and Celery Root Salad

SERVES 4

JAMES BEARD once noted that "Seafood is a natural for the composed salad." Though he grew up in Oregon eating dungeness crab, he became very fond of lobster and offered many recipes for it in his books. We adapted this one from *James Beard's Shellfish* (Thames and Hudson, 1997).

FOR DRESSING:
1½ cups mayonnaise
1 hard-cooked egg, finely chopped
2 tbsp. finely chopped capers
1 tbsp. finely chopped fresh parsley
Lemon juice
Salt and freshly ground black pepper

FOR SALAD:
2 cups cooked lobster, chopped (see page 118)
1 cup julienned peeled celery root
Salt and freshly ground black pepper
4 cups mixed greens (such as butter lettuce, arugula, and endive)
2–4 hard-cooked eggs, quartered

1. For dressing, combine mayonnaise, chopped egg, capers, and parsley in a small bowl. Mix well, then season to taste with lemon juice, salt, and pepper.

2. For salad, combine lobster and celery root in a medium bowl. Add enough of the dressing to thoroughly coat ingredients, then mix gently. Season to taste with salt and pepper.

3. Divide greens between 4 plates, top with lobster mixture, garnish with quartered eggs, and serve with extra dressing on the side.

Warm Chanterelle and Pancetta Salad

SERVES 4

IN CALIFORNIA'S Napa Valley wine country, Chris Willis and Jill Harrison make their Olio D'Oro—oil blended from California-grown Spanish, Italian, and French olives—the ancient way: with a granite crusher imported from Tuscany. Then they use it for salads like this.

¼ lb. pancetta, diced
2 shallots, peeled and minced
½ lb. chanterelles, trimmed and quartered
¼ cup pine nuts
7 tbsp. extra-virgin olive oil
1 tbsp. fresh lemon juice
2 tbsp. red wine vinegar
4 large handfuls of mixed greens (such as frisée, arugula, or red oak or bibb lettuce)
Freshly ground black pepper

1. Cook pancetta in a medium sauté pan over low heat until crisp, about 20 minutes. Drain on paper towels, then transfer to a large bowl. Pour off fat from pan (a thin film will remain). Increase heat to medium, add shallots to pan, and cook until tender, about 15 minutes.

2. Increase heat to high; add chanterelles and pine nuts and sauté until both are lightly browned, about 5 minutes. Transfer mixture to bowl with pancetta.

3. In the same pan, warm oil over medium heat, then whisk in lemon juice and vinegar and heat through, scraping up the flavorful browned bits from the bottom of the pan.

4. Add mixed greens to bowl with pancetta, chanterelles, and shallots. Add the warm vinaigrette and toss salad well. Divide between 4 plates and season to taste with pepper.

NOTE: *Storing Olive Oil*—Olive oil can easily turn rancid, so store it away from light and heat. (Don't keep it near the stove or by a window.) On the other hand, oil will turn cloudy and can spoil if kept in the refrigerator. Our best advice: Buy olive oil in small amounts and use it up quickly.

Olive Oil Renaissance

F orget California wine. These days, the talk of the valleys—Napa, Sonoma, Central—is olive oil, an old condiment with a new cachet. Olives and their oil were products of California long before it was even a state. In the 1700s, Franciscan missionaries from Mexico planted Spanish olives with as much fervor as they converted the locals. More recently, a fresh crop of growers has been planting again, but with more modest ambitions. They're certainly more secular and have a more international outlook about the olives they use. Of the numerous varieties grown in California, the three most popular are still Spanish: manzanillo, which produces oil with a sweet, intense flavor; sevillano, whose oil is strong, with a hint of artichoke; and mission, which makes a mild fruity oil with a slight peppery aftertaste. Two French varieties now growing in small quantities—picholine and lucques—produce alternately sweet, mild oils or peppery, tart ones. And at least four prominent Italian varieties are now being introduced (or reintroduced) to California—pendolino, frantoio, leccino, and maurino. Growers hope that oils made from these may one day rival the best of Tuscany. Meanwhile, it's still a boutique business: California produces only .01 percent of the world's olive oil.

Appalachian Swiss

S o much of life in Helvetia, West Virginia, revolves around food: Its cultivation and preparation draw family and friends together—and it is a way in which people who don't have much can give to each other, reports writer Sally Schneider. Food in Helvetia is generally simple fare—southern farm cooking with a strong Swiss accent, a reminder of the region's original settlers. From the South come corn bread and ham, greens, and flaky lard-crust pies. From Switzerland come the sweet-and-sour flavors of sauerbraten and sauerkraut, onion pies, dumplings, and spice cookies. Helvetia was settled by Swiss immigrants, fleeing crop failures in their native country, in 1869. They called their settlement, nestled in a lush valley near West Virginia's eastern panhandle, Helvetia—the ancient Latin name for Switzerland. Today there seems to be a great cook in every Helvetian house—Margaret Koerner, her white hair in neat braids, frying doughnuts, barefoot in her spotless kitchen; Bernadine Wooten, round and comforting in a flowered dress, plying a guest with raspberry cobbler still warm in an iron skillet. Even perfect strangers are likely to be offered food as a kind of "hello".

Irene's Sweet-and-Sour Pickles

MAKES 1 QUART

IRENE HARTFORD of Helvetia, West Virginia, proudly tells visitors that she's "made a study of pickles". She knows all about salting, balance, texture, preserving, and more. One tip that's easy to share: Use cucumbers on the small side—no bigger than three inches long.

8 *small cucumbers, washed*
Salt
1 clove garlic, peeled
1 sprig fresh dill
1 clove
1 bay leaf
3 black peppercorns
1–2 cups white vinegar
1–2 cups sugar

1. Halve cucumbers (quarter them lengthwise if they're large), then place them in a basin or large bowl and cover with a brine of 3 tbsp. salt for every 2 cups of water. Set aside for 18–24 hours.

2. Pour off brine. Arrange cucumbers, cut side out, in a dry 1-quart sterilized jar (see Note), leaving about 1" space at the top. Put garlic, dill, clove, bay leaf, and peppercorns in jar. Heat equal parts vinegar and sugar in a saucepan until sugar is completely dissolved. Pour over pickles, filling jar to within 1" of lip. Wipe rim of jar clean, place lid on jar, and screw on band until just tight.

3. Store refrigerated—or process immediately in a hot-water bath for 5 minutes (see Note), then store in a cool, dark place. The pickles will be ready to eat in about 10 days and will last 6 months. Even if you process the pickles in a hot-water bath, be sure to refrigerate after opening.

NOTE: *Sterilization and Hot-Water Bath*—To sterilize empty jars, submerge them, flat metal lids, and bands in boiling water until ready to use. (If filling more than 1 jar, remove and fill 1 at a time, leaving others in water.) For hot-water bath, place filled, sealed jars on a wire rack in the bottom of a tall 8-quart stockpot. Fill pot with hot water to cover jars by 2". Bring water to a boil and process in boiling water for the time the recipe specifies (sweet-and-sour pickles require 5 minutes of boiling). Using canning tongs, remove jar from pot and set aside to cool.

PASTA, RICE, AND BEANS

"IF THEY WANTED TO, Italians could

live a lifetime in San Francisco's North

Beach without ever speaking a word of

English. Here, they could do virtually

everything they would have done back home — paint, sing opera, play bocce, fish, buy and cook familiar vegetables, eat real pasta, even make wine: The very gutters of the neighborhood at harvesttime once ran with spillover from garage wineries."

—PEGGY KNICKERBOCKER ON PASTA (*SEE RECIPE ON PAGE 70*)

RECIPES

GNOCCHI WITH PESTO, page 70; PASTA WITH CLAMS AND BASIL, page 73; MACARONI AND CHEESE, page 74;

LINA'S TORTELLI, page 77; "CHOW MEIN", page 78; POLENTA PIE WITH GORGONZOLA, page 81; PERFECT

WILD RICE, page 82; MISS DAISY'S RED RICE, page 85; WHITE BEANS WITH LINGUIÇA SAUSAGE, page 86;

DOWN-EAST BAKED BEANS, page 89

Genoese Green

Most Italian-American communities were founded by immigrants from the south of Italy, and especially from Sicily and Naples. The original Italian population of San Francisco's lively North Beach, on the other hand, came largely from the northwestern Italian regions of Piedmont and Liguria—and particularly from the great Ligurian port city of Genoa. The most famous Genoese gift to gastronomy is the basil-and-garlic sauce called pesto (it has even been suggested, only partially in jest, that a basil leaf should appear on Genoa's city flag). Thus it is hardly surprising that pesto has long been a favorite North Beach sauce. Though blenders and food processors are now widely employed for making pesto in both Liguria and North Beach, some traditionalists (in both places) still prefer the time-honored mortar-and-pestle method. The most efficient pestles have a roughened surface on the business end. Using the same ingredients and proportions listed in the recipe at right, crush pine nuts, salt, and garlic to a paste, using firm, steady pounding and grinding motions, then gradually work in first the basil, then the cheese. Finally, drizzle in the oil and continue mortar-and-pestling until it's well incorporated. Liliano Salvetti, right, who's cooked in North Beach for more than 35 years, adds cream to take the edge off his pesto—but in Genoa, this would be considered heretical.

Gnocchi with Pesto

SERVES 4

NOT MUCH WHEAT grows on Italy's Ligurian coast, so local cooks make a pasta called gnocchi (or trofie) from potatoes bound with, well, not much wheat. North Beach Italians love gnocchi, too, sometimes saucing it with meat or tomato sauce—but more often with Genoese pesto.

4 russet potatoes
⅔ cup flour
Salt
¼ cup heavy cream

PESTO:
2 tbsp. pine nuts
Salt
2 cloves garlic, peeled
2 cups packed basil leaves
½ cup extra-virgin
* olive oil*
2 tbsp. freshly grated
* parmigiano-reggiano*
Freshly ground black
* pepper*

1. Preheat oven to 350°. Pierce potatoes with a fork, then bake until soft, about 40 minutes. Peel potatoes while they are still hot (but cool enough to handle) and mash finely.

2. To make gnocchi, combine mashed potatoes, flour, and 1 tsp. salt in a large bowl. Knead until ingredients are thoroughly mixed and dough holds together. Roll small amounts into 1" × 6" ropes, then cut ropes into ½" pieces. Use a fork to make indentations on top of each piece, then pinch gnocchi between your fingers to plump them up.

3. Make the pesto.

4. Bring a large pot of salted water to a boil. Add gnocchi to the pot carefully, so that they don't stick together. Cook until gnocchi begin rising to the top, 2–3 minutes. Remove cooked gnocchi from pot with slotted spoon and drain on a plate lined with several thicknesses of paper towel.

5. Meanwhile, warm the pesto in a large pan over medium heat. Just before serving, add cream, then gnocchi and stir gently.

PESTO: Pulse pine nuts and ½ tsp. salt together in a food processor until finely ground. Add garlic and basil and, with the motor running, drizzle in olive oil. Just before serving, transfer pesto to a large pan and stir in parmigiano-reggiano. Season to taste with salt and pepper. Makes 1 generous cup.

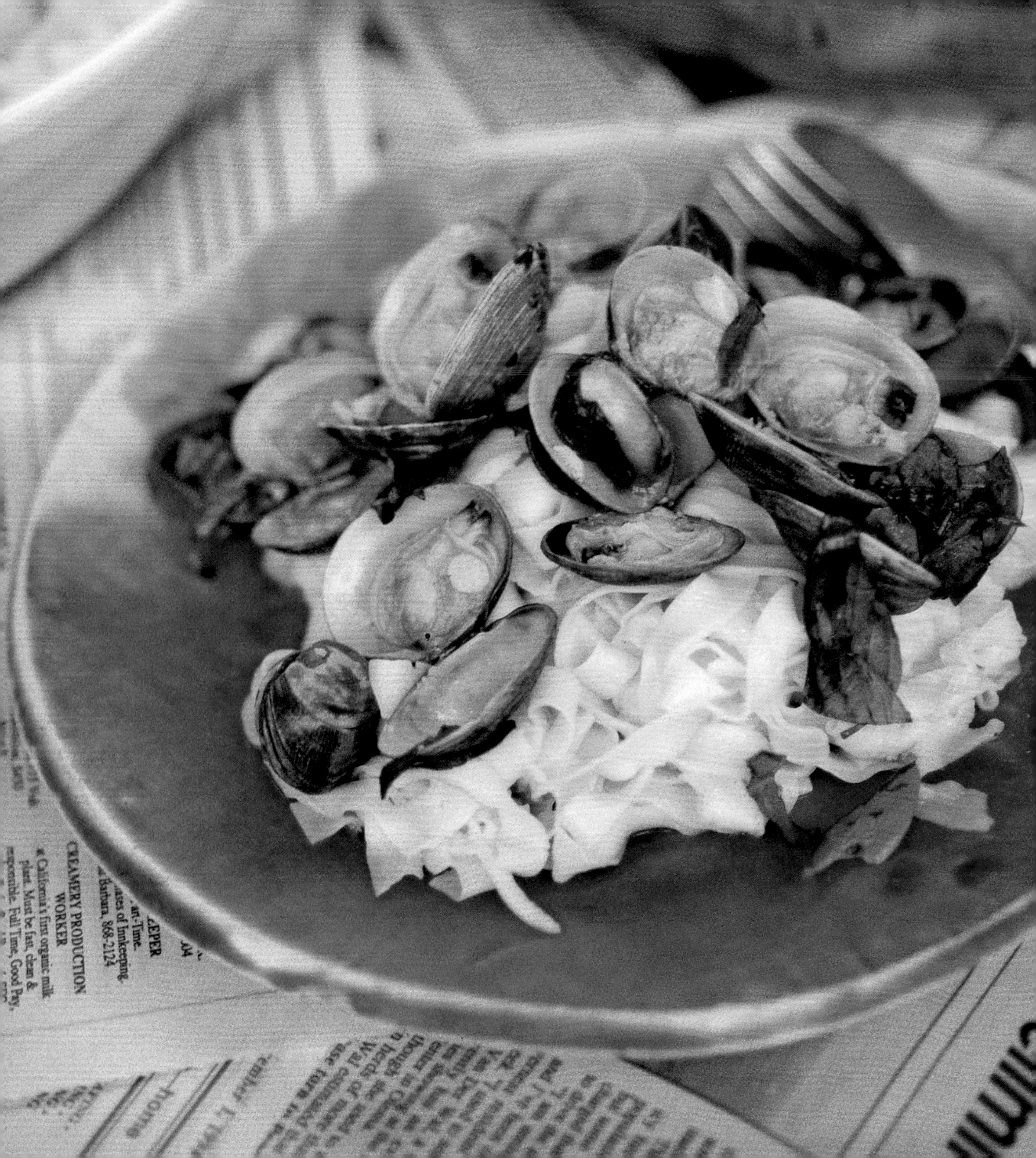

Pasta with Clams and Basil

SERVES 4

THE HOG ISLAND Oyster Company gave us this simple, savory Californian (as opposed to Italian or Italian-American) pasta recipe. Small, sweet manila clams are best, but the more commonly available littlenecks—choose the smallest you can find—are a good substitute.

⅓ cup extra-virgin olive oil
8 cloves garlic, peeled and minced
½ cup dry white wine
4 dozen manila or littleneck clams, well scrubbed (see Note)
1 lb. fettuccine
Salt
½ cup coarsely chopped flat-leaf parsley leaves
½ cup coarsely chopped basil leaves
Freshly ground black pepper

1. Heat oil in a large, heavy skillet (one with a tight-fitting lid) over medium heat. Add garlic and cook until fragrant but not brown, about 1 minute.

2. Add wine and clams, tightly cover skillet, and cook until clams open, 5–8 minutes. Shake skillet occasionally and uncover, removing clams as they open and setting them aside in a bowl. (Discard any clams that are chipped or that fail to open.)

3. Meanwhile, cook fettuccine in a large pot of boiling salted water over high heat until tender but firm, about 7 minutes. Drain pasta in a colander.

4. Transfer pasta to a large serving bowl, add parsley and basil leaves, and season to taste with salt and pepper. Add clams and toss together mixing well. Before serving, arrange some of the clams on top.

NOTE: *Choosing Clams*—Manila clams, though not native to America's Pacific Coast, are now being raised there and are much in demand. Look for small ones (1" wide), best eaten raw or steamed. Pacific littleneck clams, the most common Pacific variety, are comparable to manilas but slightly tougher in texture. On the Atlantic Coast, the smallest quahogs (1¼"–2¼" wide) are also called littlenecks, though they're not the same thing as Pacific littlenecks. They are tender and sweet, best eaten raw or steamed.

Farming the Sea

Owned by marine biologists John Finger, Terry Sawyer, and Michael Watchorn, the Hog Island Oyster Company has been cultivating and harvesting shellfish in Tomales Bay, in California's Marin County (across the Golden Gate Bridge from San Francisco), since 1982. The tides at the mouth of the bay are rich in nutrients. "The daily tidal exchange allows our oysters to become sweet and plump, really filling their shells," says Finger. Top chefs all over California love Hog Island's tasty harvest, regularly ordering the company's acclaimed sweetwater (pacific), euroflat (belon), atlantic (eastern), and kumamoto oysters—and its excellent manila clams. Tilting his head upward towards the skies over Tomales Bay, Watchorn explains the appeal of the enterprise: "Look at where we work. We don't have to commute, we get to raise our families in this gorgeous area, and we're grateful to be able to contend with natural forces rather than the corporate alternative."

American Cheese

Cheesemaking was introduced to Wisconsin by Yankee farmers from New York, Vermont, New Hampshire, and Connecticut in the 1830s; the state's first cheese factory was a farmers' cooperative established in 1841 by one Anne Pickett. Many of the earliest Wisconsin cheeses were American versions of England's classic cheddar— but in 1874, Joseph Steinwand, in the town of Colby, invented a new cheese, milder and more porous than cheddar. (It became known simply as colby.) Brick cheese, another Wisconsin creation, dating from around 1875, was named not for its shape but because it was originally pressed with actual bricks. Though comparatively mild, brick is a variation on a pungent cheese called limburger; because of its mildness, in fact, it was sometimes known as "married man's limburger". Today, a number of master cheesemakers work in Wisconsin, some of them for very large companies, bringing so much skill to bear on the manufacture of cheese that the results can rival the European cheeses that originally inspired them. One example is fourth-generation cheesemaker Sid Cook (above), president of Carr Valley Cheese, with a wheel of his prized cheddar.

Macaroni and Cheese

SERVES 6

WE DON'T MUCH HOLD with uptown versions of this classic American "comfort food"—the ones made with fancy pasta and three kinds of goat cheese—but good cheddar, Wisconsin or otherwise, does make a difference.

8 tbsp. butter
6 tbsp. flour
½ tsp. cayenne
Salt and freshly ground white pepper
3¾ cups hot milk
4 cups grated cheddar cheese
1 lb. short macaroni, cooked
½ cup heavy cream
½ cup fresh bread crumbs

1. Preheat oven to 350°. Melt 6 tbsp. butter in a heavy saucepan over low heat. Add flour and cook, stirring constantly, for about 4 minutes (flour mixture must foam as it cooks, or sauce will have a raw-flour taste). Stir in cayenne and season to taste with salt and white pepper. Whisk in hot milk, ¼ cup at a time, and cook, whisking constantly, until sauce thickens. Reduce heat to low and stir in 2 cups of cheese. Cook, stirring, until cheese melts, about 2 minutes.

2. Combine cheese sauce and cooked macaroni in a large bowl and season with salt. Sprinkle ½ cup cheese over the bottom of a buttered 8" × 11" baking dish. Put one-third of the pasta in the dish, top with ½ cup cheese, then repeat, layering pasta and cheese, ending with cheese, making three layers in all.

3. Pour cream over assembled macaroni and cheese. Melt remaining 2 tbsp. butter in a skillet. Add bread crumbs and stir to coat well with melted butter, then sprinkle over macaroni and cheese. Bake until crust is golden, about 30 minutes. Allow to rest for 15 minutes before serving.

Artist and Teacher

Lina and Armando Ferrari have lived above the Park Cheese Company factory in Fond du Lac, Wisconsin (where Armando is cheesemaker), for more than thirty years. Armando likes living "over the store", he says, so that he can check his cheeses day or night—watching temperature, humidity, any of the subtle conditions that a master cheesemaker knows can affect his art. If you sample his provolone or his parmesan, you'll realize that his efforts pay off. Armando also takes great pleasure in passing on his expertise to younger, all-American factory employees. He's a born teacher, says Lina. "It's a gift he gives."

Lina's Tortelli

SERVES 4–6

LINA FERRARI still makes this pasta specialty of her native Piacenza, but now she uses the rich dairy products that are the bounty of her new homeland, in southeastern Wisconsin. Lina makes it look easy to fold her tortelli like pretty little candy wrappers. Her neighbors often have better luck with the more classic square ravioli shape.

FOR FILLING:
1 1-lb. acorn squash,
  quartered; seeds and pith
  removed
1 egg yolk
1¼ cups freshly grated
  parmesan
Pinch freshly grated
  nutmeg
Salt and freshly ground
  black pepper

FOR PASTA:
6 egg yolks
2 cups flour
3–4 tbsp. butter, melted
Freshly grated parmesan

1. For filling, cook squash in a pot of boiling water over high heat until soft, about 10 minutes. Drain and cool, then cut away and discard skin. Mash pulp in a large bowl. Stir in egg yolk and parmesan. Season with nutmeg and plenty of salt and pepper.

2. For pasta, mix egg yolks and 3 tbsp. water in a medium bowl. Put flour in a large bowl and mix in egg mixture, moistening with up to 3 tbsp. more water, until dough just holds together. Turn out onto a lightly floured surface and knead until smooth, about 10 minutes.

3. Divide dough into 2 balls. Use a pasta machine to roll each ball into a thin sheet, then cut sheets into long 2½" strips, then into diamond shapes using a template or a ruler. Cover with a clean dish towel as shapes are cut.

4. To fill tortelli, place several diamonds, sharp points facing towards you, on a lightly floured surface and spoon about ½ tsp. filling into center of each, then fold in wide corners so that edges meet (**A**). Next, starting at the top and continuing the entire length of the pasta, fold in outside edges, enclosing seam, and pinch to seal for a ruffled effect (**B**). Repeat process until all pasta diamonds are filled.

5. Add tortelli in batches to a large pot of boiling salted water over high heat and cook until they float, about 3 minutes. Drain, then serve topped with butter and parmesan (**C**).

Noodle Evolution

Although wheat was cultivated in China as early as 2000 B.C., noodles apparently weren't invented there until early in the Han Dynasty (206 B.C. to A.D. 220)—when the Chinese started milling wheat into flour on a large scale (a technique possibly imported from Persia) instead of laboriously pounding it. Han emperors were certainly known to consume them on occasion, but from the start, noodles were mostly considered a low-class foodstuff—while rice was a luxury that only the nobility could afford, and thus a symbol of wealth and good taste. Even today, traditionalists are apt to consider noodles to be snack food, not suitable for formal dining. Chinese-style noodles came to America in the mid–19th century, brought by immigrant laborers—some of whom went on to

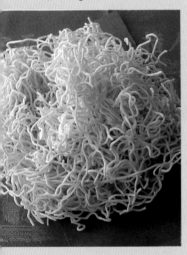

open the informal, homestyle restaurants that evolved into the Cantonese clichés many American diners grew up on. Chow mein, lo mein, and wontons (made with noodle dough) became staple dishes— even sold in cans, by companies whose connections with Chinese gastronomy were tenuous, to say the least. Today a wide range of traditional Chinese noodle varieties are available in Asian markets (as are the other ingredients to make chow mein) and in both regional Chinese restaurants and those devoted to "fusion" cooking.

"Chow Mein"

SERVES 4

THIS AMERICAN-CANTONESE specialty, ubiquitous in the kinds of Chinese restaurants most of us don't admit to frequenting anymore, has authentic Cantonese roots as a kind of fried noodle cake. This version of the real thing is called liang mian hwan, or "two sides brown", because it's crisp on the outside (and tender within).

---

4 dried shiitake
   mushrooms
½ lb. thin egg noodles
   (shi dan mian)
1 tbsp. Chinese rice wine
   (shaoxing)
3 tsp. cornstarch
½ tsp. salt
16 jumbo shrimp, shelled,
   deveined, and butterflied
½ cup vegetable oil
2 scallions, white parts
   only, julienned
6 thin slices peeled fresh
   ginger, julienned
¼ lb. Smithfield ham,
   julienned
1 lb. fresh spinach, washed
   and blanched
2 cups chicken stock
   (see page 26)
2 tbsp. light soy sauce
2 tsp. sesame oil
¼ tsp. sugar
Freshly ground black
   pepper

1. Soak shiitakes in a bowl of hot water until soft, about 20 minutes. Drain, squeeze out excess water, discard stems, and julienne caps.

2. Bring a large pot of water to a boil over high heat. Add noodles and cook for about 4 minutes, then drain, scatter on a clean surface, and let dry for 1 hour.

3. Combine rice wine, 1 tsp. cornstarch, and salt in a large bowl. Add shrimp and marinate in refrigerator for 1 hour.

4. Heat 3 tbsp. vegetable oil in a wok over high heat. Spread noodles in wok to form an 8" "cake" and fry until edges are golden, about 5 minutes. Slide noodle cake onto a plate. Add 3 tbsp. oil to wok, then return noodle cake to pan, soft side down, and fry for 5 minutes. Transfer to a serving platter and set aside. Add remaining 2 tbsp. oil to wok and stir-fry shiitakes, scallions, ginger, and ham for 3 minutes. Add shrimp and stir-fry until opaque, about 2 minutes. Add spinach, stir-fry for 1 minute, then spoon mixture onto center of noodle cake.

5. Boil stock, light soy sauce, sesame oil, and sugar in wok over high heat until reduced by one-third. Season to taste with pepper. Dissolve remaining 2 tsp. cornstarch in 1 tbsp. water, add to stock, and stir for 1 minute. Pour over stir-fried shrimp and noodles.

Polenta Pie
with Gorgonzola

SERVES 6

JOE DELGADO'S MOM knew what she was doing when she baked her polenta in a cast-iron skillet. It's an ideal cooking vessel for this and many other kinds of food. As a slow, even conductor of heat, it is sturdy enough for the stovetop or a hot oven, and it browns beautifully.

1½ cups polenta
or coarse-grained yellow
cornmeal
Salt
1 tbsp. butter
½ cup grated asiago
½ cup crumbled
gorgonzola

1. Preheat oven to 350°. Whisk polenta into 4 cups cold salted water in a large pot. Bring to a boil over medium heat, stirring constantly. Reduce heat to low and continue stirring and cooking until polenta is the consistency of porridge, 30–40 minutes.

2. Add butter and asiago to polenta. Mix well, until the butter melts, then pour into a greased cast-iron skillet or ovenproof pan, spreading polenta evenly. Sprinkle gorgonzola evenly over the top

3. Bake for 25 minutes or until gorgonzola is bubbling and brown. Remove from oven, slice into wedges, and serve—or allow to cool to room temperature before slicing and serving.

Polenta as Family Fuel

We were in San Francisco, peeling potatoes in Joe Delgado's kitchen for his baccalà salad (below), when Joe began to reminisce about his mother—who taught him to cook food, and to love it. "It was always so important for the family to get together," he told us. "We used to have a special meal, a sacred meal, every Sunday. My mother was the center. She had us all cooking. To satisfy her hungry family, she'd get us to stir up a pot of polenta. Then we'd put it in her big cast-iron skillet to bake. She always had a hunk of asiago cheese around, so we'd grate some in. If there was gorgonzola, that would be a special treat. We'd put it on top. When the polenta was baked, we'd slice it and eat it with one hand while we made the rest of the dinner."

Perfect Wild Rice

ALL WILD RICE used to be just that—wild. Today, most of what's sold as wild rice in the stores is cultivated in paddies, just like white rice. This is fine for some purposes, but the genuine article cooks much more beautifully (and in less time) and yields more flavorful results. It's more expensive—but we think it's worth the money.

1½ cups wild rice
3 tbsp. butter
4 shallots, peeled and minced
4–5 cups chicken stock (see page 26)
Salt and freshly ground black pepper

1. Wash rice thoroughly, drain, then cover with 3 cups cold water and soak for 1 hour.

2. Melt butter in a small skillet over medium-low heat. Add shallots and cook until soft, about 15 minutes. Set aside.

3. Bring 4 cups chicken stock to a boil in a medium saucepan over high heat. Add rice, cover, and allow to return to a boil.

4. Reduce heat to low and simmer until tender but firm, about 45 minutes. Add more stock if needed, or drain off any excess stock that the rice has not absorbed. Add shallots, then fluff rice with a fork and set aside, covered, for 10 minutes before serving—or keep warm in a double boiler with a towel under its lid to absorb excess moisture. Season to taste with salt and pepper.

Really Wild

Wild rice isn't rice at all, but the seeds of *Zizania aquatica*—a grass that grows high and thick in the lakes and rivers of Minnesota and Canada. Before farmers learned to cultivate it, the only way it could be harvested was painstakingly, by hand, from canoes—the same way that Chippewa Indians have done it for more than a thousand years. In this traditional practice—which is how real wild rice (the expensive kind) is still harvested—teams of two pull the zizania reeds inward and sweep the seeds off into the boat (facing page). On a good day, the canoe is paddled to shore literally filled to the brim with the light green grain—but the rice is vulnerable to wind, which can make entire harvests disappear, leaving the boats empty. When it is successfully brought to shore, the rice is parched in cast-iron drums over wood fires or natural gas—a process that lends it the lightly smoky character that has long helped make it a genuine native American delicacy.

Miss Daisy's Red Rice

SERVES 6–8

NOW BEING revived there on a small scale, rice farming was once common in South Carolina, and helped make Charleston the wealthiest city in Colonial America. It was even said that Charlestonians were like the Chinese because they honored their ancestors and ate so much rice.

4 strips bacon
1 medium yellow onion, peeled and diced
1 stalk celery, diced
1 small green pepper, cored and diced
2 cups long-grain rice
1 28-oz. can crushed tomatoes
Salt and freshly ground black pepper

1. Fry bacon strips in a heavy skillet over medium heat, turning occasionally, until crisp and golden brown, about 10 minutes. Remove from pan and drain on paper towels, reserving grease in skillet.

2. Preheat oven to 350°. Add onions, celery, and green peppers to bacon grease in skillet. Reduce heat to medium-low and cook, stirring occasionally, until vegetables are soft, about 15 minutes.

3. Increase heat to medium, add rice to vegetables and cook, stirring constantly, for 5 minutes. Add tomatoes and season to taste with salt and pepper.

4. Transfer rice mixture to a large baking dish and add 2 cups of water. Cover tightly with aluminum foil, then bake for 1 hour. Serve topped with crumbled bacon.

Kitchen Religion

Miss Daisy Brown cooks at a café attached to a BP gas station on rural Edisto Island, 40 miles south of Charleston, in the South Carolina Lowcountry. In this unassuming setting, she turns out Southern classics like squash casserole, collard greens, corn bread, barbecued spareribs—and a locally famous version of red rice. She cooks skillfully—she says she can judge the doneness of rice by the weight of a spoonful of it, or the saltiness of a dish by the color of the steam emanating from the pot—and with an old-fashioned philosophy: "Food is good," she says. "Food is love. Food is one of the best ways to bring people together and tell them you love them. I always bless the food I cook and the people who are going to eat it."

Know Your Beans

I n an attempt to settle, once and for all, the inevitable debates about whether or not to soak beans and when to salt them, we consulted food scientist Harold McGee and Chicago chef Rick Bayless (who cooks almost 12,000 pounds of beans a year), then tested their theories for ourselves. Here's what we found: To begin with, soaking beans really isn't necessary. It does minimally shorten cooking time and leach away some oligosaccharides (those pesky gas-producing sugars), but it also soaks away some of the nutrients. Cooking beans without soaking may take 20 to 30 minutes more in some cases, and requires a little more water, but the results are delicious, and the bean skins are less likely to crack. We've always been warned not to salt beans until they're cooked (salt will toughen the beans, it is said)—but we added salt to the cooking water anyway (2 tsp. salt to 1 cup beans and 2 cups water), and got delicious beans with creamy, tender insides. Some authorities say not to cover the bean pot; we found that the beans get softer if you do, but stay separate and intact if you don't. Your choice.

White Beans with Linguiça Sausage

SERVES 4–6

PORTUGUESE FISHERMEN and their families along the Rhode Island and Massachusetts coastline still prepare many traditional dishes from their homeland. This one is flavored with linguiça, a Portuguese-style sausage— but any dried, smoked pork sausage may be used instead.

3 tbsp. extra-virgin olive oil
1 medium yellow onion, peeled and minced
2 cloves garlic, peeled and minced
2 tsp. red pepper flakes
1½ tsp. paprika
Freshly ground black pepper
½ lb. linguiça, sliced ¼" thick
¼ cup tomato purée
1 lb. navy beans or other dried small white beans
Salt
2 tbsp. finely chopped fresh parsley

1. Heat oil in a large, deep skillet over medium-low heat. Add onions and cook, stirring frequently, until soft, about 20 minutes. Add garlic and cook until fragrant, about 1 minute, then season with red pepper flakes, paprika, and black pepper.

2. Increase heat to medium. Add linguiça to onion mixture and cook, stirring frequently, for 2 minutes. Add tomato purée, beans, and 4 cups water and bring to a simmer. Reduce heat to medium-low, cover, and cook until beans are tender, about 1 hour (though some types of beans may take considerably longer, depending on size and age). Season to taste with salt and garnish with parsley.

Down-East Baked Beans

SERVES 4–6

FOOD WRITER JOHN THORNE, for many years a resident of Maine, has thoroughly investigated this emblematic New England specialty, and offers this recipe in his superb book *Serious Pig* (North Point Press, 1996).

---

1 lb. dried white beans such as Maine yellow-eye, great northern, navy, or cannellini
¼ lb. salt pork, diced
1 tsp. dried mustard
½ cup full-flavored molasses
2 tbsp. dark rum
Salt and freshly ground black pepper

1. Put beans in a large pot with enough water to cover by about 2". Bring to a simmer over medium-high heat. Reduce heat to medium and simmer uncovered for 15 minutes. Drain beans, reserving cooking liquid, then transfer beans to a 2-quart bean pot or Dutch oven.

2. Preheat oven to 250°. Place salt pork in a small pot, add water to cover, then bring to a boil over high heat. Drain pork and add to beans. In a small bowl, dissolve mustard in 1 tsp. warm water. Add dissolved mustard, molasses, and rum to beans. Season with salt and pepper, and mix gently but thoroughly.

3. Heat reserved cooking liquid in a medium sauce-pan over medium heat. Pour enough of the liquid (about 3 cups) into bean pot so that beans are moist but not floating. Reserve remaining cooking liquid. Cover pot and bake, checking occasionally to ensure that beans are not drying out, adding reserved cooking liquid as needed. Cook until beans are soft, about 5 hours.

4. Remove cover, gently stir beans, and return to oven. Bake uncovered until cooking liquid thickens into a sauce. Season to taste with salt and pepper, and serve with brown bread if you like.

Serious Beans

Here is a dish," writes John Thorne (below), "where the smallest changes can reflect much tasting...and thinking. Sometimes the perceived wisdom is correct, and sometimes, correct or not, the demands of your palate insist you override that wisdom. One abiding truth regarding Maine baked beans is that a taste for them separates those who eat them from the out-of-staters whose disdain for the dish is evidenced by their lack of interest in putting in the necessary work to get it right. If you want a sure formula, open a can. Sometimes traditional instruction is right on the mark....[I]n the matter of salt...traditional recipes call for a scant amount, but when, after about two hours of cooking, the liquid was still crying out for it, I gave in and added half a teaspoon—and almost ruined the batch. The next time, I restrained myself—to discover that enough salt eventually leached from the salt pork to give the dish exactly the right amount of savor. I also discovered that half a cup of molasses was to my still-learning palate the right amount to bring out the most flavor from  a pound of beans without also making them noticeably sweet. However, since I also yearned for a little more molasses taste, I pointed it up with a little dark rum—which draws the mouth to the dry edge of that flavor instead of toward its ever-elusive sweetness."

SEAFOOD

"ONE MORNING many years ago, with less than four hours' sleep, I stood on a Nantucket beach in the predawn darkness wearing heavy rubber pants and tried, cast after cast, to catch a striped bass. I was alone and nervous, and what I kept asking myself, as the icy Atlantic Ocean sucked me repeatedly into the surf, was Why the hell am I here?"

— REBECCA GRAY ON STRIPED BASS (*SEE RECIPE ON PAGE 108*)

RECIPES

Breakfast Trout with Bacon

SERVES 4

THERE ARE TWO REWARDS for getting up early at West Branch Ponds Camps in Maine: an early start fishing in the abundant trout ponds nearby and a breakfast of just-caught fish, fried golden brown in a cornmeal crust.

4 thick slices bacon
4 8–10 oz. trout, cleaned, heads and tails on (see Note, page 108)
1 cup yellow cornmeal
Salt and freshly ground black pepper
⅓ cup vegetable oil

1. Fry bacon in a large, heavy skillet over medium heat until crisp and golden brown, about 15 minutes. Drain on paper towels and set aside, reserving bacon fat in pan.

2. Rinse fish, then dredge in cornmeal and season both sides to taste with salt and pepper. Add vegetable oil to the bacon fat, then heat pan over medium-high heat until oil is hot. Working in batches if necessary, fry fish in combined fat and oil on one side until skin is golden and crisp, about 5 minutes. Carefully turn fish (a wide, long spatula is ideal for the task) and cook other side for 5 minutes more. (If working in batches, keep cooked trout warm in an oven on low heat until all fish are done.) Serve garnished with bacon.

Fish in the Morning

West Branch Ponds Camps rises out of a clearing at the end of a rutted dirt road deep in Maine's northwestern woods. It's a fishing camp whose oldest cabins date to the turn of the century; the most modern were built in 1937. Carol Stirling, who is known across New England as one of the best of the fishing-camp cooks, dishes up simple, soulful, Yankee fare to visiting sport anglers and vacationers. Stirling's family has run the place for three generations, and she favors time-honored recipes—like trout chowder, rhubarb cobbler, and pancakes made with fresh, local blueberries. Guests often combine their trout catch for the communal good—and then share the bounty at the breakfast table.

Thanks to the Otters

D es FitzGerald decided to branch out from fish farming and try smoking seafood as a sideline in 1982—not long after otter number four took up residence in his trout stream. FitzGerald was born and raised in Washington, D.C., and got his first fishing experience after high school, on a salmon boat in Alaska. Later, he worked on a trout farm in California, and then for an environmental group in Maine. In 1978, he started his own trout farm in Lincolnville, Maine, about a hundred miles north of Portland. Then came the otters. And the owl, the raccoons, and the mink—all of which gobbled up his trout "like cheeseburgers," FitzGerald says. "We were having a disaster a month. Some years, we lost up to 8,000 fish to disease." But there were no such problems with smoking somebody else's fish and shellfish—once he got the techniques figured out. So, in 1988, FitzGerald gave up raising fish entirely, and today his Ducktrap River Fish Farm is a multimillion-dollar business, selling its wares to restaurants and markets all over the United States. Otter number four, meanwhile, is probably still eating trout.

Smoked Trout Hash

SERVES 2

WE LIKE THE SMOKED TROUT from Ducktrap Farm—cured in brine with herbs and spices (and no food coloring or nitrates) and smoked with Maine wood chips—but any good brand will do. To make a hearty breakfast or light supper, the hash is topped with a poached egg.

2 russet potatoes, peeled and diced
1 red onion, peeled and finely chopped
Salt
6 oz. Ducktrap or other smoked trout, skinned and shredded
2 tbsp. heavy cream
¼ cup chopped fresh chives
2 tbsp. butter
Freshly ground black pepper
2 poached eggs (recipe follows)

POACHED EGGS:
1 tsp. vinegar
Salt
2 eggs

1. Add potatoes and onions to a saucepan of salted water and bring to a simmer over medium heat. Cook until potatoes are just soft when pierced with a knife, about 15 minutes. Drain and transfer to a large bowl.

2. Add smoked trout, heavy cream, and chives to bowl and gently mix all ingredients together.

3. Melt butter in a large frying pan over medium heat. Add potato-trout mixture and fry, turning occasionally, until potatoes are golden brown and crisp, about 15 minutes. Season to taste with salt and pepper.

4. To serve, divide hash between 2 plates. Place 1 poached egg on top of each plate of hash and season with salt and pepper.

POACHED EGGS: Fill a medium skillet about three-quarters full with water. Add vinegar (to help eggs hold their shape) and a pinch of salt, then bring to a simmer over medium heat, adjusting heat to keep water at a gentle simmer. Crack 1 egg into a saucer, then carefully slide egg into simmering water. Repeat with remaining egg. Cook until whites are firm, about 5 minutes. (Eggs can be poached up to 1 hour in advance, stored covered with cold water, and reheated by dipping in simmering water.)

Poached Salmon with Egg-Caper Sauce

SERVES 6

DAVID LESH, of Alaska's Gustavus Inn at Glacier Bay, poaches not only salmon but also dolly varden (a subtly flavored, pink-fleshed char) and trout. He serves them with a briny egg-caper sauce or a dill mousseline ("Just an updated version of the blender hollandaise my mom used to make for vegetables," he reveals).

1 carrot, peeled and sliced
1 stalk celery, sliced
1 medium yellow onion, peeled and quartered
1 lemon, thinly sliced
2 bay leaves
6 black peppercorns
3 lbs. center-cut salmon in 1 piece
Salt
5 sprigs fresh dill
5 sprigs fresh parsley
2 cups dry white wine

EGG-CAPER SAUCE:
1½ tbsp. butter
1½ tbsp. flour
1 cup fish stock, warmed (see step 2)
½ cup heavy cream
2 hard-cooked eggs, peeled and chopped
2 tbsp. capers, rinsed and coarsley chopped
Salt and freshly ground white pepper

1. Put carrots, celery, onions, lemon slices, bay leaves, and peppercorns in a fish poacher or a large, deep roasting pan. Rub salmon with salt, then lay on top of vegetables. Add dill, parsley, white wine, and just enough water to cover.

2. Put poacher over two burners and bring to a simmer over medium heat. Cook until salmon is pink, about 35 minutes, then remove from heat. Let salmon rest in poaching liquid for 5 minutes, then transfer to a work surface, peel skin from one side, and scrape off dark flesh with a knife. Reserve poaching liquid to use in egg-caper sauce or other recipes calling for fish stock.

3. Lift off top filet of salmon, transfer to a platter, then remove salmon backbone and any other visible bones. Turn fish over, and peel skin and scrape off dark flesh as in step 2, then transfer remaining filet to platter. Serve warm with egg-caper sauce.

EGG-CAPER SAUCE: Melt butter in a small heavy saucepan over medium heat. Add flour and cook, whisking constantly, until mixture is bubbling, about 2 minutes (do not brown). Slowly whisk in fish stock and heavy cream. Bring to a simmer and cook for 30 seconds, then remove from heat and set aside to cool for 5 minutes. (Sauce will thicken as it rests.) Stir in eggs and capers. Season to taste with salt and pepper. Keep warm over low heat and serve with poached salmon. Makes 2 cups.

Small-Town Salmon

Gustavus (pronounced "gus-DAVE-us") is a community about 50 miles west of Juneau on the Icy Strait, at the entrance to Alaska's Glacier Bay. It's a small town, with only about 350 year-round residents, but it covers a lot of ground. The houses are far-flung, and the "business district" consists mostly of a few buildings near the tiny airport and another cluster of structures a mile and a half away—plus several scattered inns. At one of these, the Gustavus Inn at Glacier Bay (above), owners David and JoAnn Lesh serve one set, regionally inspired dinner every night. Salmon or halibut—which have been fished commercially in local waters since the 1880s—are often featured on the menu, but there might also be a more exotic local specialty: mysterious-looking greenish yellow rings of something sour-sweet, salty, and crunchy. Pickled bull kelp. "It's a huge seaweed we pull out of the Icy Strait," says David Lesh, adding that it goes surprisingly well with fish caught in the same waters.

Cedar-Smoked Salmon

SERVES 6

YOU DON'T NEED a smoker to lend a lightly spicy, faintly sweetish hint of the outdoors to fresh salmon. On board a friend's boat in Alaskan waters, we improvised this method with strips from cedar logs. Back home, we substituted shakes of untreated aromatic cedar (sold by the bundle at lumberyards and hardware stores).

1 untreated cedar shake
   (slat), about 6" x 12"
5 untreated cedar shakes,
   about 3" x 6"
3 lbs. center-cut salmon
   in 1 piece, cut almost
   all the way through
   into 6 steaks
Salt and freshly ground
   black pepper
1 lemon, thinly sliced
15 sprigs fresh dill
6 tbsp. butter, melted

1. Soak shakes in a pan of water overnight, then drain, or place in a large pot of water and bring to a boil over medium-high heat, then drain.

2. Preheat oven to 450°. Place large cedar shake on a cookie sheet lined with aluminum foil. Season salmon with salt and pepper, then place on cedar and slip 1 of the smaller cedar pieces, 1 or 2 lemon slices, and 2 dill sprigs into each of the cuts between salmon steaks (**A**), reserving additional dill sprigs and a few lemon slices for garnish. Brush all over with melted butter (**B**).

3. Roast salmon until pink, 20–25 minutes, then remove from oven. Remove smaller pieces of cedar from salmon and scatter them on top of fish, then wrap aluminum foil around cookie sheet, sealing salmon tightly (**C**). Set aside for 15 minutes. (For more well-done fish, return wrapped salmon to oven and roast for 5 minutes more at 450°.)

4. Unwrap salmon and, when it's cool enough to handle, finish slicing through steaks. Serve fish garnished with reserved lemon slices and fresh dill.

Smoking Sans Smoker

rom the deck of an old 92-foot wooden boat, somewhere off the coast of Baranof Island in Southeast Alaska, writer Rebecca Gray reeled in a 30-pound king salmon, the largest edible fish she had ever caught. Such a beautiful creature deserved a special preparation. Had we been on shore, we would have built a driftwood fire on the beach, fileted the fish, and let the sweet smoke slowly perfume its flesh. But as our old wooden boat, *Lotus*, was anchored for the evening in a quiet cove just around the bend from Sitka, we improvised. The 89-year-old boat's galley was simple but had an oven, and there were some cedar logs we'd found for the salon's little fireplace. Before we knew it, we were slipping sea-soaked pieces of cedar under the fish and between the steaks we'd sliced. Into the oven it went. When we peeked, our salmon was enveloped in a white cloud of cedar steam. We served our fish right on the wood, garnished with lemons and dill. Its flesh came out moist and lightly smoked. It was a fitting and honorable preparation for such a royal fish.

Fried Catfish
with Tartar Sauce

SERVES 4

CATFISH FARMING has become big business in the South; markets all over America now sell this meaty, freshwater creature—and chefs all over America now cook it. Our favorite way of preparing it, though, remains this one: fried Memphis-style in a coating of white cornmeal.

1 tsp. paprika
1 tsp. cayenne
1 tsp. salt
1 tsp. freshly ground
 black pepper
¾ cup white cornmeal
 (or, if unavailable,
 substitute yellow)
Vegetable oil
4 8-oz. catfish filets
Lemon wedges

TARTAR SAUCE:
1 cup mayonnaise
1 sweet pickle, chopped
Juice of ½ lemon
1 tbsp. grated peeled
 yellow onion
½ tsp. dried tarragon (or
 1 tbsp. fresh tarragon)
Hot sauce, such as Tabasco

1. Mix paprika, cayenne, salt, and black pepper in a bowl, and pour cornmeal into a shallow pan.

2. Pour oil into a large cast-iron skillet to a depth of ½" and heat over medium heat. Meanwhile, sprinkle catfish filets with paprika seasoning mixture, then dredge each filet in cornmeal, coating well on both sides. Shake off excess cornmeal.

3. Heat oil to 350°. (If you don't have a thermometer, add a small piece of breaded fish to the hot oil. If it sinks, the oil isn't hot enough; if the fish bubbles and floats, it is.) Add filets, a few at a time (don't crowd the skillet, fish lowers oil temperature), and cook, turning once, until golden, 3–5 minutes per side. Drain on paper towels. Serve with lemon wedges and tartar sauce.

TARTAR SAUCE: Mix together mayonnaise, sweet pickle, lemon juice, grated onion, and tarragon. Add hot sauce to taste. Cover and refrigerate for at least 2 hours. Tartar sauce may be stored in refrigerator up to 1 week. Makes 1 cup.

The Spirit of Sharing

At the Olivet Baptist Church in Memphis, the powerful connection between music, religion, community, and food is keenly felt. The choir (above) sways as it sings "Tell It to Jesus", and the pastor delivers a passionate sermon—while in the kitchen, with services piped in through loudspeakers, volunteers cook up family recipes for fried chicken, beef tips with noodles, and fried catfish for the weekly after-church feast.

Fried Salt Cod with Garlic-Pepper Sauce

SERVES 4

IN PORTUGAL, as in parts of Spain and Italy, salt cod—cod caught in northern waters, preserved in salt, then shipped to warmer climes—is a staple, appreciated even when fresh fish is available. This recipe from the Portuguese-American community of New Bedford, Massachusetts, is a version of a dish popular in Portugal's Azore Islands.

New England Spice

I n the early 19th century, Portuguese whalers began immigrating to America in large numbers from several Portuguese-ruled islands in the Atlantic—the Azores, Madeira, and Cape Verde. They landed in the Northeast and stayed to establish communities in Rhode Island and Massachusetts. Today, the Massachusetts town of New Bedford, about 60 miles south of Boston, boasts the largest Portuguese population in the United States; almost two-thirds of the area's 150,000 or so residents claim to be of Portuguese (and specifically Azorean or Madeiran) descent. It's hardly surprising, then, that for over 80 years, New Bedford has hosted an annual summertime celebration of Portuguese culture—and food. The occasion is the Feast of the Blessed Sacrament; Mass and a colorful parade are among the day's activities (see facing page). But the cooking and eating never stop—from malassadas (fried dough) in the morning to all-day feasting on salt cod and other fish, bean dishes, rabbit, pork, and more—all washed down with plenty of beer and, of course, madeira wine.

1 lb. salt cod (see Note)
1–2 cups flour
Vegetable oil for frying

GARLIC-PEPPER SAUCE:
2 tbsp. extra-virgin
 olive oil
2 tbsp. red wine vinegar
2 tsp. finely chopped fresh
 parsley
2 cloves garlic, peeled and
 sliced
Pinch cayenne
1 tsp. pimenta moída
 (Portuguese fermented
 pepper paste)

1. Put salt cod in a large bowl, cover with water, and refrigerate for 24 hours, changing water several times.

2. Put flour in a medium bowl. Drain cod, pat dry, then dredge in flour, shaking off excess. Pour vegetable oil into a large skillet to a depth of 1½" and heat over medium-high heat. Fry cod, turning once, until golden brown, about 9 minutes. Remove fish from pan, drain on paper towels, then transfer to a large platter. Serve warm with garlic-pepper sauce.

NOTE: *Buying Salt Cod and Pimenta Moída*—Buy salt cod cut from the largest pieces possible and look for a supple texture, not a firm, pressed one; it should be white to grayish white in color, not yellow. Boxed salt cod is acceptable, but unboxed is better. Hispanic groceries and fish markets carry salt cod. Pimenta moída is available at Portuguese markets and some Hispanic groceries.

GARLIC-PEPPER SAUCE: Combine olive oil, vinegar, parsley, garlic, cayenne, and pimenta moída in a small bowl and mix thoroughly. Set sauce aside to allow flavors to blend. Serve with fried salt cod. Makes about ¼ cup.

Poke

SERVES 4

YOU COULD CALL the raw fish specialty known as poke (pronounced "poky") the Hawaiian ceviche—though, unlike ceviche, it doesn't marinate long enough to "cook". "Use the best fish your pocketbook can afford," counsels Sam Choy, whose recipe this is. He adds that if you're leery of uncooked tuna, poke is also very good fried.

1 lb. fresh ahi or other
  tuna
1 medium tomato, chopped
1½ cups fresh seaweed,
  chopped (see Note)
½ cup finely chopped maui
  or other sweet onion
1 tsp. sesame oil
½ tsp. crushed red pepper
2 tbsp. shoyu (Japanese
  soy sauce)

1. Chop fresh ahi into ½" cubes. Place in a large bowl and gently toss with tomato, 1 cup seaweed, onions, sesame oil, and red pepper. Add shoyu and serve garnished with remaining seaweed.

NOTE: *Japanese Ingredients*—Fresh seaweed, sesame oil, and Japanese soy sauce are available at Asian markets and, increasingly, at supermarkets.

VARIATION: *Fried Poke*—Prepare poke as described above, up through and including the addition of shoyu, then heat 1 tbsp. vegetable oil in a wok or large skillet over high heat. Stir-fry poke for 2–3 minutes, tossing to make sure fish cooks. Serve hot, garnished with remaining seaweed.

Real Hawaiian

When Kaui Philpotts, food columnist for the *Honolulu Advertiser*, was growing up on a sugar plantation on Maui, she recalls, she didn't eat seared ahi tuna with mango salsa or any other '90s cliché of "Pacific Rim" cooking. She ate leftover rice cooked in a skillet with bits of fried egg, green onion, and fresh ginger; or fried soy sauce–marinated chicken; or musubi—triangles of seaweed-wrapped white rice with or without a filling, like oversize sushi. She'd eat tripe stew, day-old poi (the steamed and pounded corm of the taro plant), and "plate lunches" of beef stew and chicken cutlets crowding around heaps of sticky rice. This was real Hawaiian cooking—modest, down-home, neither folkloric nor self-consciously international, but derived from many sources, ancient and modern, Asian and European and Poly-nesian alike. The lighter, more sophisticated cuisine found in Hawaii's best restaurants and hotel dining rooms today can be very good indeed—but some of the best and most satisfying food in the islands today comes from chefs like Sam Choy (see page 39), who make traditional dishes better instead of replacing them with something new.

Whole Striped Bass Baked in Salt

SERVES 10

CHEF JONATHAN WAXMAN (far right) likes to roast striped bass in a crust of salt—a technique used for whole fish in parts of Italy and Spain. This works equally well with wild "stripers", like those caught off the New England coast, or the smaller farm-raised striped bass now increasingly available in fish shops around the country.

8 egg whites
5 lbs. coarse salt
1 whole wild striped bass, about 8–10 lbs., cleaned (see Note)
2 lemons, sliced ¼" thick
2 limes, sliced ¼" thick
2 blood oranges or oranges, sliced ¼" thick
1 cup fresh flat-leaf parsley leaves
3 sprigs fresh rosemary
10 fresh basil leaves
3 sprigs fresh thyme
4 sprigs fresh tarragon
6 cloves garlic, peeled and sliced
1 2-oz. piece ginger, peeled and sliced

1. Preheat oven to 400°. Beat egg whites in a large bowl until foamy, then gradually whisk in salt until mixture is only slightly moist and has the texture of cornmeal. Line a large sheet pan with parchment paper and moisten both sides with water. (If fish is too long for pan, trim tail with scissors.) Pour enough salt mixture into pan to form a fish-size bed no thicker than ¼" when patted down.

2. Lay fish on salt bed and place lemons, limes, oranges, parsley, rosemary, basil, thyme, tarragon, garlic, and ginger inside the cavity and gills, being careful not to overstuff or force in the ingredients. (The idea is for the fish to return to its natural shape.) Pat remaining salt mixture around top and sides to form a crust that entirely encloses fish.

3. Bake 8 minutes per pound of fish. The crust should be hard and light brown. Let cool slightly, then insert a knife along edge of crust. Carefully lift off crust in 1 or 2 large pieces and pull skin away from fish. Gently remove flesh in portions and serve.

NOTE: *Cleaning Fish*—Snip off pectoral fins and sharp dorsal fin with scissors. Lift back fish's collar, snip gills, and pull them out with fingers. Scale fish by scraping firmly from tail to head with the edge of a soup spoon. Remove entrails by inserting tip of knife in anal cavity and slicing to gill openings. Remove innards with fingers. Scrape out and rinse fish.

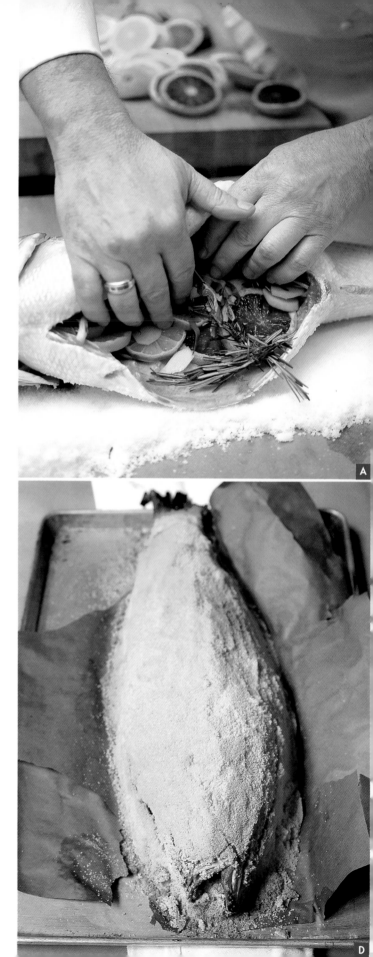

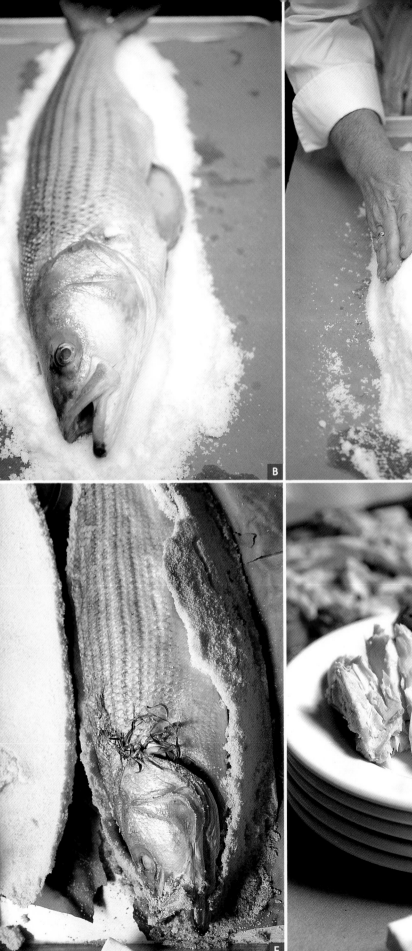

Stripers in Salt

Stuffing a striped bass (whether wild or farm-raised) helps the fish keep its shape and gives it rich, moist flavor. Chef Waxman fills the cavity of the fish with herbs and sliced citrus fruit (**A**), lays it on a bed of salt crystals mixed with egg whites (**B**), then pats the coating around the top and sides to enclose the fish (**C**). The fish is done when its crust has turned hard and light brown in color (**D**). Waxman gently cuts the top of the crust open with a knife (**E**), so that the fish may be lifted out in pieces and served. Waxman likes to accompany striped bass with nothing more than an assortment of oven-roasted vegetables (**F**).

Roast in the "R" Months

There was a time when a man who couldn't swallow at least a couple of dozen oysters at a sitting was considered kind of puny. Diamond Jim Brady allegedly ate three or four dozen at dinnertime—before the appetizers. Oysters were so plentiful in the 18th and 19th centuries that to make a class distinction about who was eating them, one had to note whether they were being washed down with champagne or beer. Oystermania continued throughout America, especially on the coasts, until the turn of the century, when over-consumption finally depleted oyster populations—above all in the once fecund Chesapeake Bay—and the bivalves became scarce and expensive. Today, oyster culture has revived in the U.S., and urban oyster bars offer dazzling selections—though they're now often sold by the piece instead of the dozen. Oysters are never inedible, just sometimes out of season. During the summer months (the proverbial months without R's)—oysters reproduce, which makes them lean and milky and less tasty than usual. When the weather and the water cool again, oysters once more grow fat and delicious. (A warning, though: In warm months, especially on the Gulf Coast, oysters are more susceptible to toxins.)

Oyster Roast

SERVES A CROWD

"WE DO IT THE WAY it was done in the old days," says South Carolina game warden Ben Moise. In the Lowcountry, an oyster roast is more an event than a dish. Moise uses both oysters from his own cultivated beds and rare wild oysters (being gathered off his island, facing page) cooking them in their own juices—tender, moist, and sweet.

Unshucked fresh oysters
Hot sauce, such as Ben's
 Oyster Sauce (recipe
 follows)

BEN'S OYSTER SAUCE:
1 cup ketchup
¼ cup cider vinegar
¼ cup horseradish
Juice of 1 lemon
1 tsp. Worcestershire sauce
½ tsp. Tabasco

1. Build a fire in a pit, using hardwood such as oak and hickory to produce a very hot ash. Place a steel plate, set up on rocks, over the fire and heat until the plate is very hot.

2. Put oysters, in their shells, on top of the steel plate. Cover them with a soaking-wet burlap bag. The water will drip off the bag and onto the plate, steaming the oysters. Keep the bag wet to prevent it from catching fire. Check for doneness by opening an oyster after about 10 minutes. The oyster should be plump, and bubbling in its own juices.

3. Using a shovel, transfer oysters to a large platter or pile them on newspaper in the middle of a table. Use gloves to handle hot oysters. Taking care to conserve hot liquor, shuck by sliding a knife along the underside of the oyster's top shell to sever it, and then under the oyster to detach it from its shell. Oysters can be eaten "naked" or with a hot sauce such as Ben's Oyster Sauce.

VARIATION: *Oysters Roasted on a Barbecue Grill*— Arrange wet oysters on the grill over a medium-hot fire. Check after 10 minutes. Use in place of pit-roasted oysters.

BEN'S OYSTER SAUCE: Combine ketchup, vinegar, horseradish, lemon juice, Worcestershire sauce, and Tabasco in a small bowl and mix well. Makes about 2 cups.

Steamed Mussels with Garlic-Butter Sauce

SERVES 4

BUY YOUR MUSSELS as fresh as possible, and with their stringy "beards" intact. If plump, sweet Mediterranean mussels aren't available, use small Atlantic or Pacific varieties rather than the oversize greenlip New Zealand mussels now often found at seafood counters.

FOR MUSSELS:
4 lbs. small to medium-size mussels
½ cup white wine
2 bay leaves
2 shallots, peeled and sliced
1 bunch parsley, washed and trimmed

FOR GARLIC-BUTTER SAUCE:
8 tbsp. butter
4 cloves garlic, peeled and minced
¼ cup chopped fresh parsley
Salt and freshly ground black pepper

1. For mussels, rinse mussels and pull off beards. Put mussels, wine, bay leaves, shallots, and parsley in a large saucepan, cover, and bring to a simmer over medium heat. Steam until mussels open, about 8 minutes. (Discard any that don't open.)

2. For garlic-butter sauce, melt butter with garlic in a saucepan over medium-low heat. Cook until garlic is soft, about 10 minutes. Add parsley, season to taste with salt and pepper, and serve as a dipping sauce for mussels.

Mussel Men

B ack in 1981, when Charlie Stevens and his partners decided that it might be a good idea to grow mussels at their Kamilche Sea Farm in Totten Inlet, in Washington State's South Puget Sound, the old-timers said it wouldn't work. The water was too warm, they said, and the mussels would die off. The old-timers were both right and wrong: The local blue mussels that Stevens and company first planted did expire—but today, mussels of a different kind are thriving in Totten Inlet. After their initial failure, the fledgling seafood farmers bought seed mussels of another type from a source in Northern California, expecting them to be just a variety of blue mussels accustomed to warmer water. These did well...but as it turned out, they weren't blue mussels at all. Instead, Stevens and company had somehow gotten ahold of a different species altogether—the Mediterranean mussel, prized by connoisseurs from Spain to Greece. In Totten Inlet, Mediterranean mussels grow bigger than the local variety, but seem to become more flavorful in the process, yielding meat that is unusually sweet and fleshy. Surprisingly, they're especially good in summer—outdoor mussels, if you will.

When Rose Pistola cooks calamari, her whole house—perfumed with long-simmered tomato sauce—smells so good it makes you want to cry, reports SAVEUR consulting editor Peggy Knickerbocker. Rose is an "old stove"—gentle, complimentary North Beach slang for someone who has put in a lot of time in front of a lot of stoves in his or her day. Old stoves are sometimes restaurant chefs (or retired restaurant chefs), but more often they are simply home cooks with many years of experience making savory dishes for themselves, their families, and their friends. Old stoves are renowned throughout the community for their culinary skills. They're old souls, legends—well aged and cured. There isn't a chance you'd have a bad meal at the hands of an old stove. Rose is full of culinary advice. "Always have basil around. I used to keep some in a jar with garlic and olive oil," she says, adding, with a twinkle, "and I never went to work without a sprig of basil in my cleavage. Men like a woman who smells like good food."

Rose Pistola's Calamari Cakes

SERVES 4

LIKE MOST GOOD COOKS, San Francisco "old stove" Rose Pistola (who even has a trendy restaurant named after her) is a conservationist: She hates to waste anything. After she makes stuffed squid (see page 117), she grinds up the unused tentacles for these tasty "leftovers".

1 cup squid tentacles, cleaned (see Note, page 117)
2 cups fresh bread crumbs
4 tbsp. freshly grated parmigiano-reggiano
4 cloves garlic, peeled and minced
4 tbsp. finely chopped fresh parsley
1 egg
Salt and freshly ground black pepper
4 tbsp. olive oil

1. Place tentacles in a food processor and pulse 6 times, until finely chopped. Transfer to a large bowl, then add bread crumbs, parmigiano-reggiano, garlic, 3 tbsp. parsley, egg, and season to taste with salt and pepper. Mix together well.

2. Wet hands to prevent calamari mixture from sticking, then form mixture into 3" cakes. Heat oil in a large skillet over medium-high heat. Fry cakes until browned, about 3 minutes per side. Drain on paper towels and serve garnished with remaining 1 tbsp. parsley.

Rose's Stuffed Calamari in "Gravy"

SERVES 6–8

THE SECRET TO COOKING squid is to either flash-fry it or let it stew gently for at least 15 minutes (as in this quintessential North Beach dish); otherwise, the squid will be rubbery. Rose Pistola's red "gravy" is similar to the sauce Lou "the Glue" cooks up for his spaghetti with calamari.

FOR "GRAVY":
½ cup extra virgin
    olive oil
2 medium yellow onions,
    peeled and finely chopped
8 cloves garlic, peeled and
    minced
1 tbsp. chopped fresh
    oregano
1 tbsp. chopped fresh basil
1 tbsp. chopped fresh
    marjoram
Salt and freshly ground
    black pepper
1 28-oz. can tomato sauce
1 6-oz. can tomato paste
½ cup chopped fresh
    parsley

FOR CALAMARI:
2 cups fresh bread crumbs
⅓ cup freshly grated
    parmigiano-reggiano
½ cup chopped fresh
    parsley
2 eggs, beaten
3 lbs. small squid bodies
    (3"–4"), cleaned
    (see Note)

1. For "gravy", heat ¼ cup olive oil in a large heavy pot over medium heat. Add onions and 6 of the minced garlic cloves and cook until soft, about 15 minutes. Add oregano, basil, marjoram, and salt and pepper to taste. Cook for 5 minutes. Add tomato sauce, tomato paste, and 2 cups water. Simmer for at least 30 minutes, stirring occasionally. When sauce is cooked, add ½ cup parsley. (Pistola simmers the sauce for as long as 4 hours. If you have the time, do so, adding a bit more water if it thickens too much.)

2. For calamari, combine bread crumbs, parmigiano-reggiano, remaining 2 minced garlic cloves, 5 tbsp. parsley, and eggs in a medium bowl and season with salt and pepper. Stuff squid with bread-crumb mixture, then close and secure tops with toothpicks.

3. Heat remaining ¼ cup olive oil in a large skillet and sauté squid in small batches until browned on all sides, 2–4 minutes. Drain on paper towels.

4. Add cooked squid to tomato sauce and cook for 15 minutes more. Garnish with remaining parsley.

NOTE: *Cleaning Calamari*—Cut off tentacles just above the eyes. Squeeze the cut end of tentacles to remove and discard beak. Set tentacles aside. Using the flat side of a chef's knife, scrape along the body from the tail to the opening. Push out and discard entrails, being careful not to break the flesh. The skin is edible, so it can be left on or removed. Reach into the body, remove transparent quill, and discard.

A Man and His Squid

L ou "the Glue" Marcelli (above)—who says he earned his nickname because he used to stick around a certain local bar as if glued to the spot—is in the galley of the Dolphin Club at Aquatic Park in San Francisco, cleaning calamari for his lunch. Lou, the club custodian, lives upstairs, and cooks for himself every day in this boat-style kitchen overlooking the bay. Today, he'll make himself pasta with calamari in red "gravy" (as sauce is apt to be known around here). It's an old family recipe, he says; the squid rings cook for only 2 minutes in the "gravy", then are tossed with cooked spaghetti. It's the kind of dish the fishermen used to whip up on their boats out in the bay. His father, who emigrated to California from Italy in 1914, was one of those fishermen. "During World War II," Lou remembers, "he fished for shark. Shark's liver was prized by bomber pilots for improving night vision." As he talks, Lou "the Glue" slides his knife smoothly along one glistening squid after another, scraping off the skin as he forces out the innards. "It should take you only 15 minutes to make this dish," he announces, looking up from his work, "and that includes cleaning the calamari."

Uncle Lobster

Once upon a time, the lobster was poor people's food. It was almost embarrassingly abundant in Colonial New England, so much so that it was used for fertilizer in the fields—and for several centuries, lobster was considered a cheap and ugly foodstuff up and down the Atlantic coastline. Then—according to one version of the story, at least—John D. Rockefeller Sr. changed the rules: In 1910, this emblematic Yankee millionaire and his family established a summer home on Mt. Desert Island, off the coast of Maine. One evening there, it is said, a bowl of lobster stew meant for the servants' table was inadvertently sent upstairs—where it was rapturously received. Either unaware of the plebeian reputation of the dish or (more likely) not much caring what people thought, the master of the house gave it a permanent place on his menu. Back in Manhattan, it soon became apparent that what was good enough for John D. was good enough for the rest of New York society—as long as it was made with lobsters from Maine. Today, Maine lobstermen—who have been known to call the object of their efforts "Uncle Lobster", out of respect—land nearly 40 million pounds of the crustacean annually, worth well over $100 million. And while it's unlikely that lobster will ever be poor folks' fodder again, the American appetite for it is increasing. Maine has recently had to institute controls on lobster fishing, in fact, limiting the number of traps that can be set and the number of licenses it issues. And to make sure that everybody understands the rules, the state now requires a two-year apprenticeship for aspiring lobstermen.

Maine Lobster with Drawn Butter

SERVES 2

FOURTH-GENERATION lobsterman Kippy Young used to say that the ideal lobster was "a snapper—one that when you pick him up, he snaps his tail a time or two." He also believed that the best way to cook lobster was to boil it in seawater. Here are some alternatives:

2 live medium lobsters
Salt
Lemon

DRAWN BUTTER:
8 tbsp. butter

1. Bring a large pot of salted water to a boil over high heat. Plunge lobsters in head-first and cook for 5 minutes per pound. Remove from pot, drain, then serve with lemon and drawn butter.

VARIATION: *Steamed Lobster*—Bring 2 cups of wine or water to a boil in a large pot with a tight-fitting lid. Put lobsters in the pot, cover tightly, and steam for 5 minutes per pound. Shake the pot to rearrange the lobsters, then continue to steam for another 5 minutes per pound. Remove from pot, drain, then serve with drawn butter and lemon.

VARIATION: *Grilled Lobster*—Split lobsters in half lengthwise by placing them on their backs, then inserting the tip of a large sharp knife just below their eyes (this will kill them quickly), and continuing to cut straight through bodies. Remove and crack claws and legs. Season split bodies with salt and pepper. Place claws, legs, and bodies (meat side up), on a grill over a medium fire. Cook, turning claws and legs once, until meat is completely opaque, about 5–7 minutes per pound. Remove from grill and serve with drawn butter and lemon.

DRAWN BUTTER: Melt butter in a small saucepan over low heat. Remove from heat and set aside. When milk solids have settled, pour off clarified butter into a serving dish.

Softshell Crab Sandwiches

SERVES 2

CRISFIELD, MARYLAND, is the softshell crab capital of the world—at least according to those folks in Crisfield, Maryland. Every spring, local watermen—as the crabbers are called—trap hard-shell blue crabs, wait for them to molt, then ship them off to market. Except, of course, for the ones they keep and fry up for themselves.

½ cup flour
Salt and freshly ground
  black pepper
2 tbsp. butter
1 tbsp. vegetable oil
2 softshell crabs, cleaned
  (see box, right)
4 pieces white sandwich
  bread
Tartar sauce
  (see page 103)
2–4 leaves bibb lettuce

1. Mix flour with a generous pinch of salt and pepper in a shallow bowl or plate.

2. Heat butter and vegetable oil in a medium skillet over medium-high heat. Dredge crabs in seasoned flour, shake off any excess, then panfry until brown and crisp, about 2 minutes on each side. Drain on paper towels.

3. Spread tartar sauce on one side of each of the 4 pieces of bread, then make up the sandwiches, using 1 crab and a leaf or two of bibb lettuce per sandwich. Serve with additional tartar sauce.

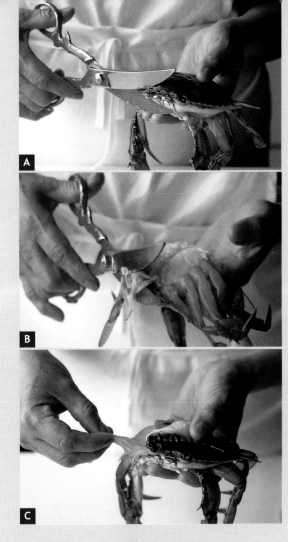

Cleaning Softshells

I f you cook softshell crabs live, they don't need cleaning; all their parts are edible. If it's been more than a few hours since their demise, however, you should ask your fishmonger to clean them for you—or do it yourself as soon as you get them home. It's easy: (**A**) Hold a crab in one hand and snip off the eyes and mouth with scissors. Squeeze out the innards through the opening. (**B**) Turn the crab over and snip away the turned-under tail, or apron. (**C**) Turn the crab over again and, with your fingers, lift up one pointed corner of the crab's outer shell and pull out and discard the gill; repeat the process on the other side, removing the other gill. The crab is now ready to be cooked.

Crab City, California

Crab in San Francisco means either Alaskan king or dungeness—and as any San Franciscan knows, dungeness is the better of the two: smaller, sweeter, more flavorful, not as chewy. (Alaskan king, usually frozen, is the stuff of cruise-ship buffets; locals won't touch it.) Named for a tiny bay on Washington's Olympic Peninsula (itself named after Dungeness, a headland in the English Channel, by British explorer George Vancouver in 1792), dungeness crab is today fished commercially from central California to the Aleutian Islands. The vast majority comes from around Eureka and Crescent City, in the northernmost reaches of California. Some connoisseurs claim that dungeness from the San Francisco area is superior to any import, even from a hundred miles up the coast. They might have a point: Crabs from the shelf outside San Francisco Bay, and from nearby Bodega and Half Moon Bays, feed on clams and mussels—giving them sweeter flesh than their northern cousins, who are more likely to nibble kelp.

Cioppino

SERVES 8

IN GENOA, ciuppin is a puréed fish soup. Genoese immigrants to San Francisco's famous North Beach neighborhood adapted the term to this hearty stew full of un-puréed seafood—most notably the celebrated dungeness crab. Our version comes from the city's Hayes Street Grill.

½ cup extra-virgin olive oil
1 large yellow onion, peeled and chopped
6 cloves garlic, peeled and chopped
2 medium carrots, diced
1 28-oz. can imported whole Italian tomatoes, drained and chopped
3 cups light red wine, preferably California pinot noir
6 cups fish stock (see page 33)
4 bay leaves
1 bunch flat-leaf parsley, trimmed and chopped
1 tbsp. lemon zest
1 tbsp. finely chopped fresh oregano
1 tbsp. fresh thyme leaves
2 tbsp. chopped fresh basil
1 tsp. cayenne
Salt and freshly ground black pepper
12 dungeness crab legs, cracked
8 mussels, well scrubbed
16 manila clams, well scrubbed
16 medium shrimp
4 black sea bass or rockfish filets (about 2 lbs. in all)

1. Heat oil in a large pot over medium heat. Add onions, garlic, and carrots and cook, stirring occasionally, until soft, about 10 minutes. Add tomatoes, wine, fish stock, bay leaves, parsley (reserve about ¼ cup for garnish), lemon zest, oregano, thyme, basil, and cayenne. Bring to a boil, then reduce heat to low and simmer, partially covered, for about 40 minutes. Strain, discarding vegetables, and return stock to pot. Season to taste with salt and pepper.

2. Add crab legs, mussels, clams, and shrimp to stock, stir gently, and cook over medium heat until mussels and clams open. (Discard any that don't open.) Add bass filets and simmer for another 7 minutes or until the fish turns opaque. Garnish with chopped parsley. Serve with toasted sourdough bread.

Building at the Jefferson
County Fairgrounds.
"Ladies on the Shore,"
by The Proper Ladies,
from Cambridge,

Shrimp and Crab Étouffée

SERVES 6–8

A DELICATE PREPARATION of seafood "smothered" in pungent sauce, étouffée is often made with crawfish—as by the "Soop Sisters" (left) at Soop's restaurant in Maurice, Louisiana. This is our interpretation of a dish we tried not far away at the Café des Amis in Breaux Bridge.

¼ lb. butter
1 medium yellow onion,
   peeled and finely chopped
1 small green bell pepper,
   cored and finely chopped
2 stalks celery, finely
   chopped
1 clove garlic, peeled and
   minced
1 tsp. salt
½ tsp. cayenne
2 lbs. medium shrimp,
   peeled and deveined
2 cups hot fish stock
   (see page 33)
2 tbsp. cornstarch
1 lb. lump crabmeat
2 scallions, finely chopped
¼ cup finely chopped fresh
   parsley

I. Melt butter in a large pot over medium heat. Add onions, green peppers, celery, garlic, salt, and cayenne and cook, stirring, until vegetables are soft, about 15 minutes.

2. Add shrimp, raise heat slightly, and cook until shrimp has turned pink, about 3 minutes. Add 1½ cups fish stock. Dissolve cornstarch in remaining stock and add to pot. Bring to a simmer, then reduce heat to medium-low, and cook until slightly thickened, about 20 minutes.

3. Add crabmeat and cook 2–3 minutes. Garnish with scallions and parsley. Serve over rice.

VARIATION: *Crawfish Étouffée*—Follow the recipe through step 2, omitting shrimp. In step 3, substitute 2 lbs. peeled crawfish tails for crabmeat.

Don't Call It 'Cajun'

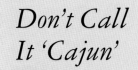 cadia was once a vast region spanning the present-day Canadian provinces of Nova Scotia, New Brunswick, and Prince Edward Island as well as part of what is now the state of Maine. Rather than swear an oath to Protestant England in 1755, many of the Catholic Acadians fled to French Louisiana. There, they became part of the region's famous cultural melting pot—and filled real, bubbling pots with their own style of cooking, which has its ancestral roots in the French farmhouse style of Quebec but is enlivened by the richness of local ingredients and influences from the Caribbean and Africa. Étouffée is a classic of the cuisine. Over time, Louisiana's Acadians became known as Cajuns—but many of their descendants prefer the older, purer term today.

Lowcountry Cookout

Exactly where the boundaries of South Carolina's Lowcountry lie may be debated. But this fabled region of swamps, beaches, abandoned rice fields, grassy savannas, and serpentine, tea-colored rivers extends roughly from Winyah Bay at Georgetown (about 60 miles north of Charleston) to the Savannah River in the south and inland from the Atlantic Ocean to the so-called Fall Line, where the topography and vegetation begin to change and the first pine-covered red clay hills appear. Ben Moise, a state game warden and noted outdoor cook, has his own Lowcountry island—a quarter-acre piece of land on the Intracoastal Waterway in the Cape Romain National Wildlife Refuge Area. He has a modest cabin there (below), with a simple cooking pavilion. Here, over a propane stove, he makes "shrimp gravy" (with bacon and tiny creek shrimp) and ladles it over hominy, and sometimes cooks the big spicy pot of shrimp, crawfish, crab, sausage, and corn on the cob known as Frogmore Stew—named for a town on the island of St. Helena, south of Charleston. It's little wonder that Moise calls his island retreat "my Valium".

Frogmore Stew

SERVES A CROWD

ON MOISE ISLAND, Ben Moise serves this Lowcountry specialty in a colander, on his long wood-plank table; everyone digs in with his hands. An even more traditional way of serving it is simply to spill the stew out onto a newspaper-lined table and let everyone help himself.

Salt
1 stalk celery per person, chopped and tied in cheesecloth
Seafood seasoning, such as Rex brand (in small bags), 1 per pot
¼ lb. smoked sausage per person, cut into 2" pieces
2 ears corn per person, shucked and broken in half
1–2 raw cleaned crabs per person (see Note)
¼ lb. raw crawfish per person
½ lb. shrimp per person

1. Fill a large stockpot half full of water, then bring to a boil over high heat. Add ¼ cup salt per gallon of water. Add celery and seafood seasoning.

2. When water is boiling, add sausage to pot and boil for 7 minutes. Next, add corn, crabs, and crawfish and continue to boil for 7 minutes more. (All ingredients should be submerged; if necessary, add more boiling water to cover.) Add shrimp and cook for 4 minutes more. Do not overcook.

3. Drain in a colander and serve shellfish, corn, and sausage in a large bowl or tub.

NOTE: *Cleaning Crabs*—Pull top shell off crab and remove gray gills. Scoop out and discard any soft fat. Crack legs with a nutcracker to expose flesh. Split crab in half down middle, then cut between each leg.

Seafood Gumbo

SERVES 6–8

GUMBO IS THICKENED with roux, a basic constituent of Acadian cooking, and with either okra (the name *gumbo* is derived from an African word for that vegetable) or, as here, with filé powder (ground sassafras leaves). Acadian gumbos are thinner than their Creole counterparts.

¾ cup vegetable oil
¾ cup flour
1 medium yellow onion, peeled and finely chopped
1 green bell pepper, cored and finely chopped
2 stalks celery, finely chopped
6 cups hot fish stock (see page 33)
1 tsp. salt
½ tsp. cayenne
1 lb. medium shrimp, peeled and deveined
1 pint or more shucked raw oysters and their liquor
1 lb. lump crabmeat
1 scallion, finely chopped
1 tbsp. finely chopped fresh parsley
Filé powder

1. Make a dark brown roux with oil and flour (see box, facing page).

2. Raise heat to medium and add onions, green peppers, and celery to roux. Cook until soft, about 15 minutes.

3. Add hot stock in a thin stream, stirring constantly. (Don't add the stock too quickly or at too low a temperature, or the roux will separate.) Add salt and cayenne and bring to a simmer, stirring frequently. Reduce heat to low and simmer for 1 hour.

4. Add shrimp, oysters, and crabmeat and cook for 3–5 minutes more. Stir in scallions and parsley. To each serving of gumbo add a small amount of filé powder to taste. Serve with white rice, if you like.

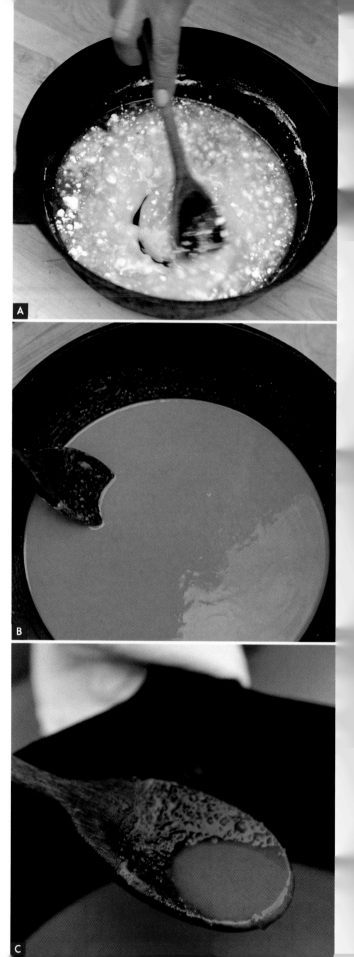

Making a Roux

arcelle Bienvenu, a cook and food writer from St. Martinville, Louisiana (the setting for Longfellow's tribute to the Acadians, "Evangaline"), once wrote a book called *Who's Your Mama, Are You Catholic, and Can You Make a Roux?*—and certainly can make a roux herself.

COMBINING flour (A) with an equal quantity of vegetable (not olive) oil in a heavy, well-seasoned, still-cold, black cast-iron frying pan. Bienvenu then turns the heat on very low. The idea is to cook the roux as slowly as possible so that while it darkens, it doesn't burn.

STIRRING the roux constantly (B) is essential until it reaches just the right color—that of a shelled pecan, says Bienvenu (though some like it even darker). She once asked her father how long it takes to cook a roux. "The time it takes to drink two beers," he replied.

FINISHING the roux (C). It has now achieved the perfect color and consistency—rich but not too thick—and is ready to serve as the base for a perfect seafood gumbo (left).

POULTRY

"ANNE SCOTT COLEMAN, a large

and graceful woman, moves across the

kitchen with an almost balletic concentra-

tion. During the holidays, she says, she

prepares as many as a hundred turkeys

for her customers. 'Everybody wants one,' she tells me, 'so we cook nonstop. We cook so many that we call them flying turkeys. They just about fly out of the house.'"

—MARY ANN EAGLE ON THANKSGIVING (*SEE RECIPE ON PAGE 149*)

Backless Birds

Living deep in the Pennsylvania countryside has many charms, reports SAVEUR Executive Editor Christopher Hirsheimer—but it also means a long drive to the nearest market for her weekend shopping. "One of the payoffs," she continues, "is that once I get to my favorite grocery store in Silverdale, I can always get free-range organic, Amish-grown chickens. I always buy several. My friend Pam Anderson, who's an editor at another food magazine (and a sometime SAVEUR contributor) taught me a great chicken trick: Using poultry shears, she removes the chicken's back by cutting along both sides of the backbone, thus producing a bird that lies flat (above)—for faster and more even roasting and easier carving. When I get home from shopping, I cut the backs out of my own chickens, then put the backs into a big pot, along with the giblets, some onions and celery, a quart of cold fresh water, some aromatic herbs, and a pinch of salt and a few peppercorns. I bring the water to a boil, then reduce it to a simmer. Two hours later, I have three cups of rich chicken stock. Oh, and the backless chickens? I roast one according to the recipe at right—and seal the others, backless, in plastic bags and stack them neatly in my freezer."

Roast Chicken

SERVES 4

SOMEWHERE along the line, chicken in America turned into chicken parts—Buffalo wings, boneless/skinless breasts, "tenders". We're here to stand up for the whole bird, roasted in a pot with vegetables. If there's a better, simpler, one-dish American meal, we don't know of it.

1 3–4 lb. chicken
1 lemon, halved
Fresh rosemary sprigs
Fresh thyme sprigs
2 cloves garlic, crushed
   and peeled
4 tbsp. butter, softened
Salt and freshly ground
   black pepper
4 small red onions, halved
8 small potatoes, halved
4 medium carrots, peeled
4 medium parsnips, peeled
Extra-virgin olive oil

1. Preheat oven to 450°. Rinse chicken, then pat dry with paper towels. Put chicken in a large cast-iron skillet or roasting pan, then squeeze lemon over chicken to cover all surfaces, inside and out, with juice. Put squeezed lemon halves, several sprigs each of rosemary and thyme, and garlic into cavity of the bird. Tie legs together with kitchen string, then rub butter all over chicken. Season liberally with salt and pepper.

2. Arrange onions, potatoes, carrots, and parsnips around chicken. Brush vegetables with a little olive oil and season to taste with salt and pepper.

3. Roast in the oven for 15 minutes, then baste chicken and vegetables with pan juices. Reduce temperature to 375° and continue to roast, basting occasionally, until skin is crisp and golden, about 45 minutes more.

4. Turn off heat and allow chicken to rest in the oven, with the oven door ajar, for about 15 minutes before carving. Garnish with additional fresh rosemary and thyme sprigs, if you like.

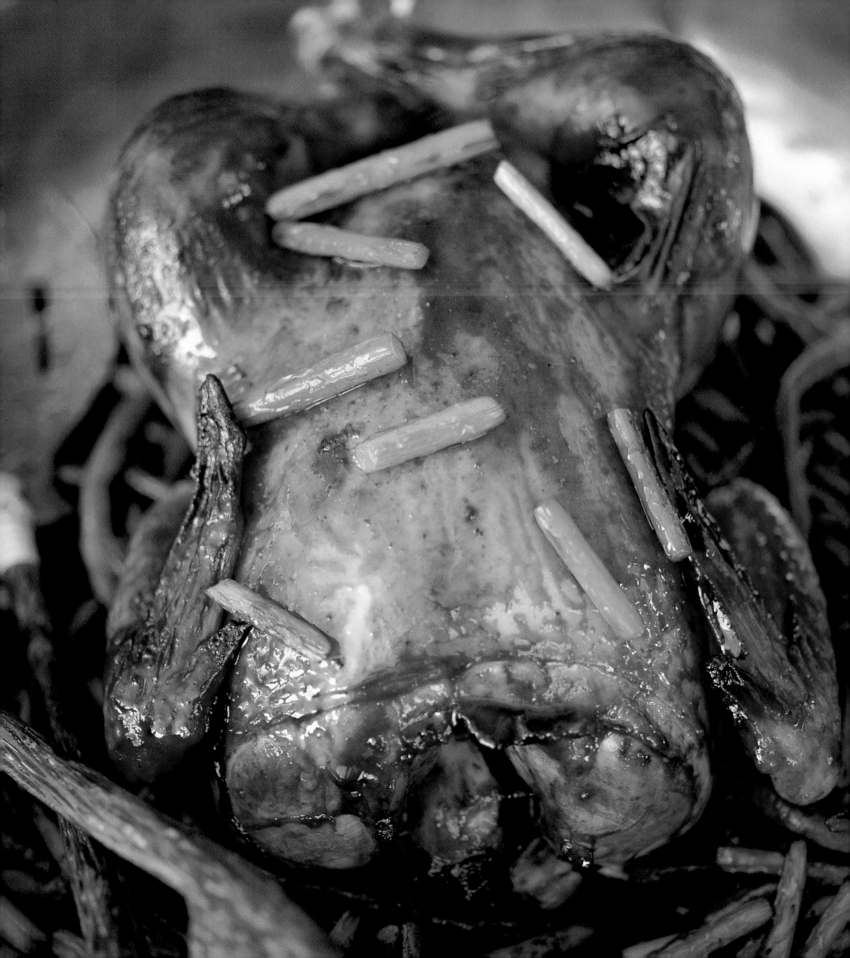

Tutu-Man's Chicken with Teriyaki Sauce

SERVES 4

KAUI PHILPOTTS, a native of Hawaii, grew up enjoying this dish, cooked by her Tutu-man, or grandfather. Peel ginger only when you're ready to use it, and slice or grate it across the grain. Use any leftover teriyaki sauce as a marinade or basting sauce for meat or vegetables.

1 3½-lb. chicken
¾ cup teriyaki sauce
   (recipe follows)
2 scallions, green parts
   only, sliced into large
   pieces

TERIYAKI SAUCE:
1 cup shoyu (Japanese
   soy sauce)
1 cup sugar
1 3" piece fresh ginger,
   peeled and sliced
4 cloves garlic, crushed
   and peeled
2 tbsp. bourbon

1. Preheat oven to 375°. Rinse chicken and pat dry with paper towels. Tuck wings under back and tie legs together with kitchen string. With a pastry brush, coat chicken inside and out with teriyaki sauce.

2. Put chicken in a roasting pan and roast for about 1 hour, basting every 15 minutes. (If you want a darker colored bird, baste more frequently.) Chicken is done when juices from leg, when pierced with a knife, run clear. Allow chicken to rest for 20 minutes before carving. Garnish with scallions and spoon a small amount of teriyaki sauce over bird.

TERIYAKI SAUCE: Stir together shoyu and sugar in a small saucepan over low heat until sugar dissolves, about 2 minutes. Add ginger, garlic, and bourbon and simmer for about 30 minutes. Remove and discard ginger and garlic. Sauce will keep in a sealed container in refrigerator for at least a month. Makes about 1½ cups.

Fields of Zest

The rainy, volcanic Hamakua Coast near Hilo on Hawaii's Big Island offers an ideal climate for the cultivation of *Zingiber officinale*, or ginger—and the Hawaiian crop accounts for about a third of the 38 million pounds of ginger consumed annually in America. Ginger plants resemble tall, dense grass, with delicately scented yellow flowers hidden in the blades. It takes about a year to grow to maturity. Baby ginger, prized in Japan, is harvested in late summer in Hawaii; full-grown plants are uprooted in January. To combat disease and pests, Hawaiian ginger farmer Takashi Wagatsuma (left) told us, workers keep their implements, boots, and bare feet scrupulously clean, and even change clothing before moving from one field to another.

Gus's Fried Chicken

SERVES 4

"THIS IS A DEAD MAN'S RECIPE," Gus Vanderbilt of Gus's Fried Chicken, outside Memphis, informed us when we asked him how he made his most famous dish. "I ain't telling." In the end, we had to work it out for ourselves. It may not be Gus's, exactly, but it's close.

Fowl Perfection

On a small country highway in Mason, Tennessee—about 40 miles from Memphis—sits a jaunty shanty of a restaurant. A yellow sign with a black chicken painted on it, surrounded by a multicolored blinking neon light, announces its name: Gus's Fried Chicken. Inside, owner Gus Vanderbilt (facing page) cranks up the volume on the jukebox and lets the sounds of Dr. Feelgood shimmy through the smoky ten-table joint. Meanwhile, his customers chugalug cold beer from quart bottles as they wait for Gus's wife, Gertrude, to cook up a batch of the best fried chicken in the world. With one hand in a yellow Playtex glove, Gertrude turns chicken pieces in their milky, saffron-colored marinade—whose secret ingredients are the pride of the place. Then she picks up the pieces with tongs and lowers them into skillets filled with roiling peanut oil. When the chicken comes to "a certain float" (as Gus explains it), she lifts the golden pieces out of the oil and transfers them to plates. The coleslaw at Gus's, frankly, is lackluster, and the baked beans are sugary. But the chicken is perfect—piping hot and peppery, crunchy and moist.

1 3½-lb. chicken, rinsed
   and cut into 8 pieces
1 quart buttermilk
3 cups flour
2 tsp. paprika
1 tsp. cayenne
Salt and freshly ground
   black pepper
Peanut oil

1. Arrange chicken pieces in a single layer in a nonreactive pan. Pour buttermilk over chicken, then cover and refrigerate for at least 2 hours, or as long as overnight.

2. Combine flour, paprika, cayenne, 2 tsp. salt, and 1 tsp. pepper in a large plastic bag and shake to mix thoroughly. Shake chicken pieces one at a time with seasoned flour in bag until well coated.

3. Pour peanut oil into a large cast-iron skillet to a depth of ¾". Heat oil over medium-high heat until very hot but not smoking, and add chicken, largest pieces first, skin side down. (Work in batches if your skillet won't hold all pieces at the same time.) Reduce heat to medium and cook, turning once, until chicken is golden brown and crispy, 12–15 minutes per side. Drain chicken on paper towels and season to taste with salt and pepper.

Mrs. Garrett's Chicken Pies

MAKES 10 PIES

IF YOU THINK chicken pot pie is a concoction of cubed carrots and shriveled peas with shreds of tired chicken in a glutinous sauce, encased in a pale and pasty crust. . . well, you obviously don't know Mrs. Garrett. These meaty, aromatic turnovers are chicken pie supreme.

FOR FILLING:
¼ cup vegetable oil
½ cup flour
1 large yellow onion,
    peeled and finely chopped
2 3-lb. chickens, each cut
    into 8 pieces
3 stalks celery, finely
    chopped
1 green bell pepper, cored,
    seeded, and finely
    chopped
2 4-oz. cans button mush-
    rooms, drained
2 scallions, trimmed and
    chopped
½ cup chopped fresh
    parsley leaves
1 tsp. cayenne
Salt and freshly ground
    black pepper

FOR PASTRY:
9 cups sifted flour
1 tbsp. salt
1¾ cups vegetable
    shortening
3 eggs, lightly beaten,
    for egg wash

1. For filling, mix together oil and flour in a large, heavy pot over medium heat and stir constantly until browned to make a roux (see box, page 129). Add onions and cook until golden, about 20 minutes. Add chicken and brown on all sides, then add celery, green peppers, and water to cover. Bring to a boil, reduce heat to low, cover, and simmer for 1 hour.

2. Remove chicken from pot and set aside to cool. Add mushrooms, scallions, parsley, and cayenne to the vegetables in the pot and season to taste with salt and pepper. Simmer, uncovered, for 30 minutes. Meanwhile, pick meat from chicken, shred, and return to pot. When vegetables are cooked, remove pot from heat and set aside to cool.

3. For pastry, combine 8 cups flour, salt, and 1 cup shortening in a large bowl and cut mixture with a pastry cutter or 2 knives until it has the consistency of coarse meal. Mix in 3 cups water, ½ cup at a time, until dough forms. Roll out dough on a floured surface into a large rectangle. Spread with ½ cup shortening and sprinkle with 2 tbsp. flour. Fold dough onto itself in 3 layers, like a letter. Spread with remaining ¼ cup shortening, sprinkle with flour, and fold into a square. Wrap in plastic wrap and chill overnight.

4. Preheat oven to 375°. Roll out dough on a floured surface and cut into ten 7" circles. Fill circles with chicken mixture. Brush edges with egg wash, then fold over to form plump turnovers. Use a fork to seal edges. Place on a baking sheet and brush with egg wash. Bake until golden, about 30 minutes.

Southern Comfort

In the storybook town of St. Martinville, Louisiana, Aline Garrett stands in the back of her shop as pots of chicken and vegetables bubble on an old black stove. Her hands are covered with flour as she folds dough into puff pastry. Garrett's daughter, Freda Garrett Harrison (below), who helps run Garrett's little savory-pie shop, let us copy her chicken pie recipe right off the wall. We originally heard about Mrs. Garrett's pies from New Orleans–based writer Gene Bourg. "These pies are just wonderful," he told us. "The crust is flaky and Mrs. Garrett seasons the chicken incredibly. They just taste good!"

Born on the Bayou

I n New Iberia, a few miles from the plain-faced storefronts and luncheonettes that constitute much of the restaurant population in the Louisiana bayou country, stands the considerably grander restaurant called Le Rosier—located in a gracious old house that reflects the neoclassical formality of its antebellum neighbor, the restored 1830s plantation house, Shadows-on-the-Teche (facing page, bottom right). On snowy linens in Le Rosier's dining room, chef Hallman Woods III (below) serves such creations as fried oys-

ters en brochette with spinach, grilled leeks with garlic-chive cream, grilled duck breast with wild-rice-and-tasso dressing, an elegant quail jambalaya, and a textbook-perfect pecan pie. These refined versions of classic local dishes, based on typical regional ingredients, might once have graced a banquet table at Shadows-on-the-Teche itself. Culinary skill runs in the family: Chef Woods's father, Hallman Woods Jr., has a reputation as one of the best natural-born cooks around this part of the bayou. He whips up hearty lunches and excellent breakfast omelettes for overnight guests at the Inn at Le Rosier, attached to the restaurant, and father and son take turns cooking for the Le Rosier dining room.

Quail Jambalaya

SERVES 4–8

JAMBALAYA IS A JUMBLE — a well-seasoned dish based on seafood, meat, poultry, or game, cooked with vegetables and white rice. The name may derive from jamón, Spanish for ham (with which jambalaya is sometimes flavored), but there is also a meatless vegetable mélange called giambalaia in Menton, near Nice—so who knows?

8 quail, butterflied
1 tsp. salt
½ tsp. cayenne
4 cloves garlic, peeled, 2 whole and 2 minced
4–5 tbsp. vegetable oil
1 medium yellow onion, peeled and finely chopped
1 green bell pepper, cored, seeded, and finely chopped
2 bay leaves
1½ cups long-grain white rice
1 lb. Cajun andouille sausage, sliced ¼" thick
3 cups hot chicken stock (see page 26) or water
Freshly ground black pepper
1 scallion, finely chopped
¼ cup finely chopped fresh parsley

1. Rinse quail, pat dry with paper towels, then season quail with salt and cayenne. Crush whole garlic cloves with the flat side of a knife. Rub crushed garlic on quail, then discard garlic. Brown quail in vegetable oil in a large, heavy pot over medium heat. Cook in batches to insure even browning, adding more oil as needed. Remove quail from pot as they brown and set aside.

2. Combine onions, green peppers, minced garlic, and bay leaves in the same pot. Cook over medium heat, stirring occasionally, until onions are golden, about 20 minutes. Add rice and andouille and cook, stirring frequently, until lightly browned, 15–20 minutes. Add quail and stock, then bring to a simmer. Reduce heat to low, cover, and cook until rice has absorbed stock, about 30 minutes.

3. Fluff rice with a fork and season to taste with salt and pepper. Just before serving, stir in scallions and parsley.

VARIATION: *Chicken Jambalaya*—Substitute 1 3-lb. chicken, cut into 8 pieces, for the quail in step 1, then proceed with the recipe. Serves 4.

VARIATION: *Chicken and Shrimp Jambalaya*—Substitute 1 3-lb. chicken, cut into 8 pieces, for the quail in step 1. Proceed with the recipe, adding 1 lb. medium shrimp, peeled and deveined, about 3 minutes before adding rice and andouille in step 2, then continue with the recipe. Serves 4–8.

Quail with Aunt Min's Gravy

SERVES 4–8

MINNIE LEE BARDIN was the best cook in Elloree, South Carolina, claims her nephew, chef Philip Bardin. As a child he was allowed to apprentice at her side, shelling butter beans, he recalls—and last Christmas he inherited her apron. But he's been making stock-based gravies and other specialties from her recipe files for years.

8 quail
Salt and freshly ground
   black pepper
¾ cup ground pecans
¾ cup flour
1 egg
1 cup milk
Peanut oil
3 cups duck or chicken
   stock (see page 26 for
   chicken stock)
½ cup heavy cream

1. Rinse quail, pat dry with paper towels, then season each liberally with salt and pepper.

2. Combine pecans and flour in a large bowl and mix well. Beat egg into milk in another large bowl. Dip 1 quail into egg wash, then roll to coat well in pecan-flour mixture. Repeat with remaining quail.

3. Preheat oven to 200°. Pour peanut oil into a large, heavy skillet to a depth of 3". Heat oil to 350° over medium heat. (Use a thermometer to check the temperature.) Fry quail until golden and tender, about 15 minutes. Work in two batches to avoid crowding the pan, keeping the first batch warm in oven while subsequent batches cook.

4. While quail cook, pour stock into a medium skillet and reduce by half over medium-high heat. Add cream and cook, stirring constantly, until sauce thickens, about 5 minutes. Season to taste with salt and pepper. Serve quail with gravy on grits, if you like.

Lowcountry Authentic

Chef Philip Bardin specializes in what he calls "Lowcountry menus with a modern twist" at the Old Post Office on Edisto Island, South Carolina—where he has cooked for the past ten years. We sampled Bardin's Orangeburg onion sausage (named for a town northwest of Charleston that is famous for its sausages), which he serves with black bean sauce, and then his fried quail with duck-stock gravy—a recipe he got from his Aunt Min, who ran the family "boarding house/hotel/dining room" in Elloree, South Carolina, for decades. We think she would have appreciated the rich chicken-stock gravy we tried with the quail, too. Is her nephew's cooking "authentic"? Bardin smiles. "'Authentic' might be too time-consuming for a restaurant," he replies. "We have a commitment to keeping things simple and uncontrived."

Roast Duck with Orange Sauce

SERVES 4–8

WILD MALLARD OR PINTAIL ducks make superb "duck à l'orange"—as this dish was once known on Continental menus. If you don't hunt (or know a hunter), farm-raised mallard ducks, available from specialty purveyors, or even supermarket ducklings work just fine.

1 orange
4 1½-lb. mallard ducks
Salt and freshly ground
    black pepper
4 cloves garlic, peeled
1 medium yellow onion,
    peeled and quartered
4 sprigs fresh rosemary
½ cup melted butter
½ cup madeira
1 cup duck or chicken stock
    (see page 26 for chicken
    stock)
1 tbsp. sugar
2 tbsp. red wine vinegar

1. Preheat oven to 500°. Zest orange, using a vegetable peeler, then julienne the zest and set aside. Cut orange into quarters. Rinse ducks, pat dry with paper towels, and season, inside and out, with salt and pepper. Tuck wings under back and stuff each duck with 1 orange quarter, 1 garlic clove, 1 onion quarter, and 1 sprig rosemary. Tie legs together with kitchen string. Put ducks in a large roasting pan and brush with butter. Roast until skin is crisp, 25–30 minutes. Remove ducks from pan.

2. Place pan over medium-high heat, skim fat, and cook just until juices are caramelized, about 5 minutes. Deglaze pan with madeira, scraping brown bits from bottom of pan. Add stock and orange zest and cook over medium heat until sauce is reduced by about one-third, 3–5 minutes.

3. Combine sugar and 1 tbsp. water in a small nonstick saucepan. Cook over medium heat until golden, 2–3 minutes. Remove from heat, then stir in vinegar and reduced sauce. Return to heat and cook for 5–8 minutes. Top ducks with sauce.

VARIATION: *Long Island Duck with Orange Sauce*— Preheat oven to 375°. Stuff 1 5-lb. long island duck with 4 cloves peeled garlic, 1 quartered orange, 1 quartered onion, and 4 sprigs fresh rosemary. Tie legs together with kitchen string, then place duck on rack over roasting pan. Roast, breast side down, 45 minutes. Turn breast up, roast 40–45 minutes more. Proceed with steps 2 and 3.

Hunting Wild Game

he sportsman and writer Charley Waterman first proposed that there were three types of hunting outdoorsmen—shooters, hunters, and dog men. According to our own wild-game authority, Rebecca Gray (top left, with husband, Ed, and their pointing dog, Bud, duck hunting in a northeastern forest), there is a certain amount of shooter in anyone who loves to eat wild birds—since it is the successful shooter who affords the hunting party a feast. Hunters travel long and hard and know a lot about their prey. Dog men like being out with their dogs almost more than the actual finding and shooting of wild birds. Anyway, it's really the dogs who do the hunting. Dog men just watch them do their magnificent job.

Roast Turkey with Corn Bread Stuffing

SERVES 10–12

THANKSGIVING is not a time for culinary experimentation. "Everybody just wants a taste of tradition that day," says Memphis caterer Anne Scott Coleman. "If we served something different, the family wouldn't eat it."

1 10–12 lb. fresh turkey
Salt and freshly ground
    black pepper

FOR STUFFING:
4 cups crumbled corn bread
    (see page 238)
2 strips bacon, chopped
2 tbsp. butter
1 small yellow onion,
    peeled and chopped
1 stalk celery, thinly sliced
1 medium tart apple,
    peeled, cored, and diced
1 bay leaf
1 tsp. dried savory
1 tsp. dried sage
1 tsp. dried marjoram
1 tsp. dried thyme
1 tsp. dried basil
Salt and freshly ground
    black pepper

6 tbsp. butter, softened

1. Preheat oven to 375°. Rinse turkey well, pat dry with paper towels, and season inside and out with salt and pepper.

2. For stuffing, spread crumbled corn bread on a cookie sheet and bake until golden, 20–30 minutes. Cool slightly, then transfer to a large bowl.

3. Cook bacon in a skillet over medium heat until brown and crisp, 8–10 minutes. Add bacon and drippings to corn bread. Melt butter in same skillet, add onions and celery, and cook for 5 minutes. Add to corn bread mixture. Stir in apple, bay leaf, savory, sage, marjoram, thyme, and basil and season to taste with salt and pepper.

4. Fill cavity of turkey with stuffing. Tuck wings under back, tie legs together with kitchen string, and rub skin with butter. Place turkey in a large roasting pan, breast side up, and roast until turkey and stuffing reach an internal temperature of 165°, 10–12 minutes per pound. Allow turkey to rest 20 minutes, then remove stuffing and carve.

A Feast from Memory

Anne Scott Coleman's kitchen is filled with the innardy scent of giblets simmering with sage and celery. Corn bread warms in the oven while yeast rolls rise in the pantry, fragrant and barmy. Sweet potato pies and pecan pies honey the air with cinnamon while languid oysters hang suspended in their bath awaiting Coleman's skillful ministrations. A turkey, flecked with butter, looks like a naked guest at the party. We are in the very maw of food. Coleman, a Memphis cook and caterer, makes Thanksgiving dinner not from recipes but from deep personal memory. "My father was the maître d' at the Memphis Country Club," she says, "so we grew up around food and cooking. There are eight of us and we always had Thanksgiving dinner at our grandmother's house. Her name was LouElla Hill, but everyone called her Mama Lou. She was a wonderful cook. I used to watch her in the kitchen, throwing in a little of this and a little of that. I guess I learned it all from her. Now I'm a throw-it-in cook too. I never measure."

They Know Turkeys

Anne and Fred Jaindl run Jaindl Family Farms in Orefield, Pennsylvania. The 13,000-acre operation (facing page) raises about a million turkeys a year. It all started in 1932, when John and Hilda Jaindl, Fred's parents, opened the Stone Tavern, a small restaurant in Allentown, Pennsylvania, serving food grown on their family farm. When Fred returned home from World War II, he expanded the farm's turkey flock, and as a result, his mother began offering—in addition to the 25-cent turkey platter already on her menu—such dishes as turkey cutlets with tomato sauce, turkey sauté with lemon and walnuts, and turkey tetrazzini. "There was nothing that woman couldn't do with turkey," says Anne.

Turkey Tetrazzini

SERVES 6

THIS CREAMY NOODLE DISH, named for Italian opera singer Luisa Tetrazzini (1871–1940), probably originated in San Francisco. Whether it was first made with turkey or with chicken is debated by aficionados.

½ lb. wide egg noodles
8 tbsp. butter
½ lb. white mushrooms, sliced
5 tbsp. flour
Salt and freshly ground black pepper
3 cups turkey or chicken stock (see page 26 for chicken stock)
1⅓ cups heavy cream
⅓ cup dry sherry
3 cups coarsely chopped cooked turkey
¼ tsp. freshly ground nutmeg
¼ cup freshly grated parmigiano-reggiano
Fresh parsley (optional)

1. Bring a large pot of salted water to a boil over medium-high heat. Add noodles and cook until tender, about 8 minutes. Drain, then transfer to a medium baking dish and toss with 1 tbsp. butter.

2. Preheat oven to 375°. Melt 2 tbsp. butter in a large skillet over medium-high heat. Add mushrooms and cook until lightly browned, 3–5 minutes. Scatter mushrooms over noodles.

3. Reduce heat to medium-low and melt remaining 5 tbsp. butter in same skillet. Sprinkle in flour, season to taste with salt and pepper, and cook, stirring constantly, for 2 minutes. Increase heat to medium, gradually whisk in stock, and simmer until sauce thickens, about 7 minutes. Add cream, sherry, and turkey, then adjust seasoning with salt, pepper, and nutmeg.

4. Spoon turkey and sauce over noodles, then sprinkle with parmigiano-reggiano. Bake until sauce is bubbly, about 20 minutes. Heat broiler and brown for 3–5 minutes. Garnish with parsley, if you like.

Goose with Chestnut Stuffing and Port Sauce

SERVES 6

AMERICAN GEESE have changed: Gone are the fatty, greasy, hard-to-digest honkers of yesteryear. Geese still have prickly personalities, but they are being bred friendlier — skinnier, meatier, but no less flavorful.

1 10-lb. fresh or fully
  thawed frozen goose
Salt and freshly ground
  black pepper

FOR STUFFING:
3 tbsp. butter
1 large yellow onion,
  finely chopped
1 clove garlic, peeled and
  minced
2 stalks celery, sliced
10 mushrooms, sliced
1 tbsp. fresh thyme leaves
2 cups roasted chestnuts,
  peeled and chopped
5 cups fresh bread crumbs
1 egg, lightly beaten
¼ cup chicken stock
  (see page 26)

FOR SAUCE:
Goose neck and giblets,
  minus liver
4 stalks celery, chopped
3 cloves garlic, peeled
1 large yellow onion,
  chopped
4 sprigs fresh parsley
5 black peppercorns
1 cup ruby port
Salt and freshly ground
  black pepper

1. Preheat oven to 450°. Wash, drain, and dry goose with paper towels, then rub, inside and out, with salt and pepper.

2. For stuffing, melt 2 tbsp. butter in a skillet over medium heat. Cook onions and garlic until soft, about 15 minutes. Add celery and cook 5 minutes more, then transfer to a bowl. Melt remaining 1 tbsp. butter in the same pan, add mushrooms and thyme, and cook 7–8 minutes more. Combine mushrooms with onion mixture, then add chestnuts, bread crumbs, egg, and stock, and mix well. Set stuffing aside.

3. For sauce, put neck, giblets, celery, garlic, onions, parsley, peppercorns, and 6 cups water in a large saucepan. Bring to boil over medium heat, reduce heat to low, skim off foam, and simmer for 2 hours. Strain, reserving stock and giblets. Discard remaining solids. Peel and finely chop giblets and set aside.

4. While stock cooks, loosely pack body and neck cavity of goose with stuffing. Tie legs closed with kitchen string. Prick legs and thighs with a fork. Roast on a rack in a roasting pan for ½ hour. Lower heat to 325° and cook for 1½–2 hours more or until thigh juices run clear. Transfer goose to a platter and allow to rest for 15 minutes, then remove stuffing and carve.

5. While goose rests, put roasting pan with drippings on top of stove (use 2 burners if necessary) over medium heat. Skim and discard fat from juices. Add port and deglaze, scraping brown bits from bottom of pan. Add giblets and stock and reduce liquid by half, about 15 minutes. Season to taste with salt and pepper. Serve sauce with goose and stuffing.

Chestnut Knowledge

L ow in fat but high in sugar, chestnuts were once a staple of American cooking— roasted, boiled, steamed, grilled, mashed, even made into flour. Then, early in this century, a blight introduced by Chinese chestnut trees planted on Long Island all but wiped out American chestnut orchards. These days, most of the chestnuts consumed in this country are imported and canned in brine or in syrup. (Italian chestnuts, good for stuffings, often come dried and need soaking and boiling like dried beans or peas.) To peel fresh chestnuts, score them crosswise on the flat side, then boil them for 4 to 5 minutes. Pull back the outer and inner skins while the chestnuts are still warm. If they still resist, boil them again, and try it once more.

MEATS

"MEL COLEMAN is a cowboy, the son

of a cowboy—the son of a cowboy's son,

for that matter. He manages more than

4,000 head of cattle, part of the family's

$55-million-a-year beef business, on

250,000 acres of public and private Colorado land. And he eats beef six days a week. He has spent much of the past 19 years convincing other people to do the same. 'Chicken,' insists the 72-year-old Coleman, 'will not thrive unopposed.'"

—CONNIE McCABE ON STEAK (*SEE RECIPE ON PAGE 158*)

RECIPES

COLEMAN RANCHES

MEL & POLLY

Kinder, Gentler Bovines

When Colorado cattleman Mel Coleman was growing up, he recalls, "Cows were for sale, not for eating. If an old one broke a leg, then Mom would fry up some steak, but it would be tougher than tough." He shakes his head. "Mom never thought to blame the cow, though." She should have, Coleman now believes—for the first secret of a perfect steak, he has since discovered, is a good cut from a healthy, well-fed, contented animal. Coleman, who once made his living wrangling and riding across Colorado, founded Coleman Natural Products, the nation's largest producer of natural beef, after his daughter-in-law complained that she couldn't buy delicious natural beef like the meat she was served at his ranch. "The idea just grew out of my saddlebag," he says. His cows are raised on pesticide-free grass and grain, with no growth-stimulating hormones or antibiotics. Twenty years ago, he adds, consumers wanted a fat-streaked piece of beef, for flavor; today they prefer a leaner cut. That's fine with Coleman, who doesn't believe that the flavor of beef is directly related to the amount of fat it contains. It's genetics and feed that make the difference, he maintains. "Man has improved the bovine," says Mel Coleman.

Panfried Flank Steak with Garlic Butter

SERVES 4

LONG BEFORE anyone had heard of "blackened" fish or meat, recalls chef Lydia Shire, proprietor of Biba and Pignoli restaurants in Boston, her father used to cook steak like this, in a cast-iron pan so hot it was smoking—thus forming a dark crust to seal in the meat's juices.

1 1½-lb. piece flank steak, about ¾" thick
Salt and freshly ground black pepper
3 tbsp. extra-virgin olive oil
2 tbsp. garlic butter (recipe follows)
1 tbsp. finely chopped fresh parsley

GARLIC BUTTER:
4 tbsp. butter
3 cloves garlic, crushed and peeled

1. Pat steak dry with paper towels, then season liberally on both sides with salt and pepper. Heat a large cast-iron skillet over high heat. When pan begins to smoke, coat with oil, then add steak (be careful; oil will spatter) and sear, until almost black, for about 4 minutes on each side (for rare). Don't move meat until ready to turn or crust will break.

2. Transfer steak to a platter and top with garlic butter. Cover loosely with foil to keep warm. Allow steak to rest for 10 minutes, then cut across the grain into ¼" slices. Spoon juices over steak and top with parsley.

GARLIC BUTTER: Heat butter and garlic in a small saucepan over medium-low heat. Cook until garlic is fragrant, about 5 minutes. Remove and discard garlic. Keep butter warm. Makes enough to top 4 servings of steak.

VARIATION: *Herb Butter*—Beat 4 tbsp. softened butter with a fork in a medium bowl until creamy. Add 1½ tsp. minced fresh tarragon, 1½ tsp. minced fresh chives, ¾ tsp. minced fresh chervil, and ¾ tsp. minced fresh parsley. Mix thoroughly and season to taste with salt and pepper. Mound butter on a piece of plastic wrap, roll to form a cylinder, twist ends of wrap, and refrigerate until firm, at least 1 hour. Slice into rounds to serve.

VARIATION: *Roquefort Butter*—Substitute 1 tbsp. crumbled roquefort, ½ tsp. cognac, and 1 tsp. dijon mustard for the herbs, then proceed as in herb butter.

A B
C D

Steak Diane

SERVES 2

THIS CLASSIC of "Continental" chafing-dish cooking may have been invented by a maître d'hôtel in Belgium in the 1920s, for a customer named…guess what. Or it may be related to the peppery sauce Diane, sometimes served with game (in honor of Diana the Huntress).

2 6-oz. steaks (such as strip, sirloin, or club), pounded ¼" thick
Salt and freshly ground black pepper
4 tbsp. butter
1 tsp. vegetable oil
2 shallots, peeled and minced
1½ tbsp. dijon mustard
1½ tbsp. Worcestershire sauce
2 tbsp. demi-glace (recipe follows)
1½ tbsp. madeira
1–2 tsp. freshly squeezed lemon juice
1 tbsp. chopped fresh parsley

DEMI-GLACE:
¼ lb. finely chopped bacon
1 medium yellow onion, peeled and chopped
1 carrot, peeled and chopped
¼ cup flour
2 tbsp. tomato paste
10 sprigs parsley
2 bay leaves
2 sprigs thyme
2½ quarts (10 cups) beef stock (see page 40)

1. Season steaks liberally with salt and pepper. Heat 1 tsp. butter and ½ tsp. oil in a large skillet over high heat. Sear one steak, 30–45 seconds per side (for medium rare), then transfer to a warmed platter, covering with foil to retain heat. Add 1 tsp. butter and remaining ½ tsp. oil to skillet. Sear second steak in the same manner. Transfer to platter and cover.

2. Melt 1 tsp. butter in same skillet over medium-high heat. Add shallots and cook, stirring, until fragrant, about 2 minutes. Stir in mustard, Worcestershire sauce, and demi-glace. Add madeira, lemon juice, and parsley. Remove skillet from heat and whisk in remaining 3 tbsp. butter. Season to taste with salt and pepper.

DEMI-GLACE: Render fat from bacon in a large saucepan over medium-low heat, about 15 minutes. Add onions and carrots and cook, stirring occasionally, for 5 minutes. Sprinkle vegetables with flour and continue cooking, stirring occasionally, for 10 minutes. Add tomato paste, parsley, bay leaves, thyme, and 2 quarts (8 cups) beef stock. Simmer, skimming occasionally, over medium heat until sauce has reduced by three-quarters, about 3 hours. Strain sauce, discard solids and return to pan. Add remaining 2 cups beef stock and simmer over medium heat until sauce has reduced by half, about 2½ hours, then strain. (Demi-glace can be stored in the refrigerator in a sealed container for up to 1 week or frozen for up to 6 months.) Makes 2 cups.

The Heat Is On

There are many ways to cook a steak—but all the best methods have one thing in common: the application of intense heat to the meat to seal in its juices. One restaurant technique that doesn't work well at home is broiling: Restaurant ranges can get as hot as 800°, while home ovens can rarely manage more than 500° or so. Here are four methods that do work at home.

PAN-GRILLING: (A) Pat dry 1½"-thick sirloin steaks with paper towels. Season with salt and pepper. Lightly oil a cast-iron grill pan or skillet with vegetable oil, then heat over medium-high heat until very hot. Add steaks. For medium-rare, sear 2 minutes per side, then reduce heat to medium and cook 3 minutes per side. Allow steaks to rest for 5 minutes before serving.

DEEP-FRYING: (B) Pat dry 1½"-thick strip steaks with paper towels. Fill a large, deep pot with vegetable oil and heat over medium heat to 375°. (A toothpick dropped in oil will quickly turn dark brown when oil is ready.) Carefully lower steaks, 1 or 2 at a time, into oil. For medium rare, cook until brown, 5–7 minutes. Remove, drain, and season with salt and pepper.

OUTDOOR GRILLING: (C) Pat dry 1½"-thick T-bone steaks with paper towels. Rub with a little olive oil and season with salt and pepper. Heat gas grill over medium-high heat, or prepare and light coals for a charcoal grill. When grill is very hot, add steaks. For medium rare, cook 10–12 minutes, turning once. Allow steaks to rest for 5 minutes before serving.

SEARING: (D) Best for thin steaks, no more than ¼" thick (like the steak Diane pictured, facing page). See instructions in step 1 at left.

Making Hash

I love making breakfast," writes SAVEUR executive editor Christopher Hirsheimer. "Not every day, of course—but give me a lazy weekend and watch me! My favorite breakfast dish is corned beef hash, topped with perfectly poached eggs. Sometimes I make corned beef and cabbage for dinner just so I can have the leftovers the next morning for hash. If I don't, then I start the night before anyway, simmering a big piece of corned beef (I prefer the bottom round) until it's so tender it falls off a fork. Then I refrigerate it and go to bed. In the morning, I shred the meat and cook 2 potatoes and 2 onions in the corned beef cooking water to add even more salty flavor. I mix the corned beef, the chopped onions, and the potatoes together and cook them to a crisp 'cake' in butter for about 5 minutes on each side. I poach the eggs ahead of time [see page 96], holding them in cold water until it's time to eat; then I reheat them quickly and put them gently on top of the golden-crusted hash."

Corned Beef and Cabbage

SERVES 4–6

THERE ARE THOSE who will inform you that corned beef and cabbage is an American invention, unknown in Ireland. In fact, the Irish have been preserving meat in corns (i.e., grains) of salt since the 11th century, and have long served this homey dish on special occasions. Be forewarned: In cooking, the meat shrinks by about half.

2 medium yellow onions, peeled
6 whole cloves
3½-lb. piece corned beef, preferably bottom round
3 large carrots, peeled and cut into thirds
2 bay leaves
8 black peppercorns
1 medium head green cabbage
4–6 russet potatoes, peeled and halved
Salt and freshly ground black pepper
Hot mustard (optional)

1. Stud onions with cloves. Rinse corned beef in cold water to remove brine. Put beef in a large pot and add onions, carrots, bay leaves, peppercorns, and enough water to cover. Bring to a boil over high heat, cover, and reduce heat to low. Simmer for 2 hours, skimming occasionally.

2. Wash cabbage, remove core and any torn leaves, then cut into 6 wedges. Add cabbage and potatoes to beef, then cover and simmer until potatoes are tender, about 25 minutes.

3. Transfer beef to a cutting board and cover with a plate weighted with heavy cans (weighting makes meat easier to slice). Transfer onions, carrots, cabbage, and potatoes to a platter. Remove cloves from onions. Strain cooking liquid, discarding bay leaves and peppercorns. Return liquid to pot and cook over high heat until reduced by one-third, 20–30 minutes. Season to taste with salt and pepper

4. Return vegetables to stock and heat through for about 5 minutes. Remove plate and cans from meat and cut across the grain, in ¼"-thick slices. Arrange beef and vegetables on warmed platter. Moisten with stock. Serve with additional stock and hot mustard if you like.

Roast Lamb with Potatoes

SERVES 6–8

ON THE GREEK MAINLAND, lamb and kid are typically spit-roasted; on the islands, however, they're more often stuffed and roasted whole (always until well-done) in communal ovens. Greek-Americans continue both traditions, although oven-roasting is more practical.

1–2 heads garlic (about 18 cloves), separated into cloves and peeled
3 tbsp. dried oregano
3 tbsp. dried rosemary
¾ cup extra-virgin olive oil
2 cups fresh lemon juice
3¼ cups red wine
Salt and freshly ground black pepper
1 8-lb. leg of lamb, bone in, trimmed of excess fat
6 lbs. russet potatoes, peeled and cut lengthwise into sixths

1. Finely chop 8 cloves garlic and place in a pan large enough to hold lamb. Add 2 tbsp. oregano, 2 tbsp. rosemary, 6 tbsp. oil, 1 cup lemon juice, wine, and salt and pepper to taste. Mix thoroughly. Place lamb in marinade, turning to coat well on all sides, then cover and refrigerate overnight.

2. Crush 6 cloves garlic and remaining 1 tbsp. oregano and 1 tbsp. rosemary together with a mortar and pestle (or mince them finely together). Season to taste with salt and pepper.

3. Preheat oven to 375°. Remove lamb from marinade, discard marinade, and pierce lamb in 8–10 places with a paring knife. Rub garlic-herb mixture over lamb, pressing it into incisions with your fingers, then coat surface of lamb with about 3 tsp. oil.

4. Mix remaining 3 tbsp. oil and remaining 1 cup lemon juice together in a bowl. Crush remaining 4 cloves garlic, place in a large roasting pan, and add potatoes. Place lamb on top of potatoes. Roast, frequently basting lamb with lemon mixture, and occasionally turning potatoes and basting them with pan juices, for 1 hour and 45 minutes for well-done. Turn off oven. Remove lamb and allow it to rest for about 10 minutes, keeping potatoes warm in oven until you are ready to carve and serve lamb.

Legacy of Lamb

T owards the end of Lent, Greeks from every corner of the New York metropolitan area start streaming into Astoria, a neighborhood in the northwestern corner of Queens with a large Greek-American community. Stores there are stocked with special pastries and cheeses, seasonal vegetables, and plenty of holiday meats—most noticeably the whole lambs and kids that dangle in the meat market windows. K&T Meats, one of Astoria's most venerated butcher shops (facing page), sells some 3,500 lambs and baby goats in the two weeks prior to Easter Sunday. (The rest of the year, they might sell 50 in a typical week.) For Greeks in America, celebrating Easter goes beyond religious observance. It's a strong link to another country and an earlier time. It's an expression of family roots and eternal rhythms.

Close to the Bone

Francis (Frank) Vitale learned how to make this lamb's-neck stew from his father, August, in his family's kitchen in Brooklyn. August in turn got the recipe from his mother, Angelina (the two are pictured above)—an immigrant from Bari, Italy, who brought with her talents as a cook and as a seamstress. She taught her son both her arts, and August went on to make his living as a fine tailor. Frank recalls that his father used to tell him how shy he was to ask the butcher for the lowly lambs' necks needed for the stew, and then pushing across the counter the 50 cents they cost. It felt like such peasant food to him. The recipe worked then, and continues to work. Its simplicity is deceptive, for its flavor derives from its long slow cooking—and the closeness of the meat to the bone. "Everyone just swoons," reports Frank, "when they eat this dish."

Lamb's-Neck Stew with Polenta

SERVES 4–6

SOME DISHES practically *are* their bones. If you boned out lambs' necks, for instance, you'd have nothing but scraps; with the meat still clinging to them, they're dinner! We think lambs' necks are one of the last great "variety meats" yet to be discovered by trendy chefs.

2 medium yellow onions,
   peeled and finely chopped
6 cloves garlic, peeled and
   finely chopped
2 tbsp. extra-virgin
   olive oil
6 lbs. lambs' necks
2 28-oz. cans whole
   Italian tomatoes
3 bay leaves
Salt and freshly ground
   black pepper
3 lbs. fresh green beans,
   trimmed and blanched

POLENTA:
1⅔ cups polenta or coarse-
   grained yellow cornmeal
Salt
4 tbsp. butter
Freshly ground black
   pepper

1. Preheat oven to 325°. Cook onions and garlic in oil in a medium skillet over medium-low heat until soft, about 15 minutes.

2. Place lambs' necks in a roasting pan. Add onion mixture, tomatoes, and bay leaves. Season with salt and pepper. Cover with aluminum foil and cook for 2 hours. Remove from oven, add green beans, stirring to incorporate, re-cover, then return to oven for 1 hour more.

3. About 45 minutes before the lamb stew is done, make the polenta.

4. Remove stew from oven, uncover, discard bay leaves, and season to taste with salt and pepper. Serve stew spooned over polenta.

POLENTA: Combine cornmeal and 7 cups cold salted water in a large pot. (Adding cornmeal to cold water keeps polenta lump-free.) Bring to a boil over medium-high heat. Reduce heat to low and cook, stirring constantly with a wooden spoon, until polenta pulls away from the sides of the pot, 30–40 minutes. Add butter and stir until melted. Season to taste with salt and pepper.

Country Ham with Redeye Gravy

SERVES 1–2

FRIED COUNTRY HAM with redeye gravy (which gets its name not from the ocular condition of those who make it early in the morning, but because the coffee, when stirred into the pan drippings, swirls like the eye of an angry red hurricane) is the centerpiece of a classic Southern breakfast; just add grits and biscuits. (If you start with a whole country ham, see below for how to prepare it.)

1 ¼"-thick slice of
   Smithfield or other
   country-style ham
   (recipe follows), with
   fat untrimmed
½ cup boiling coffee

BOILED COUNTRY HAM:
1 whole 14–16 lb.
   country ham
1 cup cider vinegar
2 cups apple juice
1 cup sugar
1 cup bread crumbs
1 cup brown sugar
2 tsp. freshly ground
   black pepper

1. Fry ham in a large skillet over medium heat, turning once, until browned on both sides, about 10 minutes. Transfer ham to a warm plate.

2. Add coffee to skillet and stir with a wooden spoon, scraping up any brown bits on the bottom of the pan. Pour gravy over ham.

BOILED COUNTRY HAM: To cook a whole country ham, cut off the hock (saving it to flavor black-eyed peas, beans, or greens), then, where the ham gets wider, use a hacksaw to cut about 8 slices ¼"-thick for frying as in recipe above. (You may ask your butcher to makes these cuts for you.) Soak remaining bulky part of original ham overnight in cold water (spiked with cider vinegar) to cover. After soaking, wash in fresh water, and scrub with a stiff brush. Rinse ham well, then put in a large pot with cold water to cover. Bring to a simmer over medium heat, then add apple juice and sugar. Reduce heat to low and simmer 15–20 minutes per lb. When done, remove from heat and allow to rest in cooking liquid until cool enough to handle. Remove from pot and trim off the hard exterior and most, but not all, of the fat. Combine bread crumbs, brown sugar, and pepper. While ham is still warm, pat mixture all over (it will harden as ham cools). To serve, slice ham from hock side in small thin slices.

The Genuine Article

I n Trigg County, Kentucky, ham is a way of life—and like life itself, not necessarily governed by scientific principles. If you ask a ham maker like Audrey P'Pool (facing page, on his smokehouse steps) how long he smokes his specimens, for instance, he's apt to reply, "I know it sounds like a smart-aleck answer, but I do it till I run out of smoke." Trigg County hams, in other words, are made by tradition rather than by recipe. That's just the sort of folksy approach that the USDA frowns upon; hams sold commercially must be produced according to consistent standards, which are concerned with hygiene but not necessarily with quality. That means that unless you visit Trigg County or some other area of the rural South that specializes in ham production, you're unlikely to encounter the real thing. There are some credible approximations, though. The Southern-style country ham originated in Smithfield, Virginia, in the mid-1600s, and today that town remains the capital of high-quality commercial country ham production. Other good examples of the genre are made in Georgia, Tennessee, even Vermont—but Smithfield remains our favorite not-quite-Trigg-County ham.

The Ham Gambit

W hen I first moved to New York City," advertising copywriter Monte Mathews told us, "a friend gave me two pieces of advice: First, if you wear an expensive watch, you can wear anything else you want; second, when you have a lot of people over, buy a cheap ham. I already had the watch, but the cheap-ham tip threw me, and my friend did not elaborate. Not long afterward, at one of my first big-city parties, what should I see center-stage on the buffet table but a giant ham, bone intact, brown as could be. And what a ham! The mingled flavors of brown sugar and orange permeated every bite, and there was a faint hint of spice in the aftertaste. Guests hovered over it, and as the evening wore on, it became unrecognizable—thoroughly picked over. My hostess, flush with the triumph of having entertained so well, was effervescent, and I, feeling particularly close to her that night, offered to stay behind and help clean up. As she washed and I dried, I begged, 'Please talk to me about your ham.' Almost conspiratorially, she instructed me to buy the cheapest ham I could find, glaze the hell out of it, and cook it for a long time. 'You can feed 30 people for $6.99!' she exclaimed. I admit that I've never been able to find a bargain quite like that—but 20 years later, I still swear by cheap ham and a great glaze. I trot one out several times a year, and it's always the hit of the party."

Monte's Ham

SERVES 20–30

ITALIAN PROSCIUTTO can cost $20 to $25 a pound; if Spain's legendary jabugo ham ever reaches these shores, it'll probably run at least twice that. Monte Mathews reports that he's never paid more than 99 cents a pound for a ham to use for this unfailingly popular party dish.

FOR HAM:
1 15-lb. smoked ham,
   on the bone

FOR GLAZE:
1½ cups orange
   marmalade
1 cup dijon mustard
1½ cups firmly packed
   brown sugar
1 rounded tbsp. whole
   cloves

1. For ham, preheat oven to 300°. Trim tough outer skin and excess fat from ham. Put ham in a large roasting pan and score, making crosshatch incisions all over it with a sharp knife. Roast for 2 hours. Remove ham from oven and increase heat to 350°.

2. For glaze, combine orange marmalade, mustard, and brown sugar in a medium bowl. Stud ham with cloves, inserting one at the intersection of each crosshatch, then brush entire surface of ham generously with glaze and return to oven.

3. Cook ham another 1½ hours, brushing with glaze at least 3 times. Transfer to a cutting board or platter and allow to rest for about 30 minutes. Carve and serve warm or at room temperature.

Pork Loin Stuffed with Apples

SERVES 8

THOUGH THIS DISH doesn't seem quite as spectacular as a roast suckling pig with an apple in its mouth, it looks wonderful coming to the table on a large platter for a special occasion (for instance, a family Sunday dinner).

¼ lb. slab bacon, cut into large dice
4 granny smith apples, peeled, cored, and sliced
1 tbsp. sugar
Salt and freshly ground black pepper
2 tbsp. butter
4 medium yellow onions, peeled and sliced
½ lb. white mushrooms, sliced
½ cup cider vinegar
3 tbsp. coarsely chopped fresh sage
1 6-lb. center-cut pork loin (9 chops), trimmed, with bones cracked

1. Cook bacon in a large skillet over medium heat until crisp and golden brown, about 8 minutes. Toss apples with sugar in a bowl. Increase heat in skillet to medium-high, add apples, and sauté until they are golden, about 10 minutes. Season to taste with salt and pepper, then transfer apples to a bowl.

2. In the same skillet, melt butter over medium heat. Add onions and cook, stirring occasionally, until golden, about 20 minutes. Add mushrooms and cook until they begin to brown, about 20 minutes.

3. Increase heat to high, add ¼ cup vinegar, and stir with a wooden spoon until vinegar evaporates, about 1 minute. Add sage and season to taste with salt and pepper. Add onion-mushroom mixture and bacon to apples and allow to cool.

4. Preheat oven to 350°. Stand the loin with the bone side facing away from you and make a 3" slit, about 1½" deep, down the middle of the front of each chop to make a pocket. Spoon about ¼ cup apple mixture into each pocket. (To stuff the whole loin, you will use about half the apple mixture.)

5. Season stuffed loin with salt and pepper, transfer to a roasting pan, and roast for 1 hour. Pour remaining vinegar and ¼ cup water into pan and scrape browned bits off bottom with a wooden spoon. Scatter remaining apple mixture around loin and continue roasting until the internal temperature of pork reaches 170°, about 1¼ hours. Transfer pork to a platter, allow to rest for 15 minutes, then slice into chops and serve with apples.

Playful Pigs

J im Dougherty (facing page), is eager to refute the popularly held myth that hogs are dirty. At his Egg & I Pork Farm in northwestern Connecticut, he gives his pigs adequate space and proper ventilation—and, he reports, they "maintain a clean area and dung in another." He adds fondly, "Hogs are also quite intelligent. They are social animals—very playful, curious, and aware of their surroundings." It is quickly apparent that he really likes his pigs. At the end of a long day, in fact, a visit to the barn is just what he needs to boost his spirits: "I like to walk in the barn just to watch the pigs. It's one of the true pleasures I have."

Family Dinner

Beneva Mayweather invited me, along with other close friends and neighbors, to partake in her family's annual reunion festivities," reports Mary Ann Eagle, a Memphis writer. "When I arrived at the redbrick house, she greeted me from behind an armful of turnip greens. 'Come on in,' she called. The kitchen was filled with family, and we all worked together, cubing potatoes for a salad, washing the greens, rolling out dough for cobblers. Smoke from the barbecue pit outside, tended by the family patriarch, 72-year-old Twillard Mayweather (below), carried the aroma of ribs inside. After a busy morning in the kitchen, we set up the buffet table in the outdoor courtyard, holding more than enough food for the 30 or so guests. I followed excited children and the adults waiting in line, then piled my plate high with Twillard's charred

and smoke-scented ribs, his daughter Emma's crisp fried catfish filets, potato salad, pungent turnip greens, and a round of the chewy cornmeal fritters the family calls 'dog bread' (because the Mayweathers' dogs love them). I joined some cousins at one of the white-draped tables set up in the courtyard. They were already in the midst of recounting family lore, and I laughed, too, as I listened to their stories—of the many times, for instance, that Twillard turned away any of his daughters' suitors who dared to come calling without a necktie. Later, we got up and served ourselves dessert from the groaning table—fresh peach cobbler, homemade vanilla ice cream, and the family's vinegar pie. We visited and ate and laughed some more, until there was nothing left but the crumbs on our plates."

Barbecued Ribs

SERVES 4–6

TWILLARD MAYWEATHER barbecues ribs in a deep pit over smoldering hickory wood for the better part of a day. The smoke that rises up into the meat as the juices drip onto the coals gives the ribs their flavor. Our version, for those without a pit, obtains similar results.

2 2-lb. racks pork
  spareribs

FOR MARINADE:
2 cups cider vinegar
½ cup Worcestershire sauce
Juice of 2 lemons
1 tbsp. spice mix (recipe
  follows)
1 tsp. cayenne

FOR SAUCE:
1½ cups ketchup
4 tbsp. butter
¼ cup cider vinegar
¼ cup brown sugar
¼ cup Worcestershire sauce
Juice of ½ lemon
1½ tsp. dry mustard
½ tsp. cayenne

SPICE MIX:
1 tbsp. paprika
¼ tsp. chili powder
½ tsp. crushed red pepper
¼ tsp. freshly ground
  black pepper
½ tsp. celery salt
⅛ tsp. garlic powder
⅛ tsp. onion powder
⅛ tsp. cayenne
¼ tsp. salt

1. Place ribs in a shallow pan. For marinade, mix together vinegar, Worcestershire sauce, lemon juice, spice mix, and cayenne, then pour over ribs, turning to coat well. Cover and refrigerate ribs for at least 2 hours or as long as overnight.

2. Preheat oven to 200°. Pour off excess marinade from pan and discard. Cook ribs in oven for 3 hours.

3. For sauce, mix together ketchup, butter, vinegar, brown sugar, Worcestershire sauce, lemon juice, mustard, and cayenne with ¾ cup water in a saucepan. Cook over medium heat, stirring occasionally, until sauce thickens, about 15 minutes.

4. To finish ribs on a charcoal or gas grill, place on a rack over a low fire. Cook, turning once, until lightly browned and crusted. This could take 5–30 minutes per side, depending on hotness of fire, distance of ribs from heat, and type of grill. When ribs have browned, baste with sauce and cook, turning once, for 5 minutes more per side. Serve ribs with additional sauce on the side.

SPICE MIX: Toast paprika, chili powder, crushed red pepper, and black pepper in a small pan over medium heat for about 5 minutes. Pulse in a spice grinder until fine, then add celery salt, garlic powder, onion powder, cayenne, and salt. Makes 2 tbsp.

Sweet-and-Sour Pork

SERVES 4

BEFORE HE GRADUATED to more authentic fare, Tom McNamee loved dishes like this one at the Happy Garden restaurant (now closed) in New York's Chinatown. This recipe comes from Wong Kee, also in Chinatown, a restaurant run by former Happy Garden employees.

3 small tomatoes
Half a lemon, sliced
1 small stalk celery, diced
1 small yellow onion,
 peeled and chopped
2 tbsp. julienned
 peeled ginger
⅓ cup pineapple juice
½ cup white vinegar
⅓ cup tomato sauce
½ cup sugar
¾ lb. pork butt, cut into
 1½" pieces
Salt and freshly ground
 white pepper
1 tsp. garlic powder
½ cup flour
5 tbsp. cornstarch
Vegetable oil
1 cup diced fresh pineapple

1. Pour 2 cups water into a medium pot. Chop 1 tomato and add to pot. Add lemon, celery, onions, and ginger, and bring to a boil over high heat. Reduce heat to medium and simmer for 20 minutes. Add pineapple juice, vinegar, tomato sauce, and sugar. Mix well, then simmer for 30 minutes more.

2. Meanwhile, season pork with salt, pepper, and garlic powder and set aside for 20 minutes. In a small bowl, mix together flour, 4 tbsp. cornstarch, and enough water (about ½ cup) to make a smooth batter. Pour oil into a skillet to a depth of 1½" and heat over medium-high heat until hot, about 350°. Dip pork in batter, shake off excess, then fry in batches until crisp and golden, about 4 minutes per batch. Drain on paper towels.

3. Quarter remaining 2 tomatoes and set aside. Combine remaining 1 tbsp. cornstarch with 2 tbsp. water in a small bowl and mix well. Add cornstarch mixture to sauce, increase heat to medium-high, and simmer for about 2 minutes. Add pineapple to sauce, cook for 30 seconds, then add quartered tomatoes and pork. Heat through, then serve with white rice, if you like.

The Happy Garden

We were stoned. God, were we stoned," recalls author Tom McNamee (below). "It was part of the job, we figured. I was a nascent A&R man. Artists-and-repertoire men were the guys who signed 'talent' to the label and produced what our boss called 'wrekkids'. You stayed up till all hours in clubs in the Village, listening to rock bands and scouting for talent, and you had an unlimited expense account. I was still wearing tweed jackets and bow ties, but my colleagues had long hair and snakeskin boots. We'd go for Chinese—usually to the Happy Garden on the Bowery, because they served till 4 A.M. and because we loved the ironic smile of our waiter, Mark. There, we'd have the classic Sino-American stuff that the Chinese themselves never ate—sweet-and-sour pork, moo goo gai pan. Marijuana food. Then one night I told Mark that we wanted to try some real Cantonese food. He gave us a doubtful look. 'American no like.' 'No. We like.' (I hoped.) Would he compose a menu for us? 'What you like?' 'Anything.' Soon, we couldn't stay away. Our tables grew bigger, the menus more subtle and complex. 'Last time you have black mushroom with fish ball, salt-and-pepper shrimp, steam squab,' Mark would say. He never forgot what we'd had before. 'Maybe you try fresh frog with garlic.' 'Fresh!' said Mark. 'Live ten minute ago.' 'Naw!' I said. So he led me into the black, stinking, rain-slimed backyard and bade me look into a dark wooden barrel. Hundreds of eyes peered back."

Bierocks

MAKES 12

ON MENNONITE farms in south-central Kansas, these meat-filled buns (pronounced "BEER-ocks"), which the Mennonites learned to make in Russia during the 18th and 19th centuries, were once served in the fields, as part of a working lunch. Today, they're enjoyed anytime.

FOR DOUGH:
1 tsp. active dry yeast
5 cups bread flour
½ cup sugar
Salt
1½ cups lukewarm milk
10 tbsp. butter, melted
2 eggs, lightly beaten

FOR FILLING:
3 tbsp. vegetable oil
1 yellow onion, peeled
    and finely chopped
1 lb. ground beef
4 cups shredded green
    cabbage
¼ lb. mild cheddar cheese,
    grated
2 tbsp. dijon mustard
Freshly ground black
    pepper

1. For dough, dissolve yeast in 2 tbsp. warm water in a small bowl. Mix together flour, sugar, and ½ tsp. salt in a large bowl. Add milk, 8 tbsp. butter, and eggs to yeast, then stir into flour (if dough is too dry, add more water). Turn dough out onto a lightly floured surface and knead until elastic, about 5 minutes. Put dough in an oiled bowl, turning it to coat with oil, then cover bowl with a clean dish towel and set aside for dough to rise until doubled, about 30 minutes. Punch dough down, then set aside to rise for 30 minutes more.

2. For filling, heat 2 tbsp. oil in a large skillet over medium heat. Add onions and cook until soft, about 15 minutes. Increase heat to medium-high, add beef, and brown for 8 minutes. Stir in cabbage, cook for 10 minutes, then add cheese and mustard and season to taste with salt and pepper. Cook for 5 minutes more, then set aside to cool.

3. Preheat oven to 350°. Return dough to floured surface and divide into 12 balls (**A**). Roll out into 6" rounds. Spoon about ¼ cup beef mixture into center of each round, then fold edges in (**B**) and pinch closed (**C**). Place, seam side down, on an oiled baking sheet and set aside to rise for 20 minutes. Bake until golden (**D**), 15–20 minutes. Brush tops with remaining 2 tbsp. butter (**E**). Serve warm or at room temperature (**F**).

Meat Buns

 ll over the world, working men (and women) eat meat or vegetables wrapped in dough—not sandwiches in this case, but sealed, savory pies—as a portable, economical lunch. Many such specialties have been imported to this country. While the Mennonites of Kansas have their bierocks, for instance, Jamaicans transplanted to America brought with them the flaky, spicy beef buns called patties; the Cornish in Michigan's Upper Peninsula make "pasties" (pronounced "PASS-tees"), stuffed with ground beef or, in lean times, potatoes (pasties were originally the luncheon fare of tin miners in the homeland, and were marked with each man's initials before baking, to avoid disputes of ownership). Jewish communities snack on knishes filled with potatoes, liver, cheese, kasha (buckwheat groats), or broccoli; the half-moon-shaped empanadas of Latin American populations may contain anything from long-cooked pork or beef to canned tuna; and the Chinese, of course, make pork buns, or bao, with a thick, soft pastry not unlike that used for bierocks. (The closest thing mainstream America has been able to come up with may be that cocktail-party staple, pigs in a blanket.)

179

Joe's Special

A LEGENDARY San Francisco regional delight, surprisingly little known outside the Bay Area, Joe's special (eggs aside) is no omelette. When it is properly made, it's a loosely bound "scramble" of a dish—simple and good.

1½ lbs. fresh spinach
Salt
2 tbsp. extra-virgin olive oil
1 medium yellow onion, peeled and chopped
½ lb. ground beef
3 eggs, lightly beaten
Grated parmigiano-reggiano
Freshly ground black pepper

1. Trim spinach and wash thoroughly (see page 48), then blanch in a pot of boiling salted water over medium-high heat for 2 minutes. Drain in a colander and cool under cold running water. Squeeze out excess water, then coarsely chop spinach.

2. Heat oil in a skillet over medium-high heat. Add onions and cook, until soft, about 10 minutes. Add beef and cook, breaking meat up with the back of a spoon, until brown, about 3 minutes.

3. Add spinach, cook for 2 minutes, then add eggs and cook, without stirring, for 30 seconds. Remove from heat, stir, and season to taste with grated parmigiano-reggiano, salt, and pepper.

Eureka! It's Joe's!

C ulinary lore is full of tales of the accidental discovery of dishes. The cupboard is bare save a few ingredients, but the cook, undaunted, whips up something wonderful and the crowd cheers; a classic is born. That's what happened (maybe) on Fourth of July weekend, 1924, when Caesar Cardini concocted his now-ubiquitous salad of romaine lettuce flavored with Worcestershire sauce and romano cheese at his Caesar's Palace in Tijuana, Mexico. That's what probably happened with Buffalo wings on October 30, 1964, when Teressa Bellissimo found that she had no food in her Anchor Bar kitchen in Buffalo, New York, except for chicken wings, hot sauce, margarine, and blue cheese. And that's what must have happened when Joe's Special was first concocted in San Francisco, out of spinach, ground beef, and eggs. In this case, however, there is much controversy over exactly when and where the serendipity that spawned this creation occurred. There are restaurants with "Joe's" in the name all over the Bay Area, and more than one of them has claimed the dish. Some scholars give the nod to New Joe's, on Geary Street; but Original Joe's, on Taylor Street, has had it on the menu since the place was opened in 1937 by Ante Rodin. Rodin is still behind the bar there, so ask him to tell you the story.

Carne Picada Burritos

SERVES 2

LONG BEFORE "wraps" became the new food fad, Kenneth Haddad was serving these burritos at El Paso's H&H Coffee Shop. The secret of their success, says Haddad, is the use of tri-tip, the tender bottom of the sirloin tip.

2 tbsp. vegetable oil
1 medium yellow onion, peeled and diced
1 lb. tri-tip beef
2 fresh jalapeños, seeded and chopped (see Note)
2 tomatoes, diced
1 clove garlic, peeled and minced
2 tsp. H&H spice salt (recipe follows)
6 large flour tortillas

H&H SPICE SALT:
2 chicken-flavored bouillon cubes
1 tsp. freshly ground black pepper
1 tsp. garlic salt

1. Heat oil in a large skillet over medium heat. Add onions and cook until soft, about 15 minutes.

2. Trim beef of any fat and cut into ½" dice. Add beef and jalapeños to onions, increase heat to high, and brown meat for 2 minutes. Stir in tomatoes, garlic, and H&H spice salt, adding more if needed. To serve, wrap in warm flour tortillas.

NOTE: *Handling Chiles*—Always wear rubber gloves, and avoid touching any exposed skin or your eyes.

H&H SPICE SALT: Grind bouillon cubes, pepper, and garlic salt together with a mortar and pestle or in a spice grinder until well mixed and fine. Makes about 1 tbsp. spice salt.

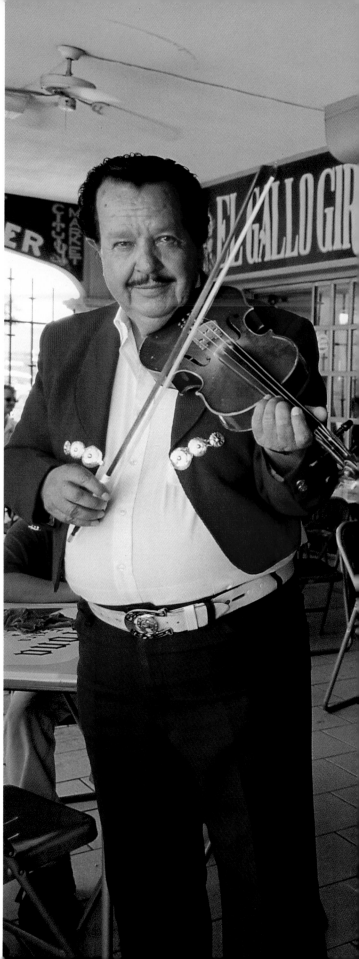

Border Food

The cities of El Paso, Texas, and Ciudad Juárez, Mexico (left), face each other across our southern border—but the typical cooking of this region isn't standard "Tex/Mex". Here, oil is used more than lard, beef more than pork, and jack cheese more than the softer Mexican cheeses. At the H&H Coffee Shop in El Paso (above), proprietor Kenneth Haddad goes further, pointing out that his food is not overloaded with sour cream and lettuce, or covered with melted yellow cheese. It is surprisingly delicate food, in fact—full of flavor and texture and is occasionally spicy but stylistically subtle.

Meat Loaf

SERVES 6–8

ONCE, WHEN ASKED what his favorite dish was, Craig Claiborne replied, "Anything with ground meat." As with any ground-meat dish, meat loaf is best (and lightest in texture) when the meat is handled as little as possible.

3 tbsp. extra-virgin
  olive oil
2 large yellow onions,
  peeled and minced
2 cloves garlic, peeled and
  minced
3 lbs. ground chuck
1 8-oz. can tomato sauce
1 egg, lightly beaten
1 cup fresh bread crumbs
Salt and freshly ground
  black pepper
3 tbsp. ketchup (recipe
  follows)

KETCHUP:

1 28-oz. can tomato purée
1 medium yellow onion,
  peeled and quartered
1 clove garlic, crushed and
  peeled
½ fresh jalapeño, seeded
  (wear rubber gloves when
  handling hot chiles)
2 tbsp. dark brown sugar
½ cup cider vinegar
Pinch cayenne
Pinch celery salt
Pinch dry mustard
Pinch ground allspice
Pinch ground cloves
Pinch ground ginger
Pinch ground cinnamon
Salt and freshly ground
  black pepper

1. Heat oil in a medium sauté pan over low heat. Add onions and garlic and cook until soft, about 15 minutes. Remove from heat and allow to cool.

2. Preheat oven to 350°. Combine ground chuck, tomato sauce, egg, bread crumbs, half the onion-garlic mixture, and salt and pepper to taste in a large bowl. Stir just enough to mix.

3. Place meat in a 3" × 11" loaf pan and round the top with your hands to form a crown. Top with remaining onion-garlic mixture and drizzle with ketchup. Bake for 45 minutes. Remove from oven and let stand about 10 minutes for easier slicing.

VARIATION: *Mushroom Meat Loaf*—Omit the tomato sauce in step 2. Substitute 2 tbsp. ketchup, ½ cup dry sherry, and 1 cup sautéed mushrooms.

VARIATION: *Horseradish Meat Loaf*—Omit the tomato sauce in step 2. Substitute 1–2 tbsp. horseradish, ¼ cup cream, and 2 tbsp. ketchup.

KETCHUP: Combine tomato purée, onion, garlic, jalapeño, and sugar in a blender or food processor. Pulse until blended, then add vinegar and 1 cup water and purée until smooth. Transfer to a medium saucepan, add cayenne, celery salt, dry mustard, allspice, cloves, ginger, and cinnamon. Cook, stirring occasionally, over low heat for 45 minutes. Season to taste with salt and pepper. (Store in refrigerator for up to 1 month.) Makes 3 cups.

Secrets of the Red Stuff

K etchup. It starts its life as an edible fruit, gets categorized by the USDA as a vegetable, and winds up at McDonald's as a condiment. Considering that it began its journey to America as ke-tsiap, a 17th-century Chinese brine of pickled fish and spices, we're talking a food with a severe identity crisis. Which seems unfair, considering what a simple food it really is. The Heinz company, which invented ketchup as we know it, says that it squeezes 24 of its own specially bred tomatoes into each bottle, along with white vinegar, corn syrup, salt, and natural flavorings (plus a secret ingredient, which SAVEUR contributor Stephanie Pierson managed to identify, while touring the Heinz factory in Fremont, Ohio, as clove oil). We like Heinz ketchup, incidentally—but we also like to make our own (above).

Carter Rochelle's Real Texas Chili

SERVES 6

PRIZE-WINNING recipes for chili may abound in the West Texas town of Terlingua, Texas, but we prefer this one from Carter Rochelle, a native Houstonian and chili connoisseur. (Competition chili must make an impact in one bite; we find it too rich and salty for a bowlful.)

6 oz. suet, cut into small pieces
3 lbs. boneless chuck, trimmed and diced
4 cloves garlic, peeled and minced
6 tbsp. chili powder
Salt and freshly ground black pepper
1 cup masa harina
4 cups beef stock, warm (see page 40)
3 tbsp. white vinegar
Cayenne
Cilantro sprigs for garnish

1. Melt suet in a large heavy skillet over medium-high heat. Remove and discard any solid pieces of suet, then add beef, in batches if necessary, and brown, turning occasionally, for 5 minutes.

2. Reduce heat to medium. Add garlic and chili powder, season to taste with salt and pepper, and mix well. Cook, stirring with a wooden spoon, for 1 minute, then sprinkle meat mixture with masa harina, and mix in thoroughly.

3. Gradually stir in stock, 4 cups warm water, and vinegar. Reduce heat to low and simmer, partially covered, stirring occasionally. Cook until meat is tender and begins to "melt" into sauce, about 4 hours; add water as necessary. Adjust seasoning with salt and cayenne. Serve garnished with cilantro.

No Beans, Y'all

M eat is cooked with chiles (literally chiles con carne) all over Mexico. At some point in the 1800s, the notion crossed the border into the American Southwest, spread throughout the southern states, and then found its way throughout this country. But Texas-style chili remains distinct, as opposed to the sometimes meatless chili of New Mexico, say, or the variety made in California, which includes tomatoes and beans and is often topped with sour cream—not to mention Cincinnati chili, flavored with cinnamon and sometimes served over spaghetti! Orthodox Texas chili is basically a ragout of cut-up (not ground) beef cooked in a little water with chiles and garlic and often seasoned with cumin and oregano. Texan purists frown on the use of tomatoes and wouldn't for a moment consider beans. The West Texas ghost town of Terlingua (population 25) hosts not one but two annual international chili cook-offs simultaneously (facing page). Both competitions draw thousands of attendees and hundreds of cooks. Their chilis run the gamut "from pleasingly punchy to bland to overbearing," notes Houston-based writer Eric Lawlor. "One was so hot it should have come with a warning label."

7

VEGETABLES

"I HAVE BEEN invited to a lot of

fascinating places in my life, but this

was a first: the opportunity to spend

a whole day paying homage to the

legume that made succotash what it is

today. 'You're going *where?*' my jealous friends demanded incredulously. 'To the National Lima Bean Festival in West Cape May, New Jersey,' I proudly replied."

—STEPHANIE PIERSON ON LIMA BEANS (*SEE RECIPE ON PAGE 206*)

RECIPES

Peas and Lettuce

Serves 4

FRESH GREEN PEAS have a remarkable intensity of flavor, with a nip of acidity, a dust of earthiness, and a touch of sweetness. These are fairly perishable qualities, however, so always cook the peas simply and quickly, boiling them briefly, as below, or steaming them lightly.

Salt
2 lbs. fresh peas in pods, to yield 2 cups shelled peas
1 pinch sugar
1 tbsp. butter
Freshly ground black pepper
4 heads baby bibb lettuce

1. Bring 3 cups salted water to a boil in a medium saucepan over medium-high heat. Meanwhile, shell peas, then add to boiling water with a pinch of sugar, and cook until peas are just tender, 1–3 minutes.

2. Drain peas in a colander, then return them to the warm pot to "dry". Toss with butter and season to taste with a little salt and a few grinds of pepper.

3. Remove the outer leaves of baby bibb lettuce and pull out the inner cores (reserving both for another use), to yield two tender middle leaves per head. Arrange these leaves on a platter and spoon peas into the 8 lettuce "cups". (Peas will slightly wilt lettuce.)

VARIATION: *Peas and Onions*—Add 1 cup boiled, peeled pearl onions to cooked peas, then spoon mixture into lettuce cups.

VARIATION: *Peas and Mint*—Add ¼ cup julienned fresh mint leaves to cooked peas, then spoon mixture into lettuce cups.

Mind Your Peas

T he green pea is an ancient legume—a venerable vegetable. Archaeological evidence suggests that it may have been cultivated nearly 12,000 years ago in such disparate places as Switzerland and Thailand, and later in India and the Middle East. The ancient Greeks and Romans ate peas. So did more recent generations of Italians, Spaniards, and French. (Ninon de Lenclos, a notorious French courtesan, considered them an aphrodisiac and ate them puréed—sometimes spiked with sherry.) Christopher Columbus is said to have introduced green peas to the Americas, planting them on Santo Domingo in 1492. Thomas Jefferson, who grew peas at Monticello, called them his favorite vegetable and catalogued more than 50 varieties. Most of the green peas we eat today come from California, and a survey done there in the late 1970s declared the pea the most "characteristic" American vegetable of all. Peas are harvested primarily between January and June, but especially in late spring. Fresh green peas remain, blessedly, largely a seasonal pleasure.

Spinach doesn't need a lot of pampering, but there are certain techniques that can help intensify its flavor:

BLANCHING (A) helps spinach hold its bright green color and improves its flavor. Simply bring a large pot of water to boil, add washed spinach (see page 48), and cook about 2 minutes. Drain, then cool under cold running water.

SQUEEZING (B) spinach dry in the palms of your hands is easy, and good enough for most purposes. If a recipe calls for very dry spinach, though, wring out small amounts in a clean tea towel.

STEAMING (C) spinach can be an end in itself as well as a step towards creamed spinach. Add washed spinach with water still clinging to leaves, to a pot, then cover and cook over medium heat for about 5 minutes. Drain or squeeze out any water.

SAUTÉING (D) is yet another fine way to cook spinach. Rub a large skillet with 1 peeled garlic clove, add some extra-virgin olive oil, and place over medium heat. When oil is hot, add 1 lb. washed, dried spinach. Cook, stirring, until tender, about 5 minutes.

Creamed Spinach

SERVES 4

MOST RECIPES for creamed spinach include a pinch or two of nutmeg. The 123-year-old Locke-Ober Restaurant in Boston, which has served this popular side dish since it opened, follows this tradition—but adds a further jolt of flavor with a splash of anise-scented Pernod.

2 lbs. fresh spinach, trimmed
Salt
1 tbsp. butter
1 shallot, peeled and minced
2 tsp. Pernod
2 tsp. flour
⅔ cup half-and-half
Pinch of freshly ground nutmeg
Freshly ground black pepper

1. Wash spinach thoroughly (see page 48), then put it, with washing water still clinging to its leaves, in a large pot over medium heat. Sprinkle with salt and cook, stirring occasionally, until spinach has wilted to one quarter of its volume, 3–5 minutes.

2. Drain in a colander and cool under cold running water. Squeeze out excess water and roughly chop. Melt butter in a skillet over medium-low heat, and add shallots and cook until soft, about 10 minutes. Add Pernod, then stir in flour with a wooden spoon or a small whisk and cook 1–2 minutes to eliminate raw flour taste. Stir in half-and-half and, when heated through, add spinach and nutmeg. Cook, stirring occasionally, until creamed spinach is thick, about 3 minutes. Season to taste with salt and pepper.

Turnip Greens

SERVES 6

IN THE SOUTH, "pot likker"—the liquid that greens are cooked in—is often served on its own, to be sipped like soup. Here, however, it is spooned right into the bowl with the greens so that they can continue to steep.

¼ lb. salt pork, coarsely
   chopped
3 lbs. turnip greens
1 lb. mustard greens
1 tbsp. sugar
1 jalapeño, halved
   (see Note, page 182)
¼ cup bacon drippings
   (optional)
Salt
Hot sauce such as Tabasco
   (optional)

1. Put salt pork in a large pot, add 6 cups water, and bring to a boil over high heat. Reduce heat to low and simmer, covered, for 40 minutes.

2. Trim turnip greens and mustard greens, discarding thick stems and discolored leaves. To remove dirt and grit, rinse as for spinach (see page 48).

3. Add greens to salt pork, stirring with a wooden spoon. When greens are submerged in liquid, add sugar and jalapeño. Add bacon drippings, if using, and season with salt (use slightly less if bacon drippings are added). Cover and simmer for 1½ hours. To serve, spoon greens and plenty of the "likker" into individual bowls. Adjust seasoning to taste with salt, and a dash of hot sauce if you like.

Greens Revolution

No soul-food meal is complete without greens—hot, wet, salty, and sometimes spicy. Greens are often the tops of root vegetables like turnips. White families in the big houses of the Old South kept the tender parts of the plant, while their slaves made do with the discards. And they did so well that greens—like many other dishes originated by slaves—soon moved into the big houses. "My hometown, Natchez, Mississippi," notes writer Sarah Gray Miller, "has more of those big, white-columned, antebellum mansions than any other place in America. And probably more greens, too. My father loves greens—he could compose entire symphonies in their honor—so my childhood memories are forever linked with that distinct half-rotten, half-sweet smell of a pot of collards simmering on an old gas stove. My dad, who was born and raised in Charlotte, eats his greens two ways: North Carolina–style, with vinegar, and Mississippi-style, with hot sauce. Pot likker is his nectar. He drinks it straight, uses it as soup stock, and pours it over corn bread. He's a purist, and usually cooks only one kind of greens at a time—but on his rebellious days, he'll throw mustards, collards, and turnips all into the same huge pot. Since greens cook down to nothing, you have to start with a pile of leaves too big to wash in any sink. Once, my father actually put ten pounds of collards into our washing machine—where they disintegrated and returned later to haunt my mother washing a load of white sheets. Now, he just throws them in the bathtub and uses a shower massager to remove stubborn grit."

A Family Affair

Ted and Susan Blew—with the help of their children, Charity, Eric, Amanda, and Jonathan (above)—grow what the market demands, at their family farm in Hunterdon County, New Jersey. And that market is usually the Union Square Greenmarket in New York City, which lately has been clamoring for their 151 kinds of hot chiles, 70 kinds of sweet peppers, 40 kinds of squash, 17 kinds of eggplants, as well as tomatoes, tomatillos, watermelons, and muskmelons. In the farm greenhouses, Susan also coddles nasturtiums, herbs (everything from borage to cinnamon basil), and 30 varieties of lettuces and other greens. In addition, the Blews raise farm hogs and cultivate about 55 acres of corn, oats, rye, wheat, and buckwheat. The Greenmarket sees at least some of everything they produce.

Grilled Vegetable Stacks

SERVES 8

ONE OF THE BEAUTIES of this dish (besides the obvious freshness and color of these seasonal vegetables from the Blew family farm) is that it looks as if you've made a huge effort, when the preparation is really quite simple.

2 medium eggplants, sliced into ¼" rounds
Salt
1 medium yellow squash, sliced into ¼" rounds
1 medium zucchini, sliced into ¼" rounds
2 medium tomatoes, sliced into ½" rounds
½ cup extra-virgin olive oil, plus additional for brushing vegetables
2 ½ tbsp. red wine vinegar
1 tbsp. coarsely chopped fresh parsley
1 tbsp. coarsely chopped fresh basil leaves
Freshly ground black pepper
¼ cup diced red bell pepper

1. Sprinkle eggplants with salt and layer in a colander. Weigh down with a plate and set aside to drain for 20 minutes. Brush salt off eggplant with paper towel and pat dry.

2. Preheat a gas or charcoal grill, or place a stovetop grill pan over medium-high heat. Lightly brush all vegetables with oil, then grill, turning once, until tender and slightly charred, about 30 seconds per side for tomatoes, 2–3 minutes per side for eggplant, squash, and zucchini.

3. Whisk together oil, vinegar, parsley, and basil in a mixing bowl. Season to taste with salt and pepper. To assemble stacks, place 1 eggplant slice on a plate, then top with a tomato slice, a second eggplant slice, a squash slice, and a zucchini slice. Repeat process to use up all vegetables, then drizzle vegetable stacks with dressing and top with diced red peppers.

Roasted Autumn Vegetables

SERVES 6–8

ROOT VEGETABLES — winter's bounty—have been misunderstood, and thus mistreated, for generations. The only way to subdue them, it was long thought, was to boil them into murky submission. But parsnips, turnips, beets, rutabagas, winter squash, and the rest greatly benefit from slow roasting, which concentrates their earthy sweetness.

8–10 lbs. of assorted vegetables such as pumpkin, butternut squash, shallots, small yellow onions, rutabagas, beets, and parsnips
Extra-virgin olive oil
Fresh herbs such as thyme, sage, and oregano
Salt and freshly ground black pepper

1. Preheat oven to 350°. Peel and seed vegetables as necessary or, if small and tender enough, simply trim them and scrub them well.

2. Coarsely cut vegetables into large pieces of approximately equal size. Arrange vegetables in a large baking pan and brush with oil. Scatter sprigs of herbs on top of vegetables. Season to taste with salt and pepper. Place in oven and roast, turning vegetables occasionally, until they are golden on the edges and tender when pierced with a knife, about 1 hour.

VARIATION: *Vegetable Rack*—Another way to roast vegetables is to use them as "rack" on which to roast a whole chicken, or a pork or lamb roast. Place a 2" layer of coarsely chopped root vegetables in a baking pan. Add a handful of chopped parsley and thyme, drizzle with oil, and season to taste with salt and pepper. Place meat on top and roast as above.

VARIATION: *Roasted Vegetable Stock*—Use leftovers from either of the above recipes to make this stock. Simmer roasted vegetables in 6 cups water, 1 cup wine, and 6 black peppercorns over low heat for about two hours. Strain stock and discard solids. Season to taste with salt. If not used immediately, refrigerate or freeze. Makes about 1 quart.

Reclaiming the Seasons

I t is entirely possible that, while standing in the produce aisle of a fluorescent-lit supermarket, we could find ourselves unable to name the month or even the season," comments garden writer Warren Schultz, who was raised on a farm in upstate New York. "The peaches say June, but the acorn squash scream October. Week after week, identical iceberg lettuces are stacked to the same height, next to the carrots, beside the broccoli. There's an incredible array of food, but no sense of bounty, no earthiness. Every speck of soil that once cradled these vegetables and fruit is gone. All traces of the human energy that went into planting and harvesting has been long since washed and waxed and trimmed away. Seduced by the promise of out-of-season tomatoes or apples, we've become jaded by constant disappointment in their flavor. Soon, we begin to take what we eat for granted. We owe it to ourselves to take back our food, and to recall its power to connect us with nature—even (or perhaps especially) if it means eating parsnips and rutabagas in their cold-weather glory instead of artificially promulgated asparagus and peas that promise nothing more than a mockery of spring."

Taming the Thistle

The first man to eat an oyster may have been very brave, but whoever first nibbled an artichoke (**A**) wasn't just fearless but ingenious. It's not immediately apparent, that is, how to address the beast. But here's some of what artichoke eaters have figured out over the years:

PARING: Americans usually discard the tasty stem of the artichoke, but in Europe and the Middle East, it is much appreciated. Use a paring knife or vegetable peeler to trim away the stem's fibrous outer layer (**B**), rub with lemon to prevent discoloration, and leave intact when cooking whole artichoke. The stem can be sliced and used in place of, or in addition to, the heart, in many recipes.

TRIMMING: The tips of the artichoke's bracts, or leaves, are barbed (this is a thistle, after all), and often needle-sharp. To avoid getting pricked, trim all full-size artichokes before handling them further. Using a very sharp or serrated knife, slice off the top ½" to 1" of the closed leaves (**C**). (Baby artichokes haven't yet developed thorns and don't need trimming.) To trim leaves, first pull away one or two layers of the tough outer leaves around the base, then use sharp scissors to cut off the ends of each outer leaf (**D**), and rub with lemon.

REMOVING THE CHOKE: It's much easier to spoon out the choke from a cooked artichoke, but some stuffed-artichoke recipes call for removing the choke before cooking. To do this, gently spread apart the trimmed leaves, pull out and discard the pale, thorny, innermost leaves, then scrape out the choke with a spoon or melon-baller (**E**) and discard it. To prepare hearts, raw or cooked (it's easier once they are cooked), remove all leaves and choke, then trim heart (**F**), rubbing cut surfaces with lemon.

COOKING: Steaming (**G**), described at right, yields the most vivid flavor, but boiling is also an option. Put artichokes in a large pot of salted water (**H**), weighting them with a heavy plate to keep submerged. Simmer over medium-high heat until tender, 30–40 minutes. Some cooks add lemon to the water to keep them green, but artichokes turn gray-green anyway. Test for doneness by carefully plucking a large outer leaf. If it pulls out easily, the artichoke is done. Scrape pulp out of leaves with a spoon (**I**), for ravioli stuffing and other uses.

Steamed Artichoke

SERVES 1

THOUGH THE ARTICHOKE is believed to have originated in the Middle East as a refinement of the cardoon, it has become an American favorite—and the Central California town of Castroville claims, apparently with good reason, to be the artichoke capital of the entire world.

1 medium artichoke, per person, trimmed
1 lemon, halved (see left)
Mayonnaise, vinaigrette, or melted butter

1. Place a steaming rack inside a large pot with a lid, and add enough water to come just under the rack. Bring water to a boil over medium heat. Place artichokes, stem down, on rack, cover, and steam until you can easily pull out a leaf, 30–40 minutes. Check water occasionally to be sure it hasn't boiled away, adding more boiling water if necessary.

2. When artichoke is cooked, remove from pot and set on a plate upside down to cool. When cool enough to handle, remove choke, or serve the artichoke as is, with mayonnaise, vinaigrette, or melted butter.

Sally's Ramps with Bacon

SERVES 4–6

RAMPS ARE WILD LEEKS, with pungent bulbs and leaf-shaped shoots. Writer Sally Schneider learned how to cook them this way at the annual ramp festival in Helvetia, West Virginia, which she attends every year.

2 lbs. ramps
½ lb. sliced bacon
Salt and freshly ground
    black pepper

1. To clean ramps, peel off the outer skin, then trim off and discard roots. Wash under cold running water to rinse away any dirt and grit clinging to the bulbs or leaves. Cut bulbs from the leaves and reserve both.

2. Fry bacon in a large skillet over medium heat, turning occasionally, until crisp and golden brown, about 15 minutes. Remove bacon from skillet, drain on paper towels, and set aside. Pour off all but about 2 tbsp. bacon grease from pan.

3. Add ramp bulbs and ½ cup water to same skillet and cook over medium heat, stirring frequently, until bulbs are soft, about 15 minutes. Coarsely chop leaves, add to skillet, and cook until wilted. Crumble in bacon and cook until ramps are soft and all liquid has been absorbed. Season to taste with salt and pepper.

Ramped Up

Ramps grow wild throughout the Appalachian Mountains. Ramp season is short, from the end of March to early May, after which these leeks grow too strong to eat. Even before that happens, ramps are notorious for their odor, which lingers on the breath and in the air near where they have been cooked—but cooked they are, in many ways: ramp chili, ramp home fries, ramps and eggs, ramp meat loaf, ramp pie, raw ramp and corn bread sandwiches. Because ramps are one of the first growing things to appear in Helvetia, West Virginia, after the harsh snows of winter, eating them is a virtual rite of spring. Finding and harvesting ramps is arduous work, as is cleaning them. Families leave before dawn on their harvesting ventures to keep the locations of their hunting grounds secret. When they get there, they find the plants grown so deeply into the stony soil that trowels, hoes, and sometimes even screwdrivers are needed to get them out, with bulbs intact. Every April, ramp suppers are held not just in Helvetia but statewide in West Virginia—in community halls, Elks' Clubs, and elementary schools. For about $7, you can eat your fill of country ham, fried potatoes, corn bread, coleslaw, beans, applesauce, and fried ramps—a celestial combination.

The Bean Queen

The town of West Cape May, New Jersey, chooses Miss Lima Bean, at its annual festival in honor of this oft-disrespected vegetable, in a manner that we believe the Miss America Pageant would do well to emulate. To enter, you write your name on a piece of paper, put it in a shoe box, and hope you get picked. One recent year, the winner was Ashley Ruberti (above), an 8-year-old Snow White look-alike who was crowned by SAVEUR Consulting Editor Sheila Lukins (above, left) with a faux-rhinestone tiara and given a green hooded lima bean sweatshirt. "I've been to the Dandelion Festival in Vineland," we heard one observer say as the ceremony proceeded, "and it's got nothing on this."

Lima Mash with Lemon and Olive Oil

MAKES 1½ CUPS

PEOPLE GO CRAZY these days for favas and lentils and cannellini beans, but it doesn't take much to make America's own lima beans into something equally special. Puréed and spread on toasted country bread, limas become a surprisingly good Mediterranean-ish appetizer.

2 cups fresh or frozen baby lima beans
2 cloves garlic, peeled and sliced
Salt
3 tbsp. extra-virgin olive oil
1 lemon
Freshly ground black pepper
Country-style bread, cut into small pieces

1. Combine lima beans, garlic, and ½ cup salted water in a medium saucepan. Bring to a boil over medium-high heat. Cover, reduce heat to low, and simmer until beans are very soft, about 15 minutes.

2. Coarsely purée beans and garlic in a food processor. Transfer to a small bowl and gradually beat in olive oil. Remove zest from lemon with a zester (or use a vegetable peeler, then finely julienne zest). Add lemon juice to taste, then season with salt and pepper. Serve in a small bowl with country-style bread on the side—or toast the bread and top with lima mash, drizzle with a little olive oil, and garnish with additional lemon zest.

VARIATION: *Mashed Beans*—For limas, you *can* substitute cooked fresh fava beans, cooked navy or cannellini beans, or cooked red lentils.

Stuffed Peppers

SERVES 4

THOUGH STANDARD European and American stuffed pepper recipes call for bell peppers (or, in Mexico, long, mild anaheim chiles), we like to stuff poblanos or similar varieties to give the dish a spicy lift. Choose colors, sizes, and levels of spiciness to suit your moods and tastes.

8 fresh poblano peppers or
   4 green bell peppers
¼ cup extra-virgin
   olive oil
1 small yellow onion,
   peeled and diced
1 clove garlic, peeled
   and minced
¼ lb. ground beef
¼ lb. ground pork
Salt and freshly ground
   black pepper
1 large tomato, peeled,
   seeded, and chopped
1 pinch ground nutmeg
1 ¼ cups cooked long-grain
   white rice
1 tbsp. chopped fresh
   marjoram leaves
1 tbsp. chopped fresh
   thyme
1 tbsp. chopped fresh
   parsley
¼ cup fresh bread
   crumbs

1. Char peppers over a gas flame or under a hot broiler, turning to blacken all over. Place in a paper bag, close tightly, and steam for 15 minutes. When cool enough to handle, rub off and remove blackened skin, taking care not to tear flesh. Cut a slit down the length of each, stopping about ½" from the tip. (If using bell peppers, simply cut off the top.) Scrape out ribs and seeds. Set aside.

2. Heat 2 tbsp. oil in a skillet over medium heat. Add onions and garlic and cook until soft and golden, about 20 minutes. Increase heat to medium-high, add beef and pork, breaking meat up with the back of a spoon, and brown for 7–10 minutes. Reduce heat to medium, season to taste with salt and pepper, and stir in tomatoes and nutmeg. Cook for 5 minutes, then remove from heat and stir in rice, marjoram, thyme, parsley, and 1 tbsp. oil. Adjust seasoning.

3. Preheat broiler. Spoon about ¼ cup filling into each pepper and place on a cookie sheet. Sprinkle with bread crumbs, drizzle with remaining oil, and broil until golden. Serve hot or at room temperature.

Chiles and Peppers

G asoline isn't a gas, and "hot peppers" aren't pepper at all. Blame the Spanish, who, discovering the pungent fruit of the *Capsicum annum*, the chile plant, apparently confounded it with true black pepper, and gave it practically the same name. (Black pepper is *pimienta* in Spanish; the chile was dubbed *pimiento*.) There may have been wishful thinking involved, since black pepper was among the most profitable spices grown in the East Indies, which Columbus, of course, was trying to find when he stumbled on the chile-growing Americas.

Chiles Rellenos

SERVES 4

IN THE HANDS OF Aída Gabilondo, a longtime resident of the border region where West Texas meets Mexico, these charred, stuffed peppers are a masterpiece of subtlety. Her recipe is an example of real border food.

8 anaheim chiles
1 lb. monterey jack cheese,
  sliced into 3" x 1" strips
2 cups flour
Salt and freshly ground
  black pepper
4 eggs, separated
Vegetable oil
3 cups red chile sauce
  (recipe follows)

RED CHILE SAUCE:
1 small onion, peeled and
  sliced
4 tbsp. vegetable oil
1 28-oz. can whole plum
  tomatoes
1 clove garlic, peeled and
  chopped
½ tsp. crushed fresh
  oregano leaves
1 tsp. sugar
Salt and freshly ground
  black pepper
1 cup chicken stock
  (see page 26) (optional)

1. Char chiles (**A**) by placing over a gas flame, turning often until skin is blackened all over. Or arrange chiles on a baking sheet and place under the broiler, turning often until blackened all over. Place hot chiles in a brown paper bag, close tightly, and allow to steam for 15 minutes. Peel off and discard skin. Cut a slit lengthwise at the top of each chile, about ½" from the stem. Use a small spoon to scrape out veins and seeds. Slip cheese slices into the chiles (**B**).

2. Pour flour into a shallow bowl and season liberally with salt and pepper. Place egg whites in a large glass bowl and yolks in a small one. Beat whites with an electric mixer (**C**) or whisk until foamy, add a pinch of salt, then continue beating until whites are stiff but not dry. Lightly beat yolks, then gently fold into whites with a rubber spatula.

3. Pour oil into a heavy skillet to a depth of 1" and heat over medium heat until oil reaches 375°. Dredge chiles first in flour, then in egg mixture (**D**), then fry in batches (**E**), turning once, until evenly browned all over, about 10 minutes. Drain on paper towels. Serve with red chile sauce (**F**).

RED CHILE SAUCE: Sauté onions in oil in a large skillet over medium heat until soft, about 15 minutes. Purée onions, tomatoes, and garlic in a blender or food processor, strain, and return to the same skillet. Add oregano and sugar, then season to taste with salt and pepper. Cook, covered, over medium heat, for 5 minutes. Thin with chicken stock if sauce is too thick. Keep sauce warm over low heat until ready to use. Makes 3 cups.

This Is Not Tex-Mex

 e abhor the idea of combination platters" says Aída Gabilondo, the author of *Mexican Family Cooking* and a leading exponent of the "border food" served on both sides of the American-Mexican frontier around El Paso, Texas, and Ciudad Juárez, Mexico. "The idea of piling three or four things on one plate came about because people were in a hurry and didn't have the help required to wash dishes for separate courses. We think every taste deserves a chance, every dish should stand alone." We saw exactly what she meant when we tasted her chiles rellenos, with their subtle bite and haunting blend of flavors. Starkly presented, adorned only with a red chile sauce to moisten them, they seemed the ultimate border-food experience.

Red Cabbage

SERVES 6

R.W. APPLE JR., chief correspondent of the *New York Times*, celebrates his family's Pennsylvania Dutch roots with a Thanksgiving feast that includes this cabbage dish (from a recipe by his friend food critic Egon Ronay).

¼ lb. smoked slab bacon, diced
1 medium red onion, peeled and thinly sliced
1 large head red cabbage, cored and shredded
2 tsp. caraway seeds
1 bay leaf
2 cloves garlic, peeled and minced
Salt and freshly ground black pepper
3¼ cups dry white wine
1 tbsp. honey
¼ cup white wine vinegar

1. Fry bacon in a large skillet over low heat, turning often, until crisp and golden brown, about 20 minutes. Increase heat to medium-low, add onions, and cook, stirring occasionally, until soft, 15–20 minutes.

2. Add cabbage and cook, stirring frequently, for 5 minutes, then add caraway seeds, bay leaf, and garlic. Season to taste with salt and pepper and cook, stirring constantly, for 5 minutes. Increase heat to medium, add wine, honey, and vinegar and simmer until cabbage is soft and cooking liquid has evaporated, about 1 hour. (Add a little water if liquid evaporates too quickly and cabbage begins to stick to skillet.)

3. Remove skillet from heat, transfer cabbage to a bowl, and allow to cool. Cover and refrigerate overnight for flavors to blend. To serve, warm over low heat, adjust seasoning with salt, pepper, and vinegar.

Lancaster Marketing

The Pennsylvania Dutch table is always laden with condiments—pickles, relishes, fresh-ground horseradish, and other pantry staples. Homemade versions of these products are sold at farm stands throughout the area. But for a truly spectacular selection, locals and visitors alike flock to the Central Market, in the heart of Lancaster, Pennsylvania, about 60 miles west of Philadelphia. Inside this huge old redbrick building, stalls sell everything from just-baked pies and old-fashioned breads to German-style sausages and the celebrated Amish chickens. (Many of the farmers here are Amish, dressed mostly in black clothes fastened with pins instead of buttons.) There's fresh produce aplenty at the Lancaster Market, too. One stand offers nothing but celery (widely used in Pennsylvania Dutch recipes), and exceptionally good celery it is. But it's those condiments that really set the market apart from other such establishments. In this part of the world, vegetables of every kind are still "put up"; cabbage is fermented into sauerkraut; pickles are an everyday art form. Dan Stoltzfus (facing page), for instance, will patiently explain to customers which of his pickles have won blue ribbons—and then sell them jars of pure, bright Pennsylvania Dutch flavor.

Pennsylvania Apples

"**A**fter a lifetime of wandering the world," R. W. Apple Jr. has noted, "it is remarkably restorative to return to one's roots and to the food of one's childhood, produced in loam enriched by generations of husbandry by frugal, industrious Amish and Mennonite farmers." The Pennsylvania Dutch, of course, aren't Dutch at all, but of German origin. ("Dutch" comes from the mispronounced "Deutsch.") Real Pennsylvania Dutch cooking, says Apple, is more like that of Alsace than of anywhere else—though, unlike the Alsatians, his people have never developed a restaurant culture, and good Pennsylvania Dutch fare is found only at home. "It is robust, boldly flavored, down-to-earth cooking," Apple observes, "not the sweet, overstarchy stuff served at roadside industrial feederies in the Amish country around Lancaster." Immigrants quickly shed their national costumes, their language, even their Old World names, he adds. (Apple used to be Apfel.) Fortunately, it takes a lot longer for them to abandon their favorite things to eat.

Mrs. Apple's Creamed Corn

SERVES 8

THIS OLD APPLE family recipe is based on dried sweet corn, a Pennsylvania Dutch staple, essential to the culture—and so much appreciated by R. W. Apple that his mother sent it to him during his years as a reporter in Vietnam. We've found that cooked dried corn, surprisingly, has all the bright flavor of corn fresh off the cob.

4 cups dried corn (see Note)
4 cups milk
3 cups heavy cream
3 tsp. sugar
3 tsp. salt
4 tbsp. butter
Salt and freshly ground
*   black pepper*

1. Place dried corn in a large bowl and cover with milk and heavy cream. Cover with plastic wrap and refrigerate overnight.

2. Transfer corn mixture to a large saucepan. Add sugar, salt, and butter. Bring to a boil, stirring frequently, over medium-high heat. Reduce heat to low and simmer, stirring occasionally, for about 30 minutes. Adjust seasoning to taste with salt and pepper just before serving.

NOTE: *Finding Dried Corn*—Pennsylvania Dutch–style dried sweet corn is available in many markets in Lancaster County, Pennsylvania, and through specialty mail-order sources.

Michael Roberts's Corn Risotto

SERVES 4

AT TRUMPS in West Hollywood (now defunct), and later at Pasadena's Twin Palms and in other venues, Michael Roberts has proven himself to be not just a skilled chef but a witty one, fearlessly and good-naturedly adding an American flair to a world of recipes—such as this one.

Kernels cut from 3–4 ears fresh corn, about 3 cups
1 scallion or shallot, peeled and minced
8 tbsp. butter
1 cup chicken stock (see page 26)
1 cup heavy cream
½ cup freshly grated parmigiano-reggiano (see Note)
12 fresh shiitake mushrooms, sliced
½ cup shelled fresh peas
Salt
Freshly ground black pepper

1. Preheat oven to 200°. Sauté corn and scallions or shallots in 4 tbsp. butter in a large skillet over medium heat for about 1 minute. Add ½ cup stock, increase heat to medium-high, and reduce liquid quickly until mixture thickens. Add cream and stir occasionally, reducing liquid again until thick, about 5 minutes. Remove from heat and stir in cheese.

2. Pulse corn mixture once or twice in a food processor to release flavors. The kernels should be broken but not puréed smooth. Put corn mixture in an oven-proof serving dish, cover with aluminum foil, and keep warm in oven.

3. Sauté mushrooms in remaining 4 tbsp. butter in a medium skillet over high heat. Add peas and remaining ½ cup stock and reduce the liquid until it thickens, about 5 minutes. Fold mushroom mixture into corn. Season to taste with salt and pepper.

NOTE: *Grating Parmigiano*—There's more than one way to grate this hard cheese. There are specialized tools to do the job, and you can always use the all-purpose kitchen grater (the side with the smallest holes). But when you need more than a sprinkle of parmigiano, add small chunks of it to the bowl of a food processor and pulse until the cheese is fluffy.

Corn Consciousness

Corn, which was probably first cultivated in southern Mexico or Central America more than 7,000 years ago, is the only cereal crop native to the New World. Over the centuries, corn has been variously planted, bred, worshiped, mashed, milled, roasted, popped, canned, boiled, baked, creamed, fried—even wrapped around hot dogs. Columbus encountered corn in 1492, but it took more than a century for the crop itself to reach Europe. Today, it is grown all over the world. The number-one producer, in fact, is China. The U.S. is second—and the only nation sensible enough to eat it on the cob, dripping with butter.

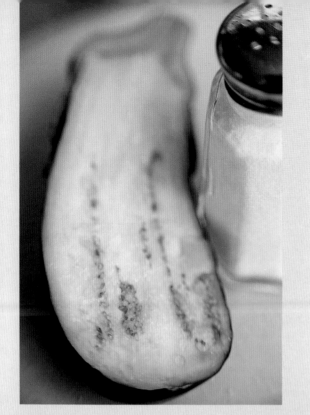

To Salt or Not to Salt?

S alting sliced eggplant for half an hour or so leaches out some of the chemical called solanine, found in the eggplant's flesh. The procedure: Sprinkle salt (coarse salt is best because less is absorbed) onto one side of the sliced eggplant. Leave it for 30 minutes, then brush it off with a damp paper towel. There's also a saltless way of obtaining the same results: Slice eggplant, arrange slices on a plate, and put it in the freezer for about four hours. When the slices thaw, just press out a lot of the moisture with the palm of your hand. This releases most of the bitterness. Is either process really necessary? If you're frying or grilling, both of which tend to concentrate the eggplant's bitter character, then yes, we recommend it. In stews and purées, however, bitterness shouldn't be a problem.

Fried Eggplant

SERVES 4–6

AFTER YEARS of appearing on American tables mostly as an ethnic specialty (as eggplant parmigiana, say, or maybe in a Szechuan-style stir-fry), eggplant is finally becoming a mainstream food in this country. The most commonly used variety is the big, purple-skinned kind.

1 cup flour
1¼ cups white wine
Salt and freshly ground
 black pepper
2 medium eggplants,
 thinly sliced into rounds
Vegetable oil
1 lemon, cut into wedges

1. Place flour in a shallow bowl. Whisk wine into flour, beating until batter is smooth and the consistency of thin pancake batter, then season to taste with salt and pepper.

2. Preheat oven to 200°. Salt or freeze eggplant slices to lessen bitterness and remove excess moisture (see left). Pour vegetable oil into a heavy skillet to a depth of 2". Heat oil to 375° or until it sizzles when you drop in a little batter. (If oil isn't hot enough, eggplant will absorb too much of it.)

3. Dip eggplant slices in batter, then drop into oil— as many at a time as you can without crowding the pan. Fry until golden, cooking on both sides, then drain on paper towels. Keep fried slices warm in oven.

4. When all eggplant slices are cooked, season to taste with salt and pepper, and serve with a squeeze of fresh lemon.

Morel Omelette

SERVES 1–2

WHILE WRITER MITCH OMER'S omelette, bursting with morels, is less refined than the classic French version, it puffs up and browns beautifully when finished in the oven. For best results, use fresh morels only.

3 tbsp. butter
1 shallot, peeled and
    minced
1 clove garlic, peeled and
    minced
8–10 small fresh morels,
    cleaned, trimmed, and
    coarsely chopped
Salt and freshly ground
    black pepper
1 tsp. finely chopped fresh
    parsley, plus additional
    for garnishing
3 eggs
1 tbsp. heavy cream

1. Preheat oven to 450°. Melt 2 tbsp. butter over medium-low heat in a medium omelette pan or non-stick skillet. Add shallots, garlic, and morels and cook, stirring frequently, for 5 minutes. Add 2 tbsp. water and continue cooking until morels are soft, 5 minutes more. Season to taste with salt and pepper, stir in parsley, and transfer to a bowl.

2. Lightly beat eggs and cream together in a medium bowl, then season with salt and pepper. Wipe out skillet, then melt remaining 1 tbsp. butter over medium-high heat. Add eggs and cook for 30 seconds, lifting cooked edges to allow uncooked egg to flow underneath. Spoon morel mixture into center of eggs (eggs should still be slightly runny). Fold omelette closed, then transfer to a nonstick or lightly buttered cookie sheet, folded side down. Bake until puffed and golden, about 3 minutes. Slide onto a warmed plate and serve garnished with additional chopped parsley, if you like.

Cult Fungus

While neither as rare nor as expensive as the black truffle, the morel is a real cult mushroom—a sort of talisman among mushroom hunters. Although morels can be found all over North America, they are particularly prolific in the Midwest, and there they are a regional passion. At the People's State Bank of Chandlerville, Illinois, for example, an image of three morels is embossed on its letterhead, checks, and deposit slips. In 1984, Minnesota designated the morel its official state mushroom. Michigan, meanwhile, has long considered itself the Morel Capital of the World, and if any Michiganders are upset over Minnesota's bit of legislative one-upmanship, they may be consoled by the fact that their own Boyne City is host to the National

Mushroom Festival, held annually on Mother's Day weekend. The festival's morel-hunting contest draws hundreds of competitors, who collect as many of the elusive fungi as they can in 90 minutes. The current record, set in 1984, is 986 morels. Another gauge of the morel's cultural importance is its cost—which, while hardly truffle-high, can range up to $24 a pound for fresh ones in season and $125 a pound for dried. Morels have recently become more easily available (at a lower price) as techniques for cultivating them have been developed, but cultivated morels don't taste as good as wild ones.

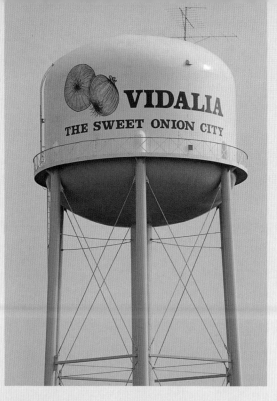

Move Over, Peaches

The vidalia onion story began in 1931, when a local farmer named Mose Coleman discovered that the onions he was growing, at his place near the southern Georgia town of Vidalia, were sweet, not hot. His neighbors, who were having trouble selling their own produce during the Depression, noticed that Coleman was moving his sweet onions at good prices, so they planted them too. In the 1940s, the state built a farmers' market in Vidalia, at the junction of several main highways, and travelers were soon carrying the onions to other parts of the state and beyond. In 1977, a local arts-and-crafts fair was transformed into the Vidalia Onion Festival, which has been held every April since then—and the onions have gained an international reputation. Vidalias are sweet, incidentally, because the area's soil and groundwater are very low in sulphur—the element that makes onions hot. You can take a vidalia seedling and plant it someplace else and it grows a hot onion.

Onion Rings

SERVES 2–4

THESE DOUBLE-DIPPED fried onion rings are made with classic Southern ingredients—buttermilk and white cornmeal—but the recipe comes from Boston chef Jasper White. Any sweet onion (such as the walla-walla, the texas 1015, or the maui) will work as well as vidalias.

*2 large vidalia or other
  sweet onions, peeled
2 cups buttermilk
1½ cups flour
½ cup white cornmeal
Cayenne
Salt and freshly ground
  black pepper
Vegetable oil*

1. Cut onions into ½"-thick slices, and separate into rings. Pour buttermilk into a bowl. Combine flour and cornmeal in another bowl and season liberally with cayenne, salt, and pepper.

2. Pour oil into a heavy skillet to a depth of 3" and heat over medium-high heat. Dip a few rings into buttermilk, shake off excess, dredge in flour mixture, shake off excess, then repeat, coating again with both buttermilk and flour mixture.

3. When oil is very hot (375°), add onions and cook until golden, about 3 minutes. Drain on paper towels and sprinkle with salt. Fry remaining onions in batches.

NOTE: *Sweetening Onions*—If vidalias or other sweet onions are unavailable, use yellow or red onions, and soak the raw onion rings in milk for one hour to sweeten them and soften their bite.

Mashed Potatoes with Butter

SERVES 4

THEY'RE THE REAL THING—pure, guileless, irresistible kitchen-table fare. They go with almost any savory main dish you can imagine, from the traditional steak or fried chicken to broiled fish or grilled vegetables. If you're tired of mashed potatoes, you're tired of life.

3 lbs. russet potatoes, peeled
    and cut into large pieces
Salt
½–1 cup milk
6 tbsp. butter
Freshly ground white
    pepper

1. Put potatoes in a medium pot and cover with cold water. Add a generous pinch of salt and bring to a boil over medium-high heat. Lower heat to medium and simmer until potatoes are easily pierced with a knife, about 20 minutes.

2. While potatoes cook, warm milk and 4 tbsp. butter in a small saucepan and bring to a simmer over low heat.

3. When potatoes have cooked, drain and return potatoes to pot, then place pot over medium heat, shaking it until potatoes become dry and mealy. Remove pot from heat and mash potatoes in pot with a potato masher (or run through a ricer, or simply mash potatoes with a fork; see right) until potatoes are finely textured and fluffy. Gradually whisk in milk mixture and season to taste with salt and pepper. Serve with remaining 2 tbsp. butter, if you like.

VARIATION: *Lighter Mashed Potatoes*—For a lighter but more potatoey flavor, reserve 1 cup potato cooking water and whisk into potatoes in place of milk.

VARIATION: *Mediterranean Mashed Potatoes*—Substitute an equal quantity of mild extra-virgin olive oil for butter.

Mash Notes

As the old saying goes (doesn't it?), there's more than one way to mash a potato. The good old-fashioned potato masher (with either a wafflelike grid or a wavy pattern at the end of a sturdy utensil handle) is pretty foolproof but tends to leave a few lumps—which some aficionados consider not just acceptable but essential. For finely textured potatoes, a ricer is best. Handheld models push potatoes through tiny rice-grain holes with a hinged plunger. There is also a conical type which rests on three legs; potatoes are pushed through the holes with a kind of pestle. A food mill—one with large holes—will also yield potatoes with a fine texture. Use a handheld mixer if you've got lots of potatoes to mash. And use a fork if you only have a few—at an intimate dinner for two, for instance. About the only means of mashing that we don't recommend is the food processor—which tends to produce something more like library paste than puréed spuds.

French Fries

SERVES 4

WE'VE NOTICED that whenever we order french fries (named, incidentally, not for France but for the fact that they're "frenched", or trimmed into lengths) in a place that knows how to make them, everybody else in the room tends to look at us enviously when they're served. That's because, we suspect, fries are as good as potatoes get.

4 lbs. russet potatoes, peeled
Peanut oil
Salt

1. Cut potatoes into lengths about ¼" × ¼" × 3" (it is easiest to do this with a mandoline). Place in a large nonreactive bowl, cover with water, and set aside in the refrigerator for about 2 hours.

2. Pour oil into a heavy-bottomed pot to a depth of 4" and heat over medium heat. Drain potatoes, then dry very thoroughly with paper towels. Check oil temperature with a kitchen thermometer. When oil reaches 325°, cook potatoes, without browning, in small batches, turning occasionally, until they are tender and their edges are slightly crisp, about 4 minutes. Drain potatoes on paper towels and allow to cool for about 20 minutes. (Potatoes may be cooked to this point several hours in advance and kept in refrigerator until ready to crisp.)

3. Reheat oil. When temperature reaches 375°, fry potatoes in small batches until crisp and golden, 1–2 minutes per batch. Drain on paper towels, sprinkle with salt, and serve.

VARIATION: *Pommes Soufflées*—Shape whole potatoes into rectangles or cylinders about 2½" long and about 1½" wide, then slice into even pieces about ⅛" thick. Place slices in a nonreactive bowl with water to cover. Proceed as in steps 2 and 3 above, but heat the oil for the initial cooking to only 250°, and for the second cooking to 400°. (Potatoes should blister slightly during the first fry and puff immediately during the second.) Pommes soufflées should be cooked until crisp. Serve immediately or set aside and then recrisp for 20 seconds in 400° oil before serving.

The Art of the Fry

Making french fries isn't complicated, but success depends on understanding some basic principles:

THE POTATO: (A) Start with good starchy ones, preferably russets (Idahos or otherwise). Peel just before slicing, then soak in water to prevent discoloration and increase crispness.

THE MANDOLINE: (B) This splendid kitchen implement produces fries of uniform size—for uniform cooking.

THE BLOT: (C) Dry potatoes *very* well before frying by blotting them with paper towels. Wet potatoes splatter and cook unevenly.

THE OIL: (D) We like the flavor of peanut oil, but olive and other vegetable oils also work well (as do lard and rendered beef fat, if you dare). Don't waste money on a deep fryer, by the way; the only equipment you'll need is a heavy pot and a kitchen thermometer.

THE FRY: (E) For great fries, fry twice. The first time cooks the potatoes; the second (seen here) crisps them to a beautiful golden brown.

THE PAYOFF: (F) Once fries are drained and salted, serve them at once—with or without mayonnaise and beer.

227

Sweet Potato Casserole

SERVES 4

GRANDMOTHER TILLMAN uses fresh sweet potatoes for this holiday treat, and she likes the kind that are about the size of baking potatoes, with smooth skin and white or deep orange flesh. These are sometimes sold as yams—but real yams, which originated in Africa and Asia, have a hairy, barklike skin and usually aren't as sweet as sweet potatoes (which come from Central America).

½ cup raisins
⅓ cup sweet sherry
3 medium sweet potatoes
⅔ cup brown sugar
4 tbsp. butter, melted
½ cup fresh orange juice
1 tsp. finely chopped
   orange zest
1 tsp. pumpkin spice
   (or ⅔ tsp. ground
   cinnamon, ¼ tsp.
   ground ginger, pinch
   ground nutmeg, and
   pinch ground allspice)
½ cup coarsely chopped
   pecans
1 cup drained pineapple
   cubes, coarsely chopped
1½ cups miniature
   marshmallows

1. Preheat oven to 375°. Soak raisins in sherry until soft, about 30 minutes. Drain raisins and transfer to a large bowl, discarding sherry.

2. Meanwhile, place sweet potatoes in a roasting pan and bake until tender, about 40 minutes. Allow potatoes to cool, then peel, purée with a food mill or food processor, and add to raisins. Add brown sugar, butter, orange juice, orange zest, and pumpkin spice and mix well. Fold in pecans and pineapple and transfer to an 8" baking dish.

3. Bake casserole for 20 minutes, then cover with marshmallows and bake until marshmallows are golden, about 5 minutes more.

Sweet Tradition

E very Thanksgiving in Natchez, Mississippi, the Tillman family—complete with aunts and uncles, a herd of cousins, and the occasional neighbor—turn up at Sarah Tillman's house for dinner. There are far too many people for a sit-down affair, so everybody gets in line, plates in hand, and fuels up at the sideboard, which is crammed with the standard holiday fare. All the food is good, reports SAVEUR associate editor Catherine Tillman—a regular at the feast—but the star of the sideboard, for her at least, is Grandmother Sarah's sweet potato casserole. "I can't help but pile on spoonful after spoonful," Catherine reports,

"burying the turkey and pushing the stuffing perilously close to the edge." The elder Tillman has been making the dish since the 1940s, and though she has tinkered with it over the years, she is convinced that she got the recipe right sometime in the '50s—probably, she says, the first time her in-laws came to dinner. The addition of marshmallows to the casserole might be seen as unsophisticated in some quarters, but it is these confections, "which turn all brown and gooey and transform an otherwise mushy mélange," that make the dish, says Catherine. Anyway, she adds, Grandmother Tillman believes that sweet potatoes and marshmallows "just belong together"—and it doesn't seem likely that she's going to change her mind anytime soon.

BREADS

"IT'S DUSK on the first day of harvest

in June 1996 on the Wenger farm in

Newton, Kansas. A slight wind tempers

the 100-degree heat; the smells of dried

grass and warm earth fill the air, and

tall, papery wheat stalks rustle in the breeze. Merle Wenger, whose ancestors moved here in the 1870s as part of a wave of Mennonite immigration, sizes up a thunderhead rolling in from the west. It's time for the Wenger family to get to work."

—JUDITH M. FERTIG ON WHEAT (*SEE RECIPE ON PAGE 242*)

RECIPES

Strawberry Jamming

Grape jelly has its partisans (many of them toting lunch boxes and equally fond of peanut butter), and life without orange marmalade is unimaginable—but when we think of jam, it's strawberry jam we have in mind. No other kind seems so luscious, so uncompromisingly *jammy*. And there's something else about it: Strawberries once implied a sense of loss and wistfulness. The fruit was fickle and perishable, the season fleeting. The plants were wild and came from mysterious dark woods. Man has long tried to tame the wild berry, and to extend its season—which always seems to end even before that sweet, sharp taste has left the tongue. Breeders have gone about this in the wrong way, creating durable but cottony, mostly flavorless year-round fruit. The right way, obviously, is to buy the best strawberries available at the height of the season—and to preserve them sweetly.

Baking-Powder Biscuits with Strawberry Freezer Jam

MAKES 12–14 BISCUITS

THESE BISCUITS should be on the American flag instead of stars, jokes SAVEUR consulting editor Marion Cunningham—an authority on culinary Americana. For the lightest biscuits, she adds, don't overhandle the dough.

1 tsp. butter
2½ cups flour
1 tbsp. baking powder
1 tsp. salt
⅓ cup vegetable shortening, chilled
1 cup milk

STRAWBERRY FREEZER JAM:
5 cups fresh strawberries, hulled, washed, and slightly crushed
4 cups sugar
1 1¾-oz. box pectin

1. Preheat oven to 425°. Grease a baking sheet with butter and set aside. Sift 2 cups flour, baking powder, and salt together into a large mixing bowl.

2. Add shortening to flour mixture in 5 or 6 large pieces, cutting it into flour with a pastry cutter, or rubbing it in with your fingers. The mixture should have the consistency of coarse meal, with no large pieces of shortening visible. Add milk and stir in with a fork just until mixture pulls away from sides of bowl. The dough will be quite sticky.

3. Turn dough out onto a lightly floured surface. Dust hands with flour and gently knead dough just until it's no longer sticky, about 30 seconds. Pat dough into a 9" circle about ¾" thick. Cut out biscuits with a cookie cutter or the rim of a juice glass and place on baking sheet. If biscuits touch each other, they will have tender sides when baked; if you prefer crisp sides, separate them a bit. Bake until tops are golden, about 12–15 minutes. Serve with strawberry freezer jam.

STRAWBERRY FREEZER JAM: Put strawberries in a bowl, stir in sugar, and set aside until sugar has dissolved, about 30 minutes. Add pectin to ¾ cup water in a small saucepan. Boil for 1 minute over high heat, stirring constantly, then stir into strawberries until mixed. Pour mixture into sterilized half-pint jars (see Note, page 64) with lids and fill to ½" from top. Keep refrigerated for up to 3 weeks—or frozen for up to 1 year. Makes 6 half-pint jars.

Georgene's Fluffy Rolls

MAKES ABOUT 2½ DOZEN

GEORGENE HALL of Memphis, Tennessee, perfected these rolls half a century ago. Although cornmeal may seem more emblematic of Southern baking, fine white wheat flour has been used for breakfast breads and other rolls in the region since Colonial times—probably on the model of an old English roll called the manchet.

1¼ cups milk
¼ cup vegetable shortening
¾ cup sugar
1 tsp. salt
1 7-gram packet active dry yeast
2 eggs, lightly beaten
4 cups flour
¾ cup melted butter

1. Combine milk, shortening, sugar, and salt in a saucepan and cook, stirring constantly, over medium heat until sugar dissolves. Remove from heat; set aside and allow to cool.

2. Mix yeast with ¼ cup lukewarm water in a large bowl; set aside until yeast dissolves and little bubbles begin to appear on the surface, about 10 minutes.

3. Pour cooled milk mixture into yeast. Stir in eggs and gradually add flour, stirring with a wooden spoon until dough is too stiff to stir, then use your hands to knead in the flour (dough will be sticky, so grease your hands with a little butter). Brush a small amount of butter on the inside of a large bowl and on one side of a sheet of waxed paper. Place dough in bowl, cover with buttered wax paper, and lay a clean, damp dish towel on top. Set aside to rise until doubled, at least 3 hours.

4. Turn dough out onto a lightly floured surface. Knead until elastic, then roll out to ½" thickness. Cut dough with a 3" biscuit cutter, dip each round into melted butter, and fold in half. Line up, round edges up, sides touching, in a baking pan. Cover with buttered wax paper and a towel, and set aside to rise, at least 2½ hours.

5. Preheat oven to 350°. Bake until golden, about 15 minutes. Rolls are best served warm.

Georgene Knows

I was raised in large part by Georgene Hall, our family cook," says Memphis writer Mary Ann Eagle. "I spent countless hours at her side, watching her pluck, cut up, and fry home-raised chickens, clean turnip greens fresh from the garden, shuck corn for buttery corn puddings, knead dough for fluffy rolls. She'd let me dip sliced tomatoes in cornmeal before she slid them into a skillet of bubbling bacon fat. And as I sat at the kitchen table, dunking my corn bread into thick buttermilk, we'd talk of the world. I was formed by food like this and by the people who cook it."

Cooking with Corn

I n short, it's a Grain of General Use to Man and Beast," wrote Thomas Ashe back in 1682, in his book *Carolina, or a Description of the Present State of that Country*. The subject was corn—Indian corn, as it was first called on these shores, to differentiate it from "corn" in the English sense of generic grain. Ashe's opinion of the vegetable's versatility notwithstanding, corn and its derivatives weren't commonly incorporated into American cookery for another hundred years or so—and even then, corn was predominantly appreciated in the South. Cornmeal, as the basis for baked goods both sweet and savory and as a coating for fried foods, is so important to the traditional cooking of the region, in fact, that it virtually defines the Southern kitchen.

Corn Bread

SERVES 6–8

DEPENDING ON where it's made and who makes it, corn bread can be composed of white or yellow cornmeal and seasoned with salt or sugar or both. Bacon fat or butter or just about any other shortening can be used to grease the container it's baked in. And that container can be loaf pan, cast-iron skillet, muffin tin, or mold. In our experience, bacon fat and a skillet yield the crispiest crust.

½ cup flour
2 tsp. baking powder
1 tsp. baking soda
1 tsp. salt
1½ cups coarse cornmeal, preferably white
1 large egg, beaten
1¾–2 cups buttermilk
2 tbsp. rendered bacon fat, butter, lard, or vegetable shortening

1. Preheat oven to 400°. Sift together flour, baking powder, baking soda, and salt in a medium bowl. Add cornmeal and stir to combine.

2. Beat together egg and 1¾ cups of buttermilk in a small bowl. Add to dry ingredients and stir until just combined. If batter is too thick, add more buttermilk. Take care not to overmix.

3. Melt bacon fat in a 9" or 10" cast-iron skillet over high heat. The skillet should be very hot. Pour batter into the skillet and bake in oven until the top is golden and a knife inserted in the center comes out clean, about 30 minutes.

VARIATION: *Fried Corn Bread*—Fry slices of leftover corn bread in rendered bacon fat, turning once, until crisp and golden on both sides. Add a slice of ham to the skillet, if you like, and heat through. Serve with maple syrup.

VARIATION: *Jalapeño Corn Sticks (left)*—Make corn bread recipe above and add 2 tbsp. sugar and 2 fresh seeded, minced jalapeños to batter. Spoon batter into a well-greased cast-iron corn-stick mold and bake until golden, 15–20 minutes. Makes about 18 sticks.

Whole Wheat Bread

MAKES 2 LOAVES

WHEN HE RAN a bakery back in Ohio, Alan Hooker was famous for his pies. At his Ranch House in California, he continued to bake as well as to cook—and his dense, full-flavored breads became a trademark of the restaurant. He liked to sweeten them slightly with honey, not sugar, Hooker once said, both for taste and for moistness.

2¼ cups milk
1 tbsp. butter
⅓ cup honey
2 tsp. salt
2 7-gram packets active
   dry yeast
5¾ cups stone-ground
   whole wheat flour
Vegetable shortening

1. Mix together milk, butter, honey, salt, and ½ cup water in a large metal bowl and warm, over a pot of simmering water, to 90°. Remove from heat and stir in yeast. Set aside until yeast dissolves and little bubbles begin to appear on the surface, about 10 minutes.

2. Add flour, ½ cup at a time, stirring with a spoon at first. Then, as dough thickens, use your hands to knead in remaining flour. Knead until thoroughly mixed, at least 15 minutes. Dough should be moist and slightly sticky. Cover with a clean dish towel and set aside in a warm place. Allow to rise until doubled in bulk, about 45 minutes.

3. Turn dough out onto a floured surface. Knead for at least 10 minutes, pressing dough flat, folding it over until all large air bubbles are squeezed out. Dough should be springy to the touch.

4. Grease 2 7½" × 3½" loaf pans with shortening and set aside. Cut dough into 2 equal pieces, then flatten each piece and fold over several times until when dough is rolled up it makes a "log" the size of the bread pan. Place dough, seam side down, in bread pans. Cover with a clean dish towel, set aside in a warm place, and allow to rise until dough is about 1" higher than pan, about 30 minutes.

5. Preheat oven to 375°. Bake for about 1 hour. Remove loaves from pans and allow to cool on a rack.

VARIATION: *Lighter Textured Wheat Bread*—Substitute 1–2 cups unbleached white bread flour for 1–2 cups of the stone-ground whole wheat flour.

Early California

S omeone, somewhere along the line, called Alan Hooker—who founded the Ranch House restaurant with his wife, Helen, in the Southern California town of Ojai in 1950—"the grandfather of California cuisine". "In truth," remembers SAVEUR editor Colman Andrews (who frequented the place for a decade), "he was more of a wise but vaguely eccentric uncle—not a direct antecedent of Alice Waters or Wolfgang Puck but a man who anticipated certain aspects of the culinary revolution that the two helped to launch, and a chef who was undeniably ahead of his time." In an age of margarine and bottled salad dressings, Hooker baked with real butter and dressed his herb-strewn salads with extra-virgin (the term still drew titters) olive oil. In a society that equated fine food with French food, he served with pride and with a sense of fun and of experiment, elaborate Indian curries and dishes inspired by recipes from Puerto Rico, Indonesia, Hungary, and Japan. And in what was largely a meat-and-potatoes cooking culture, he appreciated, bought (or grew), and imaginatively cooked fresh fruits and vegetables, and above all fresh herbs. He was passionate about food. "You know," Hooker once said of his restaurant, "this is almost a religion with me. You worship around the table."

Spicy Siblings

Bill and Pamela Penzey are a brother-sister spice trade. They travel the world persuading growers and shippers that Americans are willing to pay for the rare and select, then they bring it all home to their warehouse in the unlikely spot of Muskego, Wisconsin. They have retail shops in Brookfield and Madison, Wisconsin, and in St. Paul, Minnesota, but also sell by mail. Penzeys catalogues are gold mines (or spice boxes) of information. They tell us, for example, that the "cinnamon" we most often use is actually a spice called cassia, native to southern China and northern Vietnam. True cinnamon, lighter in color and almost citrusy in flavor, comes from Sri Lanka (formerly Ceylon), and is sold mostly in Europe and Latin America. Penzeys sell both, and either may be used to flavor breads and confections.

Cinnamon Raisin Bread

MAKES 1 LOAF

ALVIN BRENSING, miller at the Stafford County Mills Company in Hudson, Kansas—which produces the excellent Hudson Cream brand flour—shared this recipe with us. Brensing particularly enjoys the bread at breakfasttime, he tells us—toasted and generously buttered.

1 7-gram packet active dry yeast
1¼ cups lukewarm milk
1 cup raisins
3½ cups white bread flour
½ cup dark brown sugar
2 tbsp. wheat gluten
2 tsp. ground cinnamon
1½ tsp. salt
3 eggs
¼ cup melted butter

1. Mix yeast with milk in a large bowl; set aside until yeast dissolves and little bubbles begin to appear on the surface, about 10 minutes. Place raisins in another bowl, cover with warm water, and set aside to soften.

2. Combine flour, brown sugar, gluten, cinnamon, and salt in a large bowl. Beat 2 eggs into yeast, add 3 tbsp. butter, then stir into flour mixture, mixing until dough holds together (if dough is dry, add a little water).

3. Drain raisins, then knead into dough. Turn dough out onto a lightly floured surface. Knead until elastic (dough will be sticky), about 5 minutes. Place dough in a lightly buttered bowl, cover with a clean dish towel, and set aside to rise until doubled, about 1 hour.

4. Preheat oven to 400°. Return dough to floured surface and flatten into a rectangle about 9" × 11". Roll up dough to create a tight 9"-long cylinder. Pinch seam closed, then fold in outer ends and pinch closed. Shape into a loaf about 4" × 8". Put loaf, seam side down, in a buttered 9" × 4½" loaf pan. Cover with a clean dish towel and set aside to rise for 30 minutes.

5. Mix remaining 1 egg with 2 tbsp. water, brush over loaf, and bake for 10 minutes. Reduce heat to 350°, then bake for 25 minutes more. Remove loaf from pan and allow to cool on a rack.

Wheat's Triumph

The tortillas of her home state are different from everyone else's, and always have been, New Mexico-based cook and writer Sandy Szwarc told us. Back when all tortillas were made from corn, for instance, the Aztecs treated their dried corn with lime (to make its nutrients easier to digest), while Pueblo Indians in New Mexico preferred to grind dried corn with the ashes from burned desert plants. The treated corn was then mixed with water, patted into small rounds, and "baked" on heated rocks. Flour tortillas weren't made until the 16th century, when the Spanish introduced wheat to the area. By the middle of the 1880s, wheat was cheap and abundant around Taos—and before long, flour tortillas had become the local flatbread of choice. "We make them thick, airy, and on the small side," adds Szwarc.

New Mexican Flour Tortillas

THESE TORTILLAS can stand up to either a slathering of butter and honey or a pile of toppings (as for tostadas), and are favored by Pueblo Indians to soak up the savory juices of any dish. Be careful not to overwork the dough, and to cook them in a well-seasoned skillet.

4 cups flour
1¼ tsp. salt
6 tbsp. vegetable shortening

1. Sift together flour and salt into a medium bowl. Mix in shortening with your fingers until mixture resembles coarse meal. Stir in enough boiling water (about 1¼ cups) so that dough holds together.

2. Turn dough out onto a lightly floured surface and knead until smooth, about 5 minutes. Form dough into a ball, cover with plastic wrap, and allow to rest for 30 minutes.

3. Place dough on a lightly floured surface and divide into 10 balls (**A**). Use a rolling pin to roll out each ball into a ⅛"-thick round tortilla (**B**).

4. Heat a cast-iron skillet over medium heat until hot but not smoking and cook tortillas, one at a time, until slightly puffed (**C**), about 20 seconds. Flip, then cook for 20 seconds more. Wrap in a dish towel or a napkin to keep warm.

A Man and His Bread

Maria Charlotta Wikman Isaksson, a Swedish Finn, probably never anticipated that the cardamom-scented Swedish coffee bread she made in southwestern Finland would one day become a family treasure in New Jersey. In 1913, her son emerged from Ellis Island without the name he'd sailed from home with—Johanson had been summarily changed to Johnson—but with his mother's recipes safely stored in his memory. These recipes lived for a while in a kitchen in Brooklyn, but eventually made their way to bucolic Pluckemin, New Jersey, where Susan Blew started baking her great-grandmother's coffee bread soon after she got married, in 1973. The recipe had been passed on strictly by oral history. "It was a little bit of this, a little bit of that," Susan told us. "You had to see it to know how to make it." Susan and her mother set about codifying the recipe, figuring out the amounts in cups and teaspoons. Now the whole family (below) enjoys it.

Swedish Coffee Bread

MAKES 1 LOAF

SUSAN BLEW has no doubt at all about what makes this bread so special: "It's the cardamom," she declares. "When I smell it, it always reminds me of my grandfather's house." Its power to make her feel like a child again, she says, is particularly potent in the morning.

---

1 7-gram packet active
   dry yeast
1¼ cups lukewarm milk
½ cup melted butter, plus
   additional for greasing
   bowl, plus unmelted
   butter for serving
4 cups flour
¾ cup sugar, plus 2 tbsp.
   for topping
1 tsp. salt
1 tsp. ground cardamom
1 egg, lightly beaten

1. Mix yeast with ½ cup warm milk in a large bowl; set aside until yeast dissolves and little bubbles begin to appear on the surface, about 10 minutes. Stir in butter and remaining ¾ cup milk.

2. Sift together flour, ¾ cup sugar, salt, and cardamom in another bowl, then gradually add to yeast mixture, stirring with a wooden spoon. When dough becomes too stiff to stir, turn out onto a lightly floured surface and knead just until smooth and elastic, about 10 minutes.

3. Form dough into a ball, then place in a well-greased bowl and cover with a clean dish towel. Set aside in a warm place to rise until increased in bulk by one-third, about 3 hours. (This is a dense dough, so don't worry if it doesn't rise as much as expected at this stage. Press a finger into the middle and if the depression remains, it has risen sufficiently. It will continue to rise in the oven.)

4. Turn dough out onto a lightly floured surface. Divide into 3 parts and roll into 3 ropes, each about 16" long. Line up ropes on a cookie sheet and braid tightly, then cover with a clean dish towel and set aside in a warm place to rise for about 1 hour.

5. Preheat oven to 350°. Brush loaf with egg and sprinkle with remaining 2 tbsp. sugar. Bake until golden brown, 30–40 minutes. Allow to cool completely. (The bread is great fresh, but even better toasted and served with butter.)

Buttermilk Waffles

SERVES 4

PANCAKES ARE NICE, but, well, sort of flat and uninteresting. When it comes to holding maple syrup, there is no substitute for the deep grids of a perfectly crisp waffle. We don't know who invented waffles, but we do know that the Dutch first brought them, along with waffle irons, to this country in the early 17th century.

1 cup flour
1 tbsp. sugar
1 tsp. baking powder
1 tsp. baking soda
½ tsp. salt
3 eggs, separated
1 cup buttermilk
Butter
Vegetable oil
Maple syrup

1. Sift together flour, sugar, baking powder, baking soda, and salt in a large mixing bowl.

2. Beat egg yolks in a small mixing bowl, then add buttermilk and 2 tbsp. melted butter. Add to flour mixture, stirring until just combined.

3. Beat egg whites until stiff. Stir one-third of the whites into the batter, then carefully fold remaining whites into the batter in 2 batches. Batter will be airy.

4. Spread about ½ cup of batter onto the surface of a hot waffle iron lightly greased with oil, close lid, and cook until brown, about 5 minutes. Serve with plenty of butter and maple syrup.

A Sappy Story

Maple trees need four things to produce commercial quantities of sap for syrup: cold winters, a springtime snow cover, chilly night temperatures, and lots of year-round sun. This divine confluence is found only in places like southern Quebec and Ontario and the northern reaches of the states of Vermont, New York, Maine, and New Hampshire. Native Americans in these regions already had long-established methods for turning maple sap into both syrup and sugar by the time the first Europeans arrived. It is said that the Abenakis, in what is now Vermont, tossed white-hot rocks into sap-filled vats to boil down the liquid. Colonists soon learned how to process it themselves, and in 1557, André Thévet, the royal cosmographer of France, likened American maple syrup to "the good wines of Orléans or Beaune". By the 1700s, maple syrup had become a major cash crop in the eastern United States—but when cane sugar prices dropped around the turn of the 19th century, maple products suffered and eventually cheaper syrups replaced most of the real maple syrup on American tables. (A more recent blow to the industry came in early 1998, when severe ice storms felled maples throughout New England and eastern Canada.) Maple syrup is graded into three categories: Fancy or Extra-Light is the most delicate; Grade A Medium Amber or Grade A Dark Amber is a bit more robust; and Grade B, also called simply Amber or Dark Amber, is the most assertive.

9

DESSERTS

"ONE SUMMER DAY, I biked over to

Wanda Macnair's little white house in

Bremen, Maine, to watch her bake. She

was making blueberry pies that day, and

the house was fragrant with the smell of

them baking in her old metal box of an oven. Later, we sat outside in her garden, scooping warm blueberry pie out of bowls while ice cream spilled over the sides."

—MARY ANN EAGLE ON BLUEBERRY PIE (*SEE RECIPE ON PAGE 256*)

RECIPES

Pumpkin Pie

SERVES 6–8

ALMOST EVERYBODY seems to make pumpkin pie out of a can these days, and canned-pumpkin pie can be just fine. But pie made with the meat of a fresh pumpkin (not a stringy jack-o'-lantern, but a tasty eating variety like the sugar baby) attains a silky, custardy perfection.

FOR PASTRY:
1½ cups flour
¼ tsp. salt
½ cup vegetable
    shortening, chilled

FOR FILLING:
1 1½–2 lb. fresh pie
    pumpkin
⅔ cup sugar
1 tsp. ground
    cinnamon
¼ tsp. ground ginger
Pinch ground cloves
1½ cups evaporated milk
2 eggs, lightly beaten
½ tsp. salt

1. For pastry, sift flour and salt together in a large bowl. Cut in shortening with a pastry cutter or 2 knives until mixture resembles coarse meal. Add up to 5 tbsp. ice water as needed, 1 tbsp. at a time, mixing until dough holds together. Form into a ball, wrap in plastic wrap, and refrigerate for 1 hour.

2. For filling, cut pumpkin into large pieces, discarding seeds and pith. Fit a large pot with a steaming rack, add enough water to come just up to (but not over) the rack, and bring to a boil over high heat. Place pumpkin on rack, cover, and steam until pulp is soft, about 30 minutes. Cool, then scrape pulp from skin into a food processor and purée. Add sugar, cinnamon, ginger, cloves, milk, eggs, and salt and pulse until mixture is very smooth.

3. Preheat oven to 425°. Roll out dough into a 12" round on a floured surface, then ease into a 9" pie pan. Trim edges, allowing a ½" overhang, then fold edge under and crimp or flute. Fill with pumpkin filling and bake for 15 minutes, then reduce heat to 350° and continue baking until filling is set, 30–40 minutes. Allow to cool before serving.

VARIATION: *Canned-Pumpkin Pie*—Substitute 1½ cups canned pumpkin for steamed pumpkin pulp in step 2, above, and follow recipe, increasing cinnamon to 1½ tsp., ginger to ½ tsp., and cloves to ¼ tsp.

Holiday Dinners

I stayed close by when my mother cooked," SAVEUR consulting editor Peggy Knickerbocker told us one holiday season, "because I loved the smells and loved the little chores she would assign me. I'd help mash the sweet potatoes with brown sugar, orange juice, and Myers's rum, and whip the cream for the pumpkin pie. I'd lend a hand with the turkey stuffing, which my mother made the way her distant relatives did in Mississippi—with corn bread, bacon drippings, and lots of herbs. Our Uncle Dudley would inevitably come over a little early to visit his antique guitar and banjo collection, which was stashed in our basement—his hidden assets, he called the instruments, obscured from the accounting eye of his estranged wife. He'd ask my mother if she'd like him to serenade her while she cooked. (His favorite tune was 'Miss Otis Regrets'.) But she'd always say, 'I have to concentrate, Dud. Maybe a little something classical would be soothing.'"

Ask the Pie Lady

O ne day in Bremen, Maine," writer Mary Ann Eagle recalls, "I bought a blueberry pie made by Wanda Macnair. One bite and I was hooked. I had to find out how she did it." As it turned out, Macnair—who writes a gardening column for the *Lincoln County News*—has taught baking to teenage girls in an after-school program and donates hundreds of pies to the community. . . and was happy to share her pie-making secrets with Eagle. The two women spent an afternoon working together. "It is a tactile thing to make a crust," Macnair told Eagle. "I really don't think about it." She also assured Eagle in "a teacherly way" that there was no need to worry about how much water went into the dough. "If the dough doesn't hold together," she said, "just add more, very slowly, until it does." Macnair also revealed that her mother had a glass rolling pin that held ice to keep the dough chilled. But even on this warm day, with a conventional wooden rolling pin, reports Eagle, Macnair's own crust was perfect.

Blueberry Pie

SERVES 6–8

W HEN SHE BAKES at her house in Maine, Wanda Macnair uses a portable oven designed for a kerosene stove—little more than a metal box over two burners. The pies that come out of this contraption are extraordinary— but they're pretty good from a conventional oven, too.

FOR PASTRY:
2 cups flour
½ tsp. salt
⅔ cup vegetable
   shortening, chilled

FOR FILLING:
4 cups fresh blueberries
¾ cup sugar
1 tbsp. lemon juice
3 tbsp. cornstarch
1 tbsp. butter, cut into
   small pieces

1. For pastry, sift flour and salt together in a large bowl. Cut in shortening with a pastry cutter or 2 knives until mixture resembles coarse meal. Make small depressions in the mixture and drizzle in up to 5 tbsp. ice water, 1 tbsp. at a time, mixing until dough holds together. Form into a ball, wrap in plastic wrap, and refrigerate for 1 hour.

2. For filling, gently mix blueberries, sugar, lemon juice, and cornstarch together in a large mixing bowl.

3. Preheat oven to 400°. Divide dough into 2 balls. Roll out 1 dough ball into a 12" round on a floured surface, then ease into a 9" pie pan. Fill pastry with blueberries and dot with butter. Roll out remaining dough into a 12" round, place on top of berries, then fold edge under and crimp or flute. Pierce top crust with a small sharp knife in several places to allow steam to escape during baking. Bake for 10 minutes, then reduce heat to 350° and continue baking until crust is golden brown, about 30 minutes. Allow to cool before serving.

"Bluebarb" Pie

SERVES 6–8

SOME OF THE DISHES served at the annual rhubarb festival in Silverton, Colorado, are intentionally (we hope) pretty silly—but local residents, of course, also know how to use rhubarb in many sensibly delicious manners. The town's librarian, Jackie Leithauser, introduced us to this sweet-tart combination of two contrasting summer fruits.

FOR PASTRY:
2 ½ cups flour
½ tsp. salt
¼ cup vegetable
 shortening, chilled
8 tbsp. unsalted butter,
 chilled and cut into
 small pieces

FOR FILLING:
2 tbsp. cornstarch
1 ½ lbs. rhubarb stalks,
 cut into 1" pieces
1 cup sugar
½ tsp. lemon zest
¼ tsp. ground cinnamon
⅛ tsp. salt
1 cup blueberries

2 tbsp. butter, cut into
 small pieces
1 egg, lightly beaten

1. For pastry, sift flour and salt together in a large bowl. Cut in shortening and butter with a pastry cutter or 2 knives until mixture resembles coarse meal. Sprinkle in 6–8 tbsp. ice water, 1 tbsp. at a time, mixing with a fork until dough barely holds together. Add 1 or 2 tbsp. more water if dough is too dry. Knead 3 times, divide dough in half, and form into 2 balls; wrap in plastic wrap, and refrigerate for at least 1 hour.

2. For filling, dissolve cornstarch in ⅓ cup water in a medium saucepan. Add rhubarb, sugar, lemon zest, cinnamon, and salt and cook, stirring, over medium heat for 8 minutes. Remove from heat, cool slightly, and add blueberries.

3. Preheat oven to 375°. Roll out 1 ball of dough into a 12" round on a lightly floured surface, then ease into a 9" deep-dish pie pan. Trim edges, allowing a ½" overhang, then fold edges under. Roll out remaining dough into a 12" round on a floured surface. Cut dough into 6 or more strips.

4. Fill the crust with the cooled "bluebarb" filling, and dot with butter. Weave the dough strips into a top crust, crimping the edges to seal. Brush the lattice crust with egg, and bake until crust is brown, about 40 minutes. Allow pie to cool 30 minutes before serving.

Celebrating the Bitter

Though rhubarb may look like oversize red celery, it is actually a member of the buckwheat family, and a close relative of dock and sorrel. Historically regarded in Europe as something of a wonder drug, it was prescribed as a purgative and as a cure for everything from animal bites and excessive freckles to cancer. Rhubarb was introduced to the United States after the Revolutionary War, but Americans were slow to embrace it. One place in this country where rhubarb is a star, however, is the tiny town of Silverton, high in the Colorado Rockies—whose inhabitants publicly celebrate it on the Fourth of July each year. "It was either rhubarb or dandelions," local resident Gene Halaburt told us—referring to the only two crops that grow in any profusion around Silverton. "And a dandelion festival, we all agreed, just didn't cut it." In addition to a parade and fireworks, Silverton's rhubarb fête features a cooking contest that has seen such entries as rhubarb suckers, rhubarb pie with coconut meringue, rhubarb-cherry pizza, rhubarb-chile salsa, and rhubarb spaghetti sauce. One year, a contender bagged "worst in show" with a libation that was half rhubarb purée and half Budweiser beer.

Tart Pie

Lemon curd tarts have been known in Europe (especially in Britain and Ireland) for centuries, but topping a pie shell full of lemon filling with soft meringue is strictly an American conceit, dating from the 19th century. Today, a ubiquitous icon of diner food, lemon meringue pie is also frequently maligned, and all too often poorly made—with a chewy or pasty crust and a bland or starchy filling. Made well, though, it's a triumph of Yankee culinary creativity.

Lemon Meringue Pie

SERVES 6–8

THIS CLASSIC AMERICAN PIE is a popular favorite at the Gustavus Inn in Gustavus, Alaska—and, with variations, at thousands of other places around the country. Always use superfine or powdered sugar for the meringue (granulated will make it weep), and add it gradually.

FOR PASTRY:
1 cup flour
½ tsp. salt
6 tbsp. chilled butter, cut into small pieces
2 tbsp. vegetable shortening, chilled

FOR FILLING:
½ cup sugar
3½ tbsp. cornstarch
Salt
4 egg yolks
3 tbsp. butter
Juice and grated zest of 2 lemons

FOR MERINGUE:
4 egg whites
Pinch cream of tartar
½ cup superfine sugar

1. For pastry, sift together flour and salt in a large bowl. Cut in butter and shortening with a pastry cutter or 2 knives until mixture resembles coarse meal. Sprinkle in 2–3 tbsp. ice water, and knead until dough just holds together. Form into a ball, wrap in plastic wrap, and refrigerate for 1 hour.

2. Preheat oven to 400°. Roll dough into a 12" round on a floured surface, then ease into a 9" pie pan. Trim edges, allowing a ½" overhang, then fold edge under and crimp or flute. Prick dough all over with a fork. Line with aluminum foil and fill with pie weights or dried beans. Bake for 10 minutes, remove foil and beans, then bake for 10 minutes more. Set aside to cool.

3. Reduce heat to 350°. For filling, combine sugar, cornstarch, a pinch of salt, and 1½ cups water in a medium saucepan. Cook, whisking constantly, over medium-low heat for 3 minutes, then remove from heat. Lightly beat egg yolks in a bowl, whisk in 2 tbsp. of hot sugar mixture, then whisk eggs into sugar mixture. Cook, stirring constantly with a wooden spoon, over medium-low heat until thickened, about 3 minutes. Remove from heat and stir in butter, lemon juice, and lemon zest. Pour filling into pie crust.

4. For meringue, beat egg whites in a bowl. When frothy, add cream of tartar and beat until soft peaks form. Add superfine sugar and beat until whites are stiff and glossy. Spread meringue over lemon filling right to edge, leaving it slightly thicker in the middle and forming occasional peaks. Bake until brown, 15–20 minutes. Allow to cool completely before serving.

Sam's Apple Pie

SERVES 6–8

SAM WEINTRAUB, who was proprietor of the Splendid Cake Shop in Cambridge, Massachusetts, for 15 years, recommends cortland apples for this pie. "They're the juiciest," he says. As for making the crust, he echoes every baker's rule of thumb: "Don't handle the dough too much."

FOR PASTRY:
2 cups flour
½ tsp. salt
⅔ cup vegetable shortening, chilled

FOR FILLING:
3 lbs. baking apples, peeled and cored
1 cup sugar
Pinch of nutmeg
⅔ tsp. cinnamon
Salt
4 tbsp. butter, cut into small pieces
1 egg, lightly beaten

1. For pastry, sift flour and salt together in a large bowl. Cut in shortening with a pastry cutter or 2 knives, until mixture resembles coarse meal. Make small depressions in the mixture with your finger and drizzle in up to 5 tbsp. ice water, 1 tbsp. at a time, mixing until dough holds together. Form into a ball, wrap in plastic wrap, and refrigerate for 1 hour.

2. For filling, cut apples into wedges, ½" thick at the widest point. Mix sugar, nutmeg, cinnamon, and salt together in a large bowl. Add apples and mix well.

3. Preheat oven to 425°. Divide dough into 2 balls. Roll out 1 dough ball into a 12" round on a floured surface, then ease into a 9" pie pan. Fill the pastry with apples and all their juices, and dot with butter. Roll out remaining dough into a 12" round, place on top of apples, then fold edge under and crimp or flute. Poke 4 or 5 holes in top crust with your finger to allow steam to escape during baking. Beat 1 tbsp. water into egg then brush top of pie with egg wash. Bake until crust is golden brown, about 45 minutes. Allow to cool slightly before serving.

Bakery Memories

Toby Fox, associate art director of SAVEUR, whiled away many childhood hours at the Splendid Cake Shop in Cambridge, Massachusetts—run by her grandparents Sam and Irene Weintraub. (That's Toby, below, age 2, with Sam.) She still remembers the giant mixer set on the floor—she could barely peek over the edge of the bowl—and the huge sacks of flour ("You know, the 98-pound ones," Sam Weintraub clarifies) where she would curl up and take scented naps. When business was slow, Fox was even allowed to punch the buttons on the cash register while her grandmother ran the front of the shop. All that was a long time ago—the bakery closed in 1968—but Weintraub, now 90, has never stopped baking. His specialty? "Chocolate eclairs, yule logs, jelly rolls,

apple pie, blueberry pie, Boston cream pie, pecan pie, lemon meringue pie, cranberry muffins, blueberry muffins, corn muffins, jelly doughnuts, honey-dipped doughnuts, chocolate doughnuts. Do you want me to continue?" When Fox called him recently to ask how he made his perfect apple pie, one of the things he told her was to "poke four or five holes in the crust with your finger. Nothing fancy." "My finger?" Fox asked doubtfully. "You listen to Grampy," he replied, the way he always does. "You'll see. It'll be good."

The Cookie Bake

On the first Saturday in December, every year for the past 50 years, thousands of homemade Christmas cookies have gone on sale at Trinity Church in Solebury, Pennsylvania. Even with a limit of two boxes per customer (each box weighs a pound and contains about 50 cookies), they are usually sold out within 45 minutes. This annual Cookie Bake—both the sale itself and the flurry of preparing for it—is a tradition that continues to conjure up the feel of the rural agricultural community that Solebury used to be. Cookie Bake had its origins just after World War II, when a small group of women at the Episcopal church started baking cookies to sell at their annual bazaar. Now, over a hundred men, women, teenagers, and children work cookie-making shifts over a six-day period, turning out about 20,000 cookies in all. In 1996, they made $1,700—but the parishioners of Trinity Church stopped baking for the money a long time ago. Now, they say, they bake for the life of their community.

Christmas Butter Cookies

MAKES ABOUT 1 DOZEN

THIS BASIC COOKIE recipe from Trinity Church turns into almond rounds, snowmen glazed with colored sugar, or stars brushed with egg wash (facing page).

1¼ cups flour
½ tsp. baking powder
⅛ tsp. salt
8 tbsp. unsalted butter, softened
1 cup sugar
1 egg
½ tsp. vanilla extract

1. Sift flour, baking powder, and salt together in a bowl and set aside. Beat butter in a bowl with an electric mixer on medium speed. Gradually add sugar and beat until mixture is light and fluffy. Beat in egg and vanilla, then reduce speed and gradually add flour mixture until just combined. Divide dough in half and wrap in plastic wrap. Refrigerate for at least 1 hour.

2. Preheat oven to 325°. Roll out half of dough ⅛" thick, on a lightly floured surface, cut into desired shapes, arrange 1" apart on buttered nonstick cookie sheets, and decorate as you like. Bake for 5 minutes, rotate baking sheet, and bake until golden, about 5 minutes more. Transfer cookies to a wire rack to cool, then finish decorating. Repeat with remaining dough.

VARIATION: *Almond Rounds*—Toast blanched almond halves until golden. Roll out dough ⅛" thick, then cut with a 2¼"-wide circular cutter. Arrange on a buttered nonstick baking sheet. Beat 1 egg with ½ tsp. water in a bowl. Brush cookies with egg wash, top with 3 almond halves and cinnamon sugar, and bake.

VARIATION: *Snowmen*—Roll out dough ⅛" thick and cut with a snowman cutter. Arrange on a buttered nonstick baking sheet. Beat 1 egg with ½ tsp. water in a bowl. Brush cookies with egg wash and bake. Mix ¼ cup confectioner's sugar with 1–2 tbsp. water and divide between 2 small bowls. Tint liquid in one bowl with red food coloring and the other with black. Use a small brush to decorate baked snowmen.

VARIATION: *Stars*—Roll out dough ⅛" thick and cut with a star-shaped cutter. Arrange on a buttered nonstick baking sheet. Beat 1 egg with ½ tsp. water in a bowl. Brush cookies with egg wash and sprinkle with nonpareils (sugar pellets) before baking.

White Peaches Poached in Sauternes

SERVES 4

WHEN THEY FIRST RIPEN, white peaches have an undertone of raspberries; within a few days they start to suggest muscat grapes. To complement the peaches' lusciousness, make your poaching liquid with good-quality wine and a bottled water without a strong mineral flavor.

1 bottle (3¼ cups)
  sauternes or barsac
2 cups bottled spring water
  (nonsparkling)
1 cup sugar
4 large ripe white peaches

1. Mix together sauternes, water, and sugar in a deep saucepan. Bring to a simmer over medium heat.

2. Lower peaches into simmering liquid and blanch just long enough to loosen their skins, about 2 minutes. Remove peaches with a slotted spoon, then carefully peel and place in a deep bowl. Immediately cover peaches themselves with plastic wrap to keep them from turning brown.

3. Continue to simmer poaching liquid until it has reduced by half and thickened slightly, about 30 minutes. Remove saucepan from heat and allow syrup to cool completely.

4. Pour the cooled syrup over peaches and set aside to macerate for 2–4 hours before serving.

White Peach Reverie

Early in June each year," remembers SAVEUR Executive Editor Christopher Hirsheimer, "my grandfather would drive more than a hundred miles down the Central Valley to Fresno. He knew a farmer there who had babcocks, which were pretty much the only white peaches grown commercially back then. The harvest season was short—only a couple of weeks—making it, of course, that much sweeter. The farmer himself would pick and pack the peaches in a single layer, lining up the flat wooden crates on the back seat of my grandfather's big Buick. At home, we'd keep them on the back porch, which was a bit cooler than the kitchen, and eat them till those crates were empty."

Poached Quinces in Pastry

WE TRIED BAKING quinces as we would apples, but found that they remained stubbornly firm inside. Our solution: Poach them first, then bake them in light pastry.

Intoxicating Quinces

According to some food historians, the quince, not the apple, was the forbidden fruit that tempted Eve—and indeed, quinces can inspire love at first whiff; they smell like vanilla, jasmine, guava, and pineapple all at once. On the other hand, Eve probably wouldn't have liked them if she'd bitten into one raw. Uncooked quinces are grainy, bland, and unpleasantly tannic, even painful to the tooth. Cooked, on the other hand, they are a wonderment—delicate, tender, and tart, with just a hint of spice. Bake them whole. Poach them in wine, as in the recipe at right. Slip slices of one into an apple pie. Stew them with a vanilla bean, or with cinnamon and a sprinkling of sugar. High in pectin, quinces were once widely used to flavor and solidify jellies and jams. Then Charles Knox invented powdered gelatin in the 1890s and the quince fell out of favor. Fresh American-grown quinces are still available, though, in high-end grocery stores, at Hispanic and Korean markets, and at some greenmarkets nationwide from September through November each year. They're worth sniffing out.

FOR PASTRY:
2 cups flour
1 tsp. salt
12 tbsp. chilled butter, cut into small pieces
4 tbsp. vegetable shortening, chilled

FOR QUINCES:
1 cup sugar, plus additional for dusting (optional)
2 cups white wine
1 vanilla bean, halved lengthwise
4 large quinces, peeled, quartered, and cored

1 egg, lightly beaten
Fresh mint (optional)

1. For pastry, sift together flour and salt in a large bowl. Cut in butter and shortening with a pastry cutter or 2 knives until mixture resembles coarse meal. Sprinkle in 5–6 tbsp. ice water and knead until dough just holds together, wrap in plastic wrap, and refrigerate for 1 hour.

2. For quinces, mix together sugar and wine in a medium pan, then add vanilla bean and quinces. Cover and bring to a simmer over medium heat. Gently simmer for 30 minutes, then remove pan from heat and allow quinces to cool in the poaching liquid.

3. Preheat oven to 375°. Roll out dough about 1/8" thick on a floured surface and cut into 10" circles. Cut 12 "leaves" out of dough scraps. Put 4 poached quince quarters together to form a whole quince and place in the middle of a dough circle. Wrap dough circle around fruit to cover completely. Press the "leaves" on top. Repeat with remaining quinces and dough. Refrigerate for 1 hour. Beat 1 tbsp. water into beaten egg, then brush pastry with the egg wash.

4. Bake until golden brown, about 45 minutes. Meanwhile, reduce poaching liquid by half over medium heat. Remove and discard vanilla bean.

5. Spoon sauce on individual plates and place baked quinces on top. Garnish with fresh mint and dust baked quinces with additional sugar, if you like.

Ice Cream (Various Fruit Flavors)

MAKES 1 QUART

IN THE OLD DAYS, ice cream was just that: sweetened pure cream, beaten and frozen in a pot over ice or saltpeter. We still like to keep it as simple as possible.

1½ cups whole milk
1½ cups heavy cream
1 vanilla bean, halved
  lengthwise
4 egg yolks
¾ cup sugar

1. Put milk and cream into the top of a double boiler. Add vanilla bean and cook over gently boiling water over medium heat until mixture comes to a simmer, about 30 minutes. Remove vanilla bean.

2. Meanwhile, beat egg yolks in a mixing bowl, gradually adding sugar while beating, until mixture is thick, smooth, and pale yellow.

3. Slowly whisk 1 cup of the hot milk mixture into the yolks. Then gradually add the egg-milk mixture into the remaining milk in the double boiler, stirring constantly with a wooden spoon. Cook over medium heat until mixture is thick enough to coat back of a spoon, about 15 minutes. Allow to cool. Cover, then refrigerate for at least 4 hours. Pour into an ice cream maker and process according to manufacturer's directions.

VARIATION: *Strawberry Ice Cream*—Combine 2 cups thinly sliced hulled fresh strawberries, ⅓ cup sugar, and the juice of ½ lemon in a mixing bowl. Set aside to macerate for 2 hours. Slightly mash strawberries, stir into chilled cream base, and process as above.

VARIATION: *Blackberry Ice Cream*—Combine 2 cups fresh blackberries, ¾ cup sugar, and the juice of ½ lemon in a mixing bowl. (Add more sugar if berries are tart.) Set aside to macerate for 2 hours. Stir into chilled cream base and process as above. Just before mixture is set, add 1 cup halved fresh blackberries.

VARIATION: *Peach Ice Cream*—Combine 2 cups chopped ripe peaches, ½ cup sugar, and the juice of ½ lemon in a mixing bowl. Set aside to macerate for 2 hours. Drain and stir juice into chilled cream base. Set peaches aside in refrigerator. Process ice cream as above. Just before mixture is set, add peaches.

Cool Dish

Myth has it that Marco Polo brought the secret of freezing sorbet without ice to Italy from China in the 13th century, and that Catherine de Médicis took Italian ices to France a few centuries later. Whatever really happened, by the end of the 18th century, creamy elaborations of Italian ices had become the rage among the upper classes all over Europe—while across the sea, George Washington served them on special occasions. But it took New Jerseyite Nancy Johnson to bring ice cream home to the rest of us. In 1846, she invented the hand-cranked ice cream maker—and Americans have been celebrating summer with this chilly confection ever since. We're talking about the real, old-fashioned thing here: Sherbet is too sweet; frozen yogurt isn't rich enough; those trendy herb sorbets leave your mouth tasting like turkey stuffing. And that chunky, rippled stuff is too, well, chunky and rippled. We prefer ice cream pure and simple, flavored with the season itself—with, say, strawberries in June (facing page, top left), blackberries in July (facing page, top right), and drippy, messy peaches (facing page, below) to keep us happy throughout oppressive August.

The Grunt, the Slump, and the Betty

Now, pay attention, because we're only going to say this once: A betty is the same thing as a crisp. A cobbler—sometimes known as a bird's-nest pudding in New England—is similar, but has a crust on top. A grunt is an old Colonial dish of berries covered with dough and steamed. Sometimes the names *grunt* and *slump* are used interchangeably, but a slump is often made with apples, with bits of dough baked on top. Where did these names come from? No one really knows.

Apple Brown Betty

SERVES 6

TO PERK UP THE FLAVOR of bland apples, counsels SAVEUR contributing editor Marion Cunningham—who shared this recipe with us—add lemon juice and grated lemon rind to the fruit. Better yet, of course, use the ripest, most flavorful apples and forget the citrus.

6 tbsp. butter
2 cups fresh bread crumbs
1½ lbs. tart apples,
 peeled, cored, and cut
 into ¼" slices
½ cup brown sugar
½ tsp. ground cinnamon
Juice and grated rind
 of ½ lemon (optional)
Heavy cream

1. Preheat oven to 350°. Grease a 9" baking dish or a 1½-quart casserole (preferably with a lid) with 1 tbsp. butter.

2. Melt remaining 5 tbsp. butter in a small pan over medium heat. Lightly toss bread crumbs and melted butter together in a medium bowl. Spread about ⅓ of the crumb mixture in the baking dish.

3. Combine apples, sugar, cinnamon, and lemon juice and rind (if needed) in a medium bowl. In the baking dish, fan out half the apple mixture over crumbs. Add another layer of crumbs, a layer of apples, and a final layer of crumbs.

4. Pour 1 cup hot water slowly and evenly over crumbs. Cover baking dish with lid or foil and bake for 25 minutes. Uncover and bake 20 minutes more. Serve topped with heavy cream.

Strawberry Shortcake

SERVES 4

SOME COMMERCIAL VERSIONS of shortcake are built around little sponge-cake molds. We favor the non-commercial biscuit-based interpretation of this definitive American dessert—and instead of making individual small shortcakes, we like to construct an heroic big one.

4 cups strawberries,
    washed, hulled, and
    halved
6 tbsp. sugar
1½ cups flour
2 tsp. baking powder
1 tsp. salt
6 tbsp. chilled butter, cut
    into small pieces
¾ cup milk
Whipped heavy cream
    (optional)

1. Put strawberries in a medium bowl, sprinkle with 5 tbsp. sugar, and set aside to macerate for 30 minutes at room temperature.

2. Preheat oven to 400°. Sift flour, baking powder, salt, and remaining 1 tbsp. sugar together into a mixing bowl. Cut 4 tbsp. butter into flour mixture with a pastry cutter, or use your fingers to work it in, until mixture resembles coarse meal. Mix in milk. Turn out dough onto a lightly floured surface, knead several times, then shape dough into a large biscuit, 2" thick and 6" in diameter. Bake on an ungreased cookie sheet until just golden, about 15 minutes.

3. Cool biscuit slightly, then slice it in half horizontally. Spread remaining 2 tbsp. butter on cut sides. Place bottom half of biscuit on a plate and spoon half the strawberries and juice on top. Cover with other half of biscuit and spoon remaining strawberries over top. Serve with whipped cream, if you like.

Very Berries

hen colonists arrived in the New World, they found fields carpeted with small crimson strawberries. In 1838, this native East Coast variety was crossed with a larger, West Coast berry, to produce a more sizeable but unfortunately less flavorful fruit. Ralph Waldo Emerson once took time out from his busy philosophizing schedule to bemoan the cultivated strawberry. "Bluntly," he opined, "[strawberries] lose their flavor in garden beds." And he never even tasted the strawberry of the late 20th century. Our advice: Buy the best local varieties, by varietal name if possible, at the height of their season. Specifically, look for earliglow, sparkle, and jewel in the Northeast and Midwest; cardinal in the South, totem and redcrest in the Northwest; and chandler out West. In winter, if you're desperate, look for camarosa, a new California variety.

Pumpkin Walnut Cake with Candied Oranges

Soul Secrets

Christopher Hirsheimer, SAVEUR executive editor, recalls her grandmother as "a big-hearted woman, generous and loyal to a fault with her friends and family." In the matter of recipes, however, she fell short of holiness. "Ask her for the secret of her pumpkin walnut cake, and she'd sweetly change the subject. If pressed, she might comply, but you took your chances: A subtle but key ingredient could be missing. I never did find out what ended a 30-year friendship between my grandmother and her best friend Em, but I have a feeling it had something to do with a recipe for devil's food cake."

SERVES 8

HER GRANDMOTHER never gave her the real, un-abridged recipe for this cake, says Christopher Hirsheimer, but she was eventually able to figure out its secrets herself.

FOR CAKE:
1 cup softened butter, plus additional for greasing pan
2½ cups flour, plus additional for dusting pan
1 tsp. baking soda
1 tsp. baking powder
½ tsp. salt
½ tsp. freshly ground black pepper
1 tsp. ground cinnamon
¼ tsp. ground ginger
1 pinch ground allspice
1 cup sugar
3 eggs
1 cup pumpkin pulp
1 cup coarsely chopped walnuts
½ cup coarsely chopped candied orange slices (recipe follows)

FOR GARNISH:
¼ cup walnut halves
1 tsp. butter
2 tbsp. sugar
½ cup candied orange syrup (recipe follows)

CANDIED ORANGE SLICES WITH SYRUP:
2 tbsp. black peppercorns
10 whole allspice berries
3 cups sugar
2 seedless oranges (such as valencias), thinly sliced

1. For cake, preheat oven to 350°. Grease and flour a 7¼" (7-cup) angel food cake pan. Sift together flour, baking soda, baking powder, salt, pepper, cinnamon, ginger, and allspice into a large bowl and set aside.

2. In another large bowl, beat remaining 1 cup butter until fluffy. Gradually add sugar, then beat in eggs, one at a time, and fold in pumpkin. Slowly add dry ingredients to butter mixture, mixing just until smooth. Stir in walnuts and candied orange.

3. Spoon batter into pan. Bake until a toothpick inserted in center comes out clean, about 1 hour. Cool in pan for 10 minutes, then unmold and cool on rack.

4. For garnish, toast walnuts in a dry skillet over medium heat until brown, about 3 minutes. Stir in butter, remove from heat, and toss walnuts with sugar. Transfer cake to a platter, drizzle with candied orange syrup, and garnish top with walnuts and candied orange slices.

CANDIED ORANGE SLICES WITH SYRUP: Wrap peppercorns and allspice berries in a small square of cheesecloth, tie into a bundle, then put in a medium saucepan with sugar and 3 cups of water. Bring to a boil over medium heat and add oranges. Place the lid of a smaller saucepan on orange slices to keep them submerged. Simmer until the rinds become very soft and the syrup begins to foam, about 1½ hours. Remove slices from syrup and allow to cool on wax paper. Discard spices and reserve syrup. Makes about 12 orange slices and 1½ cups syrup.

Very Moist Chocolate Layer Cake

SERVES 10

WRITER ROBBIN GOURLEY learned the alchemy of baking from her grandmother Mattie, a North Carolinian known for her luscious cakes. This recipe comes from Gourley's book (with Joy Simmen Hamburger), *Cakewalk*.

FOR CAKE:
1 cup milk
4 oz. unsweetened chocolate, coarsely chopped
1 cup vegetable shortening, plus additional for greasing pans
2 cups flour
½ tsp. salt
1 tsp. baking soda
1 cup firmly packed dark brown sugar
1 cup sugar
3 eggs
1 tsp. vanilla extract

FOR ICING:
2 cups sugar
¼ cup light corn syrup
½ cup milk
8 tbsp. unsalted butter, cut into small pieces
2 oz. unsweetened chocolate, coarsely chopped
¼ tsp. salt
1 tsp. vanilla extract

1. For cake, heat milk in a small saucepan over medium heat until it just begins to simmer. Remove from heat, add chocolate, and cover. Set aside for 5 minutes, then stir until smooth.

2. Preheat oven to 350°. Grease 3 9" cake pans and line with rounds of greased wax paper. Sift flour and salt together in a mixing bowl. Dissolve baking soda in ⅓ cup hot water.

3. Put shortening, brown sugar, and sugar in a mixing bowl and beat with an electric mixer until fluffy. Add eggs one at a time, continuing to beat well. Add flour and chocolate mixtures in alternate batches, beginning and ending with flour. Beat in vanilla and dissolved baking soda. Divide batter equally between pans and smooth it. Bake for 30 minutes or until a toothpick stuck into cakes comes out clean. Allow to cool for 10 minutes, then turn cakes out of pans and onto cooling racks.

4. For icing, mix together sugar, corn syrup, milk, butter, chocolate, and salt in a saucepan and cook over low heat until butter and chocolate are melted and icing is smooth. Increase heat to high and boil icing until mixture reaches 220° on a candy thermometer, 1–2 minutes.

5. Pour icing into a small mixing bowl. Beat at medium speed until slightly cooled. Add vanilla, increase speed to high, and beat until icing is smooth and soft. Working fast before it sets, spread icing on top of 1 cake layer. Top with second layer, then spread icing on top of that one. Finally, spread icing evenly over top and sides of assembled cake.

The Chocolate Tree

At first glance, the connection between a chocolate cake like the one at left and the lumpy, lilac-tinged mass inside a cacao pod is difficult to imagine. But the former begins with the latter. Cacao, which probably originated in Brazil's Amazon basin, is grown in equatorial climates all over the world, the bulk of it in West Africa, Malaysia, and Brazil. (Like wine grapes, cacao beans develop different characteristics in different regions.) There are three basic types of cacao: the sturdy, high-yielding forastero, responsible for most of the world's production; the fragile criollo, native to Venezuela and considered the most complex in flavor and aroma; and the trinitario, a cross between the two. Freshly harvested cacao pods are split open and fermented before being dried in the sun (where they gain their rich brown color). The beans are then grated, cleaned, roasted, and milled into chocolate liquor, which in turn becomes cocoa powder or eating chocolate—and the next thing you know, it's likely to end up in an irresistible chocolate cake.

Fruitcake Weather

Fruitcake is as much about the gathering of ingredients, the making of the thing, and the giving of it, as it is about the eating. Every year, just after Thanksgiving, cooks all over America start gathering ingredients—green angelica, glacéed cherries, candied orange peel, crystallized ginger, and the like—and gathering themselves for baking. In his unexpectedly sentimental memoir *A Christmas Memory*, Truman Capote recalls that his elderly cousin in rural Alabama used to call this time of year "fruitcake weather". To some people, of course, fruitcake weather isn't something to be looked forward to. They dread it, in fact—or, rather, dread the heavy, lumpy confections, which are often more doorstop than delicacy. But fruitcake can be as light and subtly flavored as its maker wants it to be and knows how to make it.

Golden Fruitcake

MAKES 2 CAKES

FRUITCAKE DOESN'T have to be dark, dense, heavy, and aged for a year or more down in the cellar or under somebody's bed. Some interpretations, like this one, inspired by the sweet golden bounty of California orchards, are light in texture and color, and best eaten young.

1½ cups sliced almonds
¾ cup candied lemon peel, minced
¾ cup candied orange peel, minced
1 cup golden raisins
1 cup dried apricots, minced
1 cup dried peaches, minced
1 apple, peeled, cored, and grated
1 cup orange liqueur, such as Grand Marnier
1 cup flour
1 tsp. baking soda
1 tsp. ground mace
1 tbsp. ground ginger
¼ tsp. ground cloves
½ tsp. salt
1 cup fresh white bread crumbs
1 cup softened butter, plus additional for greasing pans and aluminum foil
1 cup sugar
4 eggs
1 cup sour cream
½ cup lemon juice
2 tbsp. vanilla extract

1. Spread almonds in a single layer on a baking sheet and toast until golden, about 5 minutes per side. Combine almonds, lemon peel, orange peel, raisins, apricots, peaches, apple, and orange liqueur in a large bowl and macerate at room temperature for 2 hours.

2. Sift flour, baking soda, mace, ginger, cloves, and salt together into a large bowl. Stir in bread crumbs and set aside.

3. Preheat oven to 350°. Beat butter with an electric mixer in a large bowl, gradually adding sugar and beating until mixture is light and fluffy. Beat in eggs, one at a time, then beat in sour cream, lemon juice, and vanilla. Slowly add dry ingredients, mixing until combined. Gently fold in macerated fruit and liqueur, then spoon into 2 well-greased fluted 4-cup tube pans.

4. Cover pans with lids or greased aluminum foil and place in a deep roasting pan. Add enough hot water to come one-third up sides of pans. Bake until a toothpick inserted in center comes out clean, about 1 hour and 45 minutes. Unmold cakes while warm; allow to cool before serving. (Store, wrapped in plastic wrap, in refrigerator.)

Apricot Soufflé

SERVES 2–3

WE DISCOVERED this dessert at Café Jacqueline, on Grant Avenue in San Francisco—where proprietor Jacqueline Margulis makes a specialty of soufflés. If blenheim apricots (see right) are unavailable, use the sweetest locally grown variety you can find. Avoid bland, cottony fruit.

¾ cup heavy cream
2¼ tsp. flour
¼ cup sugar, plus
   additional for dusting
   soufflé dish
8 large fresh apricots; 4
   diced, 4 sliced
1 tsp. kirsch
3 extra-large eggs,
   separated, at room
   temperature
Pinch cream of tartar
1 tsp. butter
Confectioners' sugar

1. Preheat oven to 450°. Combine cream, flour, ¼ cup sugar, and diced apricots in a large saucepan. Bring to a simmer over medium heat and cook, whisking, until thick, about 3 minutes. Remove from heat, add kirsch, then whisk in egg yolks, one at a time.

2. Beat egg whites in a mixing bowl until foamy. Add cream of tartar and continue to beat until very stiff.

3. Butter a small soufflé dish (6½" in diameter and 2½" deep), dust with sugar, and spread ¼ cup apricot mixture on bottom. Add about a third of the egg whites to remaining apricot mixture and gently fold whites and apricots together. Repeat, carefully folding in remaining egg whites in two more batches. Do not overmix. Spoon over apricot mixture into soufflé dish.

4. Make sure oven rack is low enough to allow soufflé room to rise as much as 2" above rim of dish, then bake soufflé until lightly browned on top, 12–15 minutes. Dust generously with confectioners' sugar and arrange sliced apricots on top. Serve immediately. (Soufflé will continue to cook as it rests, so recommend to guests that they start eating from the outside and work their way into the middle.)

Trouble in Paradise

The center of the apricot industry used to lie near the California coast, in the Santa Clara Valley—an area that in the 1920s and 1930s, the golden age of the California apricot, was affectionately known as the Valley of Heart's Delight. In the 1960s, however, laments writer David Karp, computers moved in and the Valley of Heart's Delight became the Valley of Silicon. Most growers moved over the Diablo Mountains to the San Joaquin Valley. On the Santa Clara side of the range, where once there were 20,000 acres of apricots, 2,000 remain. George Bonacich (facing page, top left) owns 35 of these acres, farming apricots on his family's Forge Ranch in Hollister. His grandparents started growing the blenheim, an English apricot variety, here in 1923. The blenheim's yield is low and it's a fragile fruit—but warm days and cool nights in Hollister allow it to mature slowly into delectable sweetness. This makes it perfect for drying—and if you are so lucky as to be able to taste one plucked right off the tree, you'll find it a honeyed but tangy indulgence. "They are finicky," Bonacich says of these apricots, "but nothing beats a blenheim."

Gimme a Man?

Medieval European monks were, apparently, the first to bake with ginger, including it in a heavy dough of dark rye or wheat flour, strong buckwheat honey, and a variety of spices. By the 1400s, gingerbread of this sort had become a staple throughout Northern Europe. By the 1600s, eggs and butter or lard were being added and the dough was cut into squares, shaped into animal or human figures, or pressed into elaborately carved wooden or terra-cotta molds that portrayed saints or biblical events. English colonists introduced gingerbread to America. "We ate gingerbread all day long," wrote the Virginia diarist William Byrd in 1711, referring to a day he spent training for the local militia. Germans who emigrated to Pennsylvania added their Lebkuchen, a shaped and decorated spice cookie, to the American gingerbread repertoire; Moravians in North Carolina rolled gingerbread dough paper-thin to make crisp cookies; and Swedish settlers brought along their recipes for pepparkakor, which are the cookies we know as gingersnaps. Abraham Lincoln never cared much about food, reports culinary historian Meryle Evans, but he made an exception for his mother's gingerbread. One day, Lincoln recalled, as he sat under a hickory tree ready to gobble down three freshly baked gingerbread men, a young lad from a neighboring family, poorer than his, came along: "'Abe,' he said, 'gimme a man?' I gave him one. He crammed it into his mouth in two bites and looked at me while I was biting the legs off my first one. 'Abe,' he said, 'gimme that other'n.' I wanted it myself, but gave it to him, saying, 'You seem to like gingerbread.' 'Abe,' he said, 'I don't s'pose anybody on earth likes gingerbread better'n I do—and gets less than I do.'"

Lafayette Gingerbread

SERVES 8

LEGEND HAS IT THAT this gingerbread cake was first made for General Lafayette, in the 1780s, by George Washington's mother. Mary Ball Washington reportedly studded her version with sweet raisins and orange rind.

½ cup softened butter
½ cup dark brown sugar
1 cup unsulphered molasses
3 eggs
3 cups flour
2 tbsp. ground ginger
1 ½ tsp. ground cinnamon
1 tsp. ground mace
1 tsp. ground nutmeg
1 tsp. baking soda
1 cup buttermilk
⅓ cup fresh orange juice
1 tbsp. grated orange zest
1 cup raisins
Whipped heavy cream
   (optional)

1. Preheat oven to 350°. Cream butter and brown sugar together in a large bowl. Stir in molasses, then beat in eggs, one at a time. Sift together flour, ginger, cinnamon, mace, nutmeg, and baking soda into a medium bowl. Combine buttermilk, orange juice and zest, and raisins in another bowl. Beat ⅓ of flour mixture into butter mixture, then beat in ⅓ of buttermilk mixture. Repeat process twice, until all of flour mixture and buttermilk mixture have been combined into butter mixture.

2. Pour batter into a greased, floured 9" × 13" baking pan. Bake 40–45 minutes or until a toothpick inserted in center comes out clean. Serve with whipped cream, if you like.

Hazelnut Brownies

MAKES 16 BROWNIES

TO ROAST HAZELNUTS for this recipe (which we adapted from one favored by Oregon's Hazelnut Marketing Board), spread shelled nuts in a shallow pan and put in a 275° oven for 20 to 30 minutes, until the skins crack. Rub the hazelnuts with a rough cloth to remove skins.

FOR CREAM CHEESE FILLING:
4 oz. softened cream cheese
¼ cup sugar
1 egg
2 tsp. lemon juice
½ tsp. vanilla extract
¼ cup finely ground roasted hazelnuts

FOR BROWNIE BATTER:
1 cup semisweet chocolate morsels
4 tbsp. butter
¾ cup flour
2 tbsp. cocoa
½ tsp. baking powder
¼ tsp. salt
¾ cup sugar
2 eggs
1 tsp. vanilla extract
½ cup coarsely chopped roasted hazelnuts

1. For cream cheese filling, combine cream cheese and sugar in a mixing bowl and beat with an electric mixer until smooth. Add egg, lemon juice, and vanilla and continue beating until well mixed. Use a spatula to fold in hazelnuts. Cover and refrigerate.

2. For brownie batter, melt chocolate morsels and butter in the top of a double boiler over simmering water over medium heat. Remove from heat and set aside.

3. Sift together flour, cocoa, baking powder, and salt in a medium bowl and set aside.

4. Preheat oven to 350°. Combine sugar, eggs, and vanilla in a large mixing bowl and beat with an electric mixer until smooth and lemon-colored, about 2 minutes. Beat in melted-chocolate mixture, then add flour mixture and continue beating until mixture is smooth. Fold in hazelnuts with a spatula.

5. Spread half the chocolate batter into an 8" square baking pan. Spread cream cheese filling over chocolate. Gently spread remaining brownie batter over cream cheese layer. Pull a spatula through layers to create a marbleized effect. Bake for about 40 minutes. Allow to cool before cutting into 2" squares.

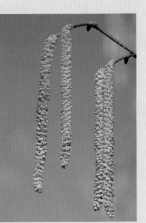

Hazelnuts Are Filberts

Hazelnuts are grown commercially in only four regions of the world: Turkey, Italy, Spain, and Oregon. In the last of these, where they are raised in orchards scattered through the Willamette Valley, in the western portion of the state, they are also known as filberts. Only about 3 percent of the world's hazelnut crop comes from Oregon, but that 3 percent is widely considered to be the best of the best—larger, healthier, tastier hazelnuts than anybody else's. This is no surprise to Oregonians, used to being able to grow everything from perfect Christmas trees and world-class iris bulbs to pungent spearmint and voluptuous blackberries. Oregonians take their hazelnuts for granted—by whatever name.

10

COCKTAILS

"THE COGITATION and introspec-

tion that bourbon does in the cask, with

the caramelized sugars in the charred

oak releasing that honey flavor, give the

whiskey remarkable depth. Just as you

can get flashes of dusty Spanish sunlight

in a good brandy de Jerez, you can get that

mild Middle South climate—the sweet air

over pastureland, the clean spring water,

the sunbursting corn—out of bourbon."

—DAVID GRINSTEAD ON BOURBON (*SEE RECIPE ON PAGE 298*)

RECIPES

The Martini

SERVES 2

WHEN ERNEST HEMINGWAY "liberated" the bar at the Ritz Hotel in Paris in 1944, he bought martinis for everybody. The hotel later named the room—the most famous "American bar" in the city—after him. There, bartender Colin Field (left) makes an excellent martini.

4 oz. dry gin
Dry vermouth
Large pitted green olives

ROASTED ALMONDS:
8 tbsp. unsalted butter
1 lb. raw almonds
Salt

1. Fill 2 stemmed cocktail glasses with crushed ice and allow to chill. Meanwhile, pour gin over plenty of ice in a cocktail shaker. Stir, but not too briskly, or you'll break up the ice and dilute the gin. Empty ice from glasses and strain gin into the chilled glasses. Float a single squirt of dry vermouth from a perfume vaporizer over the top of the gin and add one or more olives to each glass.

VARIATION: Add 3 drops vermouth to gin in the cocktail shaker, strain into chilled cocktail glasses, and add one or more olives to each glass.

HORS D'OEUVRE

ROASTED ALMONDS: Clarify butter by melting it in a pan over very low heat until almost all the sizzling noises have stopped and a white foam forms. Pour the clear yellow liquid butter through a tea strainer, and discard the milky solids. Set aside. Preheat oven to 375°. Bring a large pot of water to a boil.

Drop in almonds and cook for 1 minute. Drain, then squeeze almonds out of their skins (this is painstaking work) and place them in a single layer on a cookie sheet. Drizzle with clarified butter and bake until lightly roasted, 10–15 minutes. Sprinkle with salt to taste. Makes 1 lb.

The Martinians

The martini is a very serious matter. Any bartender who can't make it right might as well retire—and according to one master of the bartender's craft, the cocktail has even spawned a new breed of man: the Martinian. "Tennessee Williams was a Martinian," says Mauro Lotti, longtime head bartender at Le Grand Hotel in Rome. "He would come to the bar with his funny little dog, who would jump up on the bar stool as soon as I finished making Tennessee's martini. The dog would delicately poke his nose into the glass, pull out the stick with the olive on it, and toss it to the floor, where he would eat it. Another Martinian was Richard Burton. Burton's martini was extremely large, and I served him many of them over the years. He came in late one night with Elizabeth Taylor. She was carrying an enormous bouquet of roses. He ordered his usual martini and she ordered champagne. Their conversation became so heated that she stood up and started hitting him with her roses. He clutched his martini and through it all didn't spill a drop."

The Mai Tai

SERVES 2

CREDIT FOR CREATING the mai tai usually goes to
"Trader Vic" Bergeron, who concocted it at his Hinky
Dinks restaurant in Oakland, California, in 1944. Tast-
ing it, a guest supposedly proclaimed it "Mai tai roa!",
Tahitian for "Out-of-this-world, the best!" The name stuck.

2 oz. dark rum
2 oz. light rum
1 oz. orange curaçao
1 oz. orgeat (almond
    syrup)
Grenadine
1 lime, juiced, rinds
    reserved
Sprigs of fresh mint

RUMAKI:
4 slices bacon, halved
    crosswise
8 canned water chestnuts
4 chicken livers, cut in
    half
Soy sauce
1 tsp. grated fresh peeled
    ginger
1 tbsp. brown sugar

1. Fill a cocktail shaker with ice. Add dark rum, light
rum, curaçao, orgeat, 2 dashes grenadine, and lime
juice. Shake well; strain into 2 ice-filled old-fashioned
glasses, and garnish with reserved lime rind and a
sprig of fresh mint.

HORS D'OEUVRE

RUMAKI: Preheat oven to 400°. Lay bacon on a
cookie sheet and bake for 10 minutes, until cooked
but not crisp. Remove pan from oven and drain off
any fat, then blot bacon and pan with paper towels.
Place 1 water chestnut in the middle of each piece of

bacon, then top each with
half a chicken liver. Place
a drop of soy sauce, a pinch
of ginger, and a sprinkle of
brown sugar on top of each
liver. Wrap bacon around
water chestnuts and livers
and secure with a skewer.
Return pan to oven and
bake until bacon is crisp
and golden. Makes 8.

Caribbean Spirit

Rum is a spirit distilled from either fermented sugarcane juice or molasses (a by-product of sugar refining). It's manufactured on almost every Caribbean island where sugarcane—*Saccharum officinarum,* introduced to the New World from the Canary Islands by Columbus—is grown, and it inspires fierce national pride wherever it is made. When he invented the mai tai, recalls Victor J. Bergeron in his *Trader Vic's Bartender's Guide* (and anybody who says he didn't invent it, he notes, "is a dirty stinker"), he based it on a 17-year-old Jamaican rum from J. Wray Nephew. Owen Tulloch, master blender at that distillery, now called Wray & Nephew, considers rum "a friendly companion"— and notes that his firm's white overproof is the best-selling rum on the island. It is believed to have elixir-like powers, is used to christen newborns and to purify the dead, and is even sprinkled on the foundations of houses to rid them of evil spirits.

The Margarita

SERVES 2

OUR THEORY IS that, whoever invented the margarita, it was based on a stylish cocktail of the 1930s called the sidecar—which is virtually the same drink, but with brandy in place of tequila and with (in some versions, anyway) powdered sugar (!) instead of salt on the rim.

2 large limes, juiced, rinds reserved
4 oz. premium tequila
4 oz. Cointreau or triple sec
Margarita salt or kosher salt

GUACAMOLE:

1 small white onion, peeled and finely chopped
1 jalapeño, seeded and minced (or more to taste)
4 tbsp. finely chopped fresh cilantro
Salt
2 medium Haas avocados
1 small tomato, coarsely chopped

Tortilla chips (optional)

1. Fill 2 stemmed cocktail glasses with crushed ice and allow them to chill. Meanwhile fill a cocktail shaker with ice and add the lime juice, tequila, and Cointreau. Shake well. Empty the ice from the glasses, rub the rims of the glasses with the pulp side of one of the lime rinds, then dip the moistened rims into a saucer of salt. Strain the margaritas into salt-rimmed glasses and garnish each with a slice of lime, if you like.

HORS D'OEUVRE

GUACAMOLE: Combine half the onions, half the jalapeño, and half the cilantro in a mortar or food processor, season with about ½ tsp. salt, then pulse or grind into a smooth paste. Transfer to a medium bowl. Cut avocado in half lengthwise, then remove and discard pit. Make crosshatch incisions in avocado pulp with a paring knife. Scoop pulp out with a spoon, then combine with onion mixture. Mix well with a wooden spoon. Stir in remaining onions, jalapeño, and cilantro, then gently mix in tomatoes. Season to taste with salt. Transfer to a serving bowl and serve with tortilla chips, if you like. Makes about 2 cups.

Margarita Mythology

According to one story, the margarita—that classic cocktail of tequila, lime juice, and Cointreau or triple sec—was invented by a Texan named Margarita Sames, who mixed it up for houseguests at her villa in Acapulco in the late 1940s. Another version credits it to the Caliente Race Track near Tijuana. Still another traces it to the now-defunct Tail o' the Cock restaurant in Los Angeles, where it was supposedly named after some long-forgotten starlet. Don't try to spread these tales around Ciudad Juárez, across the Mexican border from El Paso, Texas, however. Local cocktail connoisseurs in that lively border town know for certain that the drink was first concocted at Juárez's Kentucky Club in the 1940s. One night, it seems, a bullfighter was pounding back shots of straight tequila there while his date—whose name you can guess—expressed a longing for something a bit more ladylike. The bartender improvised an icy mixture of tequila, lime juice, and Controy (a Mexican imitation of Cointreau) in equal parts—and named it after the fetching Margarita. The drink became a local tradition. In the old days, movie stars used to flock to Juárez for quickie divorces. One of these was Marilyn Monroe, who flew in to detach herself from Arthur Miller in 1961. When the deed was done, they say, she dropped by the Kentucky Club to celebrate by buying a round of margaritas for the house.

The Mint Julep

KENTUCKIANS ARE particular about their mint juleps. Some swear the mint must be gathered in early morning, while the dew is still thick. Others insist on sterling cups. But all agree on the texture of the ice: well crushed, of course.

Bourbon and Horses

In the late 1700s, German and Scots-Irish farmers in Pennsylvania, who made whiskey from the rye they grew, refused to pay taxes on their product to the fledgling U.S. government. They took up arms in rebellion, and the government sent in troops. Some farmers fled the tumult, landed in Kentucky, planted corn instead of rye, and created America's only native spirit—bourbon. The next thing anybody knew, it was Kentucky Derby time, and everybody was drinking bourbon in the form of mint juleps. Bourbon is only one of the two definitive ingredients in this fabled beverage. Mint-grower Bill Dohn and his wife and sons, official suppliers of the herb to Churchill Downs in Louisville (where the Derby is run), put in long hours harvesting mint on their ten-acre suburban farm in the two weeks leading up to Derby Day—the first Saturday in May—each year. Traditionally, the mint julep is served in an icy cold silver cup (facing page)—but even at Churchill Downs, we hear, they use a commemorative glass. The accompaniment of choice for juleps is the Benedictine sandwich—named not for the order of monks but for Louisville caterer Jennie C. Benedict, who invented the green-tinged filling in the 1890s.

½ cup sugar
1 large bunch fresh mint, trimmed of any bruised leaves
12 oz. bourbon

BENEDICTINE SANDWICHES:

6 oz. cream cheese
1 medium cucumber, peeled, seeded, and grated
1 medium yellow onion, peeled and grated
2 tbsp. mayonnaise
¼ tsp. Tabasco sauce
Salt
Green food coloring
16 slices of thinly sliced sandwich bread

1. To make simple syrup, mix together sugar and ½ cup water in a small saucepan and bring to a boil over medium heat, stirring until sugar has completely dissolved. Remove from heat and allow to cool.

2. Rub the rims of 4 pre-chilled mint julep cups with a few sprigs of fresh mint. Pack the cups with crushed ice so that it mounds over the top. Pour 1 oz. simple syrup and 3 oz. bourbon into each cup, over the ice, and garnish generously with sprigs of mint.

HORS D'OEUVRE

BENEDICTINE SANDWICHES: Put cream cheese in a bowl and mash with a fork until smooth. Wrap cucumber in cheesecloth, then squeeze out and discard juice. Add cucumber to cream cheese and mix thoroughly. Wrap grated onion in cheesecloth and squeeze juice into cream cheese mixture, then discard onion. Mix mayonnaise and Tabasco sauce into cream cheese mixture. Season to taste with salt, then add 1 drop green food coloring and mix well. Spread mixture on 8 slices of bread, then top each slice with another slice. Trim off crusts, and cut into finger sandwiches. Makes 16 sandwiches.

PROPER ATTIRE
JACKETS REQUIRED
AFTER 5:00 PM
ALL DAY SUNDAY

NO RESERVATIONS

The Sazerac

SERVES 2

THE FABLED GALATOIRE'S on Bourbon Street in New Orleans bottles its own Sazerac (invented at the city's now-defunct Sazerac Coffee House), made, idiosyncratically, with bourbon. This, the original version, is made with rye.

4 dashes Angostura bitters
8 dashes Peychaud bitters
1 tsp. Pernod
3 oz. rye whiskey
2 tbsp. simple syrup (see page 298, step 1)
Twists of lemon peel

OYSTERS AND BACON EN BROCHETTE:
4 slices bacon
1 cup flour
1 egg
1 cup milk
Salt and freshly ground black pepper
Tabasco sauce
8 small oysters, shucked
Vegetable oil
Fresh parsley, finely chopped
1 lemon, cut into 8 wedges

1. Put 2 dashes Angostura bitters and 4 dashes Peychaud bitters in each of 2 old-fashioned glasses. Tip the glasses and swirl bitters around to coat the sides, then pour out and discard the excess. Mix together Pernod, whiskey, and simple syrup in a cocktail shaker with about 10 ice cubes. Shake the mixture briefly, then strain into the ice-filled, bitters-coated glasses. Garnish each drink with a twist of lemon.

HORS D'OEUVRE

OYSTERS AND BACON EN BROCHETTE: Blanch bacon in a pot of boiling water for 10 seconds. Drain, pat dry, then cut each slice in half crosswise. Put flour on a plate. Beat egg with milk and season to taste with salt, pepper, and Tabasco sauce. Pat oysters dry with paper towels. Dredge oysters in flour, then dip in egg mixture. Reserve flour. Thread 1 oyster with 1 slice of bacon on each of 8 bamboo skewers. Pour vegetable oil into a heavy skillet to a depth of 4". When oil is hot (about 350°), roll brochettes in flour,

taking care to coat thoroughly on all sides. Fry brochettes in batches, turning occasionally, until crisp and golden, about 3–5 minutes. Drain on paper towels, season with salt, then sprinkle with finely chopped parsley. Serve with lemon wedges. Makes 8 brochettes.

Durable and Eccentric

G alatoire's is not a restaurant," says Henri Schindler, a New Orleans native, carnival float designer, Mardi Gras historian, and all-around bon vivant. "It's a religion. It's a refuge that gives you peace and consolation. It's another world, a place where you can go and know that things will never change." Galatoire's is one of America's oldest and most eccentric dining rooms (it was built in the 1830s and has been Galatoire's since 1905, when Jean Galatoire bought and named it after himself), and is as much a part of New Orleans culture as the St. Louis Cathedral or, for that matter, Mardi Gras. Until her retirement a couple of years ago, the most familiar face in the room was that of Yvonne Galatoire Wynne, who ruled the place at lunchtime. (Above, busboy Barry Patterson sets tables for lunch.) Miss Yvonne's old-school attitude was a mix of authoritarianism and compassion. She reportedly lobbied other family members to keep menu prices low. "My father always used to say that a poor soldier gets as hungry as a rich banker."

The Ramos Gin Fizz

SERVES 2

THIS FROTHY, REFRESHING brunch cocktail was invented by New Orleans bar owner Henry Ramos in 1888. In 1935, the city's Fairmont Hotel (then called the Roosevelt) trademarked it, and Fairmont bartender Tony Ortiz (facing page) taught us how to make it the right way.

Gin Origins

Gin was originally *genever* or *jenever*—Dutch for juniper, the spirit's defining flavoring. Invented in 1650 by Prussian-born Franciscus Sylvius, a physician at the University of Leiden in Holland, gin was initially recommended as a cure for cold feet and insomnia. British soldiers fighting in Holland in the 17th century dubbed gin "Dutch courage", because they thought it inspired fearlessness in the indigenous armies. When Holland's William of Orange became King William III of England, he banned French brandy, and the English gin industry was born. Pilgrims brought gin to America on the *Mayflower*, but it was only when our boys came home from World War I that it really caught on.

1 tsp. fresh lemon juice
1 tsp. fresh lime juice
1 tsp. orange-flower water
3 oz. dry gin
1 small egg white
2 tbsp. powdered sugar
¾ cup milk

RASPBERRY CAKE:
½ packed cup light brown sugar
2 tbsp. flour
1 tbsp. butter
½ oz. semisweet chocolate, finely chopped
1 cup flour
¾ cup sugar
½ tsp. baking powder
¼ tsp. baking soda
¼ tsp. salt
⅓ cup buttermilk
1 egg, lightly beaten
½ tsp. vanilla extract
⅓ cup butter, melted, and cooled
1¼ cups fresh black or red raspberries

1. Combine lemon juice, lime juice, orange-flower water, gin, egg white, powdered sugar, and milk with plenty of ice in a cocktail shaker. Shake very well and strain into 2 tumblers.

BRUNCH SUGGESTION

RASPBERRY CAKE: To make topping, mix together brown sugar, flour, and butter in a bowl. Use your hands to mix thoroughly. Add chocolate, mix well with a wooden spoon, and set aside. To make cake, preheat oven to 375°. Sift flour, sugar, baking powder, baking soda, and salt together into a medium bowl. In a separate bowl, whisk together buttermilk, egg, vanilla, and melted butter. Add

buttermilk mixture to flour mixture and mix with a wooden spoon. Pour batter into a lightly greased 8" round springform cake pan. Sprinkle raspberries over cake, then cover with topping. Bake until well browned, 40–45 minutes. Serve warm. Makes one 8" cake.

The White Spider

BRITISH FASHION JOURNALISTS who frequented the Algonquin Hotel's original Blue Bar used to favor this old-style cocktail. While imbibing it (or anything else), they had to abide by the strict rules of the establishment: Don't use crude language and don't be a bore.

1 small egg white
2 tsp. superfine sugar
½ cup fresh lemon juice
3 oz. gin
1½ oz. Cointreau

MINIATURE ALGONQUIN
WELSH RAREBITS:
1 cup grated cheshire or
   cheddar cheese
1 tbsp. beer
2 tsp. butter
2 tsp. Worcestershire sauce
¼ tsp. dry English
   mustard
Cayenne
1 egg yolk, beaten
   (optional)
4 slices white
   sandwich bread

1. Fill 2 stemmed cocktail glasses with crushed ice and allow to chill. Make a sour mix by mixing together egg white, 1½ tsp. sugar, and lemon juice in a large glass. Set aside.

2. Mix together half of the sour mix (reserving the rest for the next round), gin, Cointreau, and remaining ½ tsp. sugar in a large mixing glass filled with ice. Shake the drink vigorously. Empty the ice from cocktail glasses and strain the white spider into the chilled glasses.

HORS D'OEUVRE

MINIATURE ALGONQUIN WELSH RAREBITS: Preheat broiler. Mix together cheese, beer, butter, Worcestershire sauce, mustard, and a pinch of cayenne in a small heavy saucepan. Cook, stirring with a wooden spoon, over medium heat, until cheese mixture is melted, then remove from heat. If you are using egg yolk, stir it in. Cut 1"–2" rounds out of bread slices, discarding scraps. Arrange bread rounds on a baking sheet and toast in the broiler on one side only, then turn over so the toasted side is down, and spoon a little cheese mixture on top of the bread. Brown under broiler for about 30 seconds. Makes 8–12.

Blue Initiate

T he original Blue Bar in the Algonquin Hotel, on West 44th Street in Manhattan, was a little room filled with the ghosts of the famous and the antics of living characters," longtime Blue Bar-tender David Grinstead recalled in the pages of SAVEUR. "It seemed fitting that I first entered this enchanted space like an initiate, crawling through a tiny door off the corridor by the women's loo. That was how bartenders got in to work their shift." The bar itself was a worn mahogany plank that spanned one end of a small room. In front of it stood seven stools. The little lobby-entrance door, enclosing the tiny bar inside like a treasure in a box, drew customers in. The concealed hatch meant the bartenders appeared as if from a stage trap. The effect was magical. "The Blue Bar was nothing if not literary," Grinstead continued, "and working there was a wonderful education for a writer like myself. I got to quiz old Algonquin hands who'd known Thurber and Parker, Bankhead and George S. Kaufman, Edmund Wilson, Laurence Olivier and Vivien Leigh, and the Angry Young Men. And I learned to hold up my end of a conversation with anyone." What happened to the Blue Bar was, simply, that it closed. The hotel was sold and the new owners shuttered the bar, ostensibly to use it as a luggage storage and office space. At last call on the last night, March 10, 1990, many people cried. The hotel now has a "Blue Bar" in another room. Don't believe a word of it.

The Ultimate Acquired Taste

Gaspare Campari started inventing cocktails in the cellar of his Milan caffè in the early 1860s, selling his homemade libations upstairs. One day, he came up with what he decided was a Dutch-style bitter, composed of alcohol, sugar syrup, distilled water, and an infusion flavored with oranges, rhubarb, ginseng, and, of course, secret herbs. The recipe for what became known by his name supposedly hasn't changed since. William Sertl, SAVEUR travel editor, remembers that when he first got out of college, he used to order Campari on any occasion, just to let the world know that he'd graduated. Moved East. Even spent a summer in Europe. "I still drink Campari," he says, "but for a different reason now: I like it. I like the spicy, bitter taste. I like the rosy hue. I'm grateful that Campari, the ultimate acquired taste, has proven to be every bit as sophisticated as I once longed to be."

The Americano

SERVES 2

TO BE PERFECTLY FRANK, the americano isn't an American drink at all—its name may be a pun on *amer,* French for bitter—but it's the kind of civilized, international aperitivo Americans (among others) drink in Italy.

3 oz. *Campari*
3 oz. *Italian sweet*
  vermouth
Soda water
2 *orange slices*

POTATO CHIPS:
3 lbs. *russet potatoes, peeled*
Peanut oil
Salt

1. Fill 2 old-fashioned glasses with ice cubes. Divide Campari and sweet vermouth between the two glasses, add soda water to taste, stir well, and garnish with orange slices.

HORS D'OEUVRE

POTATO CHIPS: Slice potatoes into rounds about 1/16" thick (it is easiest to do this with a mandoline). Put potatoes in a large nonreactive bowl and cover with water. Pour enough oil to come 4" up the side of a heavy-bottomed pot. Heat over medium-high heat. Drain potatoes, then dry thoroughly with paper 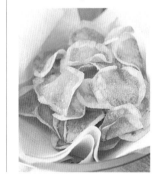 towels. Check oil temperature with a thermometer; when oil reaches 375°, fry potatoes in small batches until they are crisp and golden, about 3 minutes per batch. Drain chips on paper towels, sprinkle with salt, and serve warm or at room temperature. Serves 2–4.

Photography Credits

PERMISSIONS: 60–61: Lobster and celery root salad recipe adapted from *James Beard's Shellfish*, edited by John Ferrone, a book published by Thames and Hudson. Copyright ©1997 by John Ferrone; used by permission of the publishers. 88–89: Excerpt and Down-East baked beans recipe from *Serious Pig* by John Thorne with Matt Lewis Thorne. Copyright © 1996 by John Thorne. Reprinted by permission of North Point Press, a division of Farrar, Straus & Giroux, Inc. 240–41: Whole wheat bread recipe from *Vegetarian Gourmet Cookery* by Alan Hooker, Cole Publishing Group, Inc., 1993; used by permission of the publisher. 254–55: Pumpkin pie recipe adapted from *The Fannie Farmer Cookbook* by Marion Cunningham; Alfred A. Knopf, Inc., 1996; used by permission of the publisher. 272–73: Apple brown betty recipe adapted from *The Fannie Farmer Cookbook*, by Marion Cunningham; Alfred A. Knopf, Inc., 1996; used by permission of the publisher. 278–79: Very moist chocolate layer cake recipe adapted from *Cakewalk: Spoonfuls from a Southern Kitchen* by Robbin Gourley and Joy Simmen Hamburger. Copyright © 1994 by Robbin Gourley and Joy Simmen Hamburger; used by permission of Doubleday, a division of Bantam Doubleday Dell Publishing Group, Inc.

Menus

Spring Dinner
•

Lobster and Celery Root Salad (page 60)

Poached Salmon with Egg-Caper Sauce (page 99)
Peas and Lettuce (page 193)

Lemon Meringue Pie (page 260)

Easter Dinner
•

Cooked and Raw Vegetable Salad (page 52)

Roast Lamb with Potatoes (page 165)
Sally's Ramps with Bacon (page 205)

Strawberry Shortcake (page 275)

Fourth of July
•

Margaritas (page 297)
Guacamole (page 297)

Gus's Fried Chicken (page 138)
Barbecued Ribs (page 174)
Down-East Baked Beans (page 89)
Corn Bread (page 238)

Blueberry Pie (page 256)
Ice Cream (page 271)

Summer Lunch
•

Chilled Lima Bean Soup (page 26)

Whole Striped Bass Baked in Salt (page 108)
Stuffed Tomatoes (page 56)

White Peaches Poached in Sauternes (page 267)

Harvest Dinner
•

Sazeracs (page 301)
Oysters and Bacon en Brochette (page 301)

Lina's Tortelli (page 77)

Roast Duck with Orange Sauce (page 146)
Perfect Wild Rice (page 82)
Roasted Autumn Vegetables (page 201)

Poached Quinces in Pastry (page 268)

Thanksgiving Dinner
•

Cranberry Bean Soup (page 29)

Roast Turkey with
Corn Bread Stuffing (page 149)
Mashed Potatoes with Butter (page 225)
Michael Roberts's Corn Risotto (page 217)
Sweet Potato Casserole (page 229)
Turnip Greens (page 197)

Pumpkin Pie (page 255)
Sam's Apple Pie (page 263)

Holiday Dinner
•

Pumpkin Soup with Sage (page 30)

Warm Chanterelle and
Pancetta Salad (page 63)

Goose with Chestnut
Stuffing and Port Sauce (page 153)
Parsley Salad (page 55)
Red Cabbage (page 213)

Golden Fruitcake (page 280)
Christmas Butter Cookies (page 264)

Sunday Brunch
•

Ramos Gin Fizzes (page 302)

Breakfast Trout with Bacon (page 95)
Corned Beef Hash (page 162)
Baking-Powder Biscuits
with Strawberry Freezer Jam (page 234)
Swedish Coffee Bread (page 246)
Raspberry Cake (page 302)

Sunday Supper
•

Spinach Salad (page 48)

Lamb's-Neck Stew with Polenta (page 166)
Steamed Artichokes (page 202)

Pumpkin Walnut Cake
with Candied Oranges (page 276)

Cocktail Buffet
•

Americanos (page 306)
Martinis (page 293)
Roasted Almonds (page 293)
Potato Chips (page 306)

Monte's Ham (page 170)
Georgene's Fluffy Rolls (page 237)

Rumaki (page 294)
Miniature Algonquin Welsh Rarebits (page 305)
Lima Mash with Lemon and
Olive Oil (page 206)

Add a Salad, Make a Meal

Index

Table of Equivalents

THE EXACT EQUIVALENTS IN THE FOLLOWING TABLES HAVE BEEN ROUNDED FOR CONVENIENCE.

LIQUID AND DRY MEASURES

U.S.	METRIC
¼ teaspoon	1.25 milliliters
½ teaspoon	2.5 milliliters
1 teaspoon	5 milliliters
1 tablespoon (3 teaspoons)	15 milliliters
1 fluid ounce (2 tablespoons)	30 milliliters
¼ cup	65 milliliters
⅓ cup	80 milliliters
1 cup	235 milliliters
1 pint (2 cups)	480 milliliters
1 quart (4 cups, 32 ounces)	950 milliliters
1 gallon (4 quarts)	3.8 liters
1 ounce (by weight)	28 grams
1 pound	454 grams
2.2 pounds	1 kilogram

LENGTH MEASURES

U.S.	METRIC
⅛ inch	3 millimeters
¼ inch	6 millimeters
½ inch	12 millimeters
1 inch	2.5 centimeters

OVEN TEMPERATURES

FAHRENHEIT	CELSIUS	GAS
250	120	½
275	140	1
300	150	2
325	160	3
350	180	4
375	190	5
400	200	6
425	220	7
450	230	8
475	240	9
500	260	10